Studia Fennica
Litteraria 1

The FINNISH LITERATURE SOCIETY (SKS) was founded in 1831 and has, from the very beginning, engaged in publishing operations. It nowadays publishes literature in the fields of ethnology and folkloristics, linguistics, literary research and cultural history.

The first volume of the Studia Fennica series appeared in 1933. Since 1992, the series has been divided into three thematic subseries: Ethnologica, Folkloristica and Linguistica. Two additional subseries were formed in 2002, Historica and Litteraria. The subseries Anthropologica was formed in 2007.

In addition to its publishing activities, the Finnish Literature Society maintains research activities and infrastructures, an archive containing folklore and literary collections, a research library and promotes Finnish literature abroad.

STUDIA FENNICA EDITORIAL BOARD
Anna-Leena Siikala
Rauno Endén
Teppo Korhonen
Pentti Leino
Auli Viikari
Kristiina Näyhö

EDITORIAL OFFICE
SKS
P.O. Box 259
FI-00171 Helsinki
www.finlit.fi

Changing Scenes

Encounters between European and Finnish Fin de Siècle

Edited by Pirjo Lyytikäinen

Finnish Literature Society · Helsinki

Studia Fennica Litteraria 1

The publication has undergone a peer review.

VERTAISARVIOITU
KOLLEGIALT GRANSKAD
PEER-REVIEWED
www.tsv.fi/tunnus

The open access publication of this volume has received part funding via Helsinki University Library.

© 2003 Pirjo Lyytikäinen and SKS
License CC-BY-NC-ND 4.0 International

A digital edition of a printed book first published in 2003 by the Finnish Literature Society.
Cover Design: Timo Numminen
EPUB: eLibris Media Oy

ISBN 978-951-746-439-0 (Print)
ISBN 978-952-222-990-8 (PDF)
ISBN 978-952-222-768-3 (EPUB)

ISSN 0085-6835 (Studia Fennica)
ISSN 1458-5278 (Studia Fennica Litteraria)

DOI: http://dx.doi.org/10.21435/sflit.1

This work is licensed under a Creative Commons CC-BY-NC-ND 4.0 International License. To view a copy of the license, please visit http://creativecommons.org/licenses/by-nc-nd/4.0/

A free open access version of the book is available at http://dx.doi.org/10.21435/sflit.1 or by scanning this QR code with your mobile device.

BoD – Books on Demand, Norderstedt, Germany

Contents

FOREWORD 7

Pirjo Lyytikäinen
THE ALLURE OF DECADENCE
French reflections in a Finnish looking glass 12

Riikka Rossi
FINNISH NATURALISMS
Entropy in Finnish Naturalism 31

Viola Parente-Čapková
FREE LOVE, MYSTICAL UNION OR PROSTITUTION?
The dissonant love stories of L. Onerva 54

Jyrki Nummi
BETWEEN TIME AND ETERNITY
K. A. Tavaststjerna's *Barndomsvänner*.................... 85

Päivi Molarius
"WILL THE HUMAN RACE DEGENERATE?"
The individual, the family and the fearsome spectre of
degeneracy in Finnish literature of the late 19th and
early 20th century 121

Vesa Haapala
I AM FIRE AND WATER
Self and modernity in Edith Södergran's
"Vierge moderne" (1916) 143

Leena Kaunonen
THE FEMININE IN PAAVO HAAVIKKO'S
WINTER PALACE...................................... 169

Auli Viikari
POETICS OF NEGATION................................ 191

CONTRIBUTORS 218

Foreword

The late 19th and early 20th century was a period of dynamic modernisation and internationalisation in Finnish literature and art. Society became more outward-looking, though the existence, as a nation, of the Grand Duchy still politically tied to Russia was threatened by tsarist attempts at Russification. Writers and artists travelled to Paris and Berlin and immersed themselves in European culture, their aim being to play a closer role in international cultural debate. Whereas the available resources had previously been channelled into laying the foundations of a national culture, artists and writers were now keen to capture the spirit of the times by adopting the new contemporary trends. They were eager to avoid the dangers of backwardness and isolation at a time when culture was driven by a greater inner impetus than ever before, despite the growing external threat.

The past century had seen sweeping changes. Until the 19th century, there was no Finnish culture to speak of in the demanding sense of the word: before that, the culture in Finland was for the most part that of Sweden, apart from the folk culture existing in oral form. The development of a specifically Finnish national culture got under way in earnest in the course of the 19th century, but not until the end of the century did culture in Finnish really find its feet. The stimulus for this was provided by Finland's annexation to Russia. When Finland became an Autonomous Grand Duchy of the Russian Empire in 1809, it was forced to rethink its status. Swedish dominated the former province of Sweden almost entirely at that time, even though the ordinary people spoke mostly only Finnish. Under the new regime, people were, however, receptive to the nationalist ideals borrowed primarily from Germany. The Finns had no wish to become Russians, there was no reverting to Swedish dominance, and the only way to become a nation was by integrating the educated circles and the common folk. The creation of a national culture in Finnish became the goal of Finland's educated Swedish speakers. Although the collection and publication of the priceless treasures of folk poetry in Finnish provided the stimulus for and faith in the national project, the work was slow and the country poor, worn down by repeated famines and watched over by the sometimes stern eye of Russia. Not until the closing decades of the 19th century did the situation take a decisive turn for the better.

In training an educated class that now spoke Finnish, the school system gradually created a wider readership for literature in this language. Meanwhile, linguistic antagonism was driving Finnish and Swedish speakers into opposing camps, and literature in Finnish and Swedish began to grow apart. At around the turn of the century, Swedish speakers found themselves on the national periphery, and for them, cosmopolitanism and contacts abroad took the place of nationalist zeal. A rift emerged between Finnish culture in Swedish and nationalist culture in Finnish. K. A. Tavaststjerna, a prominent Finnish writer in Swedish, joined the ranks of the realists and described relations between the nation at large and the educated classes as problematic. He was nevertheless overshadowed in Finnish-speaking circles by the leading writers in Finnish.

Literature in Finnish became more international during the period of realism and naturalism in the 1880s, in line with contemporary trends in France and the Nordic countries. Even so, the political lobby on behalf of Finnish left such a strong mark on cultural life that the literature coloured by Naturalistic strivings was in many cases read in the spirit of nationalism. The earlier description of the people that was part of the pro-Finnish ethos in a way maintained its position and was enriched by portrayals of the urban working class, but the tone and the emphasis shifted. Descriptions of the middle-class, often petty-bourgeois milieu now began to enter literature in Finnish, too. Writers set about analysing relations within the family and between the individual and society, and pointing out social evils. Of the realists, Minna Canth to a great extent turned her attention to the workers and small-town bourgeoisie: the position of women and social injustice are themes running through her work. By contrast, Juhani Aho sought to live up to the role of national writer bestowed upon him by placing his characters in a rural Finnish setting, in the heart of the Finnish countryside, even when his themes had nothing to do with the national project. The conflict between modern and pre-modern is already raging in the works of Aho: it threatens the rustic idyll and the rural way of life as the epitome of the Finnish ethos and allows aspects of French Naturalism to creep into his accounts.

By the dawn of the new century, literature in Finnish had become both national and more pan-European than ever. Writers, like other artists, had lively foreign contacts, and literature was closely influenced or produced in dialogue with international trends. On the other hand, the transition from realism to new, symbolistic modes of expression and ways of thinking stressing the internal or intellectual rather than the external and social paved the way in novel fashion for history and myth, and hence for the use of the national past or mythology.

The national themes were further fuelled by the political situation. The position of autonomous Finland as a Russian dominion came under greater pressure when the striving to strengthen the Finnish national identity began to be regarded by the Russians as a threat rather than as a means of severing Finland from Swedish influence, and when the nationalist movements in Russia set about Russifying all the nations in the Empire. In reaction to this, the nationalist movement in Finland and the search for national symbols grew stronger. The roots of the Finnish nation were now sought in Karelia, the eastern periphery idealised by the Finns and home of the poetry that went to make up the national epic, the Kalevala. For here, it was assumed, the true Finnish ethos was still alive. This initially nostalgic Karelianism nevertheless soon gave way to art uniting the national and the universal in which the emphasis on 'Finnish' could be combined with contemporary international trends. The Symbolism born in France, seeking a more profound reality by allegorical means rather than giving realistic, everyday descriptions was well suited for this purpose.

In Finland the Symbolists embraced Finnish mythology as a source of universal symbols; thus the national was combined with the universal heritage. The stories and characters in the Kalevala were used, especially in the poetry and poetic dramas of Eino Leino, to depict both current political moods and modern ideals. The most remarkable synthesis of contemporary ideals and Symbolism was his play *Sota valosta* (1900) in which Väinämöinen, cast as a popular leader and poet, and other heroes from the Kalevala try to rescue ancient Finnish society, which is in danger of destruction, but are at the same time clearly Nietzschean, *fin de siècle* individualists; the entire play is set in the Kalevalaic era yet is at the same time an allegory of modern times. Yet in his great masterpiece *Helkavirsiä* (1903) Leino developed the art poem based on the Kalevalaic metre and created heroes of his own who had national roots yet rose to mythical greatness.

Not all the Symbolistic literature in Finland drew on national myths, however. The young Volter Kilpi based his early works representing symbolistic lyrical prose on themes taken from the Bible, Antiquity, and tales of medieval chivalry, but he evoked an echo in only a few young writers and Finnish writers in Swedish oriented towards international imagery. The Symbolistic search for beauty, likewise the cosmopolitan Decadence that accompanied it, were alien to the broader reading public, and the only literature to enjoy prestige was that of a nationalist nature or commenting on the current historical situation. The relationship with the ordinary people was, however, also a problem for the Symbolists raised to the status of interpreters of the nation, such as Leino.

In being transformed into the alter egos of Symbolistic artists and into Nietzschean supermen, the Kalevalaic heroes parted company with the Finnish people, even though they were ostensibly still Finnish heroes. Artists began distancing themselves from the ordinary man, the simple peasant, who was now regarded as part of a threatening mass. They thus focused by veiled means on threats associated in the most highly-industrial parts of Europe with the birth of the workers' movement and the urban proletariat, thought to have a degenerating effect on mankind, but also with mass production and the ascendancy of bourgeois values in cultural life. The ingenious heroes, who in literature were usually artists, sought to stand out above the masses condemned as lower mortals and lacking in the higher, idealistic aspirations and respect for individuality.

Ideas such as this had already won a foothold in Finland before the political and social developments really provided any substance for fearing any concrete threat from the masses. It was thus easier, when the opportunity arose, to interpret events by viewing the people as wild barbarians, or as a monstrous threat to civilisation as a whole. In Finland the workers' movement first demonstrated the power of the masses in a way that conflicted with the goals of the educated classes in the general strike of 1905. In this new social and ideological atmosphere, Finnish literature finally rejected, once and for all, the idea based on nationalist aspirations and the Runebergian ethos of an alliance between the people and the educated class and of common goals on the issue of the national awakening. In place of the idealised peasant, the lower classes of society began to be viewed as an irrational threat to civilisation. Instead of innocent, the masses were regarded as corrupt.

This decline had previously been attributed to the changes brought by modernisation. Cast in the role of scapegoat in the descriptions of country life was the wood-processing industry with its timber sales and loggers, its mills and merchants placing modern luxury goods within reach of the masses and tempting them to dispense with thrift. Little by little, however, as new European ideals reached Finland, another, profounder reason was put forth: the masses were primitive; it was no longer believed that they had ever been good. Instead, they were depicted as wild, as beasts, as dangerous barbarians. Meanwhile, the intelligentsia and decadent Western culture were seen as powerless. Various European doctrines analysing and explaining degeneration spread to literature and influenced the human image. The wild primitivism of the masses, the inferiority of the entire Finnish race or the degeneration of members of the intelligentsia could all be motivated by resorting to popular contemporary theories. The accounts of degeneration were made all the more forceful by the onslaught in literature of a new naturalism with even fewer illusions after the period of Symbolism and accompanying Decadence.

The six articles in *Changing scenes* represent the ongoing reassessment of *fin de siècle* literature in Finnish research. The period was seen in earlier research as something of a national renaissance or golden age and interpreted in the light of its national symbols and meanings. Only recently has more attention been paid to its international dimensions and its role in the modernisation of Finnish culture. In particular the spotlight has been trained on the reflection in Finnish literature of manifestations of the degeneration thinking so common in Europe at that time. Research has also picked out works and writers such as L. Onerva that featured less in earlier studies.

The article by Pirjo Lyytikäinen outlines manifestations of *fin de siècle* Decadence in Finnish literature. Previous research has paid almost no attention to these, because decadence did not fit the image of Finland's emerging national literature. The article also serves as an introduction to the modernist themes of *fin de siècle* literature and is based on her monograph *Narkissos ja sfinksi* (1997) addressing Finnish Symbolism and Decadence. The Naturalism that preceded and paved the way for Decadence, and that is not so provocative in Finnish literature as in, say, French, is discussed by Riikka Rossi. Her article demonstrates that many works previously classified as Realist can be read within a Naturalist frame of reference, thus yielding completely new readings of them. Viola Parente-Čapková draws a portrait of L. Onerva, the leading (woman) writer influenced by the Decadent trend of the *fin de siècle*. Adopting a feminist perspective, the article examines the theme of love in the early works of Onerva, above all her best-known novel, *Mirdja*. *Fin de siècle* love discourse is analysed above all with reference to male-female relations and their social aspects. Päivi Molarius investigates the degeneration debate of the early 20th century and its manifestations in Finnish literature. The ideas rooted in the 19th century on the degeneration of the human race persisted and metamorphosed in the 20th century, drawing stimuli from new scientific or pseudo-scientific models. Degeneration themes in literature in Finnish are illustrated by numerous examples, but with special reference to the works of the female writer Maila Talvio.

Finnish literature in Swedish is the subject of two articles. Jyrki Nummi evaluates the relationship of the debut novel *Barndomsvänner* (Childhood Friends) by K. A. Tavaststjerna to the Modernism in Finnish prose. The novel has previously been examined in the Finnish prose tradition in Swedish as the first modern novel in the framework of Realism and Naturalism. Nummi also points out the lyrical features of the novel that tie it to the romantic tradition of lyric poetry in Swedish. Vesa Haapala discusses the poem "Vierge moderne" in the debut collection by the Modernist lyricist Edith Södergran. He contributes to international debate by putting forth a new interpretation of this acclaimed and contested poem. He is, for example, interested in the way even this early poem already condenses the metaphorical strategies of identity formation so fundamental in her late works and their links with the aesthetics of Nietzsche.

Also in the anthology is an article by Leena Kaunonen and another by Auli Viikari examining the poetry of the distinguished Finnish modernist Paavo Haavikko (b. 1931). The article represents the latest research into the Finnish modernism of the 1950s.

Translated by Susan Sinisalo

PIRJO LYYTIKÄINEN

The Allure of Decadence
French reflections in a Finnish looking glass

Eighteenth-century France could still regard its own (Europe's leading) culture as young and as having recently emerged from barbarity,[1] but by the following century concepts and ideas of cultural decadence gained the upper hand, at least in literary representations. Particularly towards the end of the century, writers and artists began to regard themselves as representatives of a late stage of culture, and the concept of "things come late" even spread to countries such as Finland, where national culture was still under construction. Literary Decadence,[2] ambivalently merging descriptions of decay, wallowing in its imagery, presenting shocked reactions to decay and idealising it while developing a "decadent" style which questioned the essence and nature of the work itself, exerted its influence on young cultures, where national objectives combined with an openness to influences from the centres of European culture.

Literary Decadence was one of the varied discourses of decay of the late 19th century, outlining in different ways the presumably inevitable decaying stage of Western civilization. These discourses addressed in like manner the threats of modern technology, theories on the spiritual and physical degeneration of the human race, and the metaphysical pessimism of fashionable philosophers. Literary Decadence, on the other hand, proceeded from the world which had been presented by Naturalism, in which all things ended in repugnance, dissolution, illness and death, or dying alive.[3] Both nature and man were represented as processes of disintegration and decay. In Decadence, that which was beautiful and continued to thrive found its place in the shadow of death.[4]

Emile Zola, the leading figure of Naturalism, was also a leader in depicting decay, taking as his themes all possible forms of decadence in the social, genetic, moral, erotic, and spiritual domains. In his works, however, decadence is generally bound to the conventions of a realistic mode of representation. The discourse most characteristic of Decadence differs from naturalistic depictions of decay by its shift into fantasy and internalisation. In prose, the narrator observing from the outside now gave way to representations of the principal character's narcissistic self-reflection and imagination. J. K. Huysmans' novel *A rebours* (1884), which became the Bible of Decadence, demonstrated this transition and served as a compilation of the characteristics of Decadence. This was also associated with a difference in the depiction of characters. In Decadent prose the protagonists (civilised male intellectuals) reflect on their own state of decadence, choosing transgression, pleasure and decay, while in Naturalism environmental and genetic determination made tragic victims out of the principal characters (usually common people or women).

In literary Decadence depictions of decay were combined with its romanticisation and its transfer from the everyday world to the exotic or mythical realms of fantasy. In this sense, Decadence is also Symbolism, or rather its negative reverse face, where the ecstasy of beauty is contorted into sickness, grotesque visions or representations of perversion and transgression. The model for Decadent poetry was set by Charles Baudelaire's "La charogne" which realises the "aesthetic of the carcass" by making things ugly and repugnant aesthetic: " ... and the sky viewed the handsome carcass on the ground / like a bud unfolding". On the other hand, Decadent characters are aroused and excited more by images of sado-masochistic violence than by visions opening on to the ethereal.

There is a provocative aspect to aestheticising the evil and the ugly. *Épater le bourgeois*, the tendency to shake and overturn prevailing values is an aspect of Decadence – a strategy which has remained important in modern art. On the other hand, the provocative nature of Decadence is often associated with resignation – it is resigned to inevitable decay rather than seeking to change the world. Weakness, fatigue and illness, of which the decadent era and its people suffer in the visions of Decadence, can only lead to destruction. The beauty produced by them in art and literature is the overripe fruit of an overly refined neurotic culture worshipping nuance and form. It is the rotten core of the fruit that the Decadents themselves are masochistically digging out.

In the Nordic countries the idea of an overly refined, neurotic culture of decay and a decadent style reflecting it was represented not only in the cult works of Decadence but also in *Essais de psychologie contemporaine* (1883) by the fashionable writer Paul Bourget. In this work the degeneration of Western civilization is seen as the disintegration of the social organism caused by modern individualism. Modern people observe and enjoy the nuances of their own souls; they are no longer involved in nation building. They are neurotic and weak, while also incapable of creating any new kind of beauty.[5] Since decay is inevitable in any case, it is to be made into a virtue. The refinement of an overripe civilisation and the visions of beauty engendered by it may be the products of illness, but they are also the apex of modern civilisation.

In Finland, Decadence did not appear in any markedly programmatic form or in distinct schools, but its themes and style were present in literature at the beginning of the 20th century. Naturalism had already presented "decadent" characters: seducers, aesthetes, tramps and dilettantes. These types lived on in prose ascribed to Neo-romanticism or Symbolism.[6] In a country of two official languages such as Finland, Decadence was also bilingual. In literature written in Swedish in Finland Decadence tended towards cosmopolitan themes and presented itself in terms of ennui and melancholy rather than as a flood of mythical images of degeneration, while Decadence expressed in Finnish, especially in its early stages, cloaked itself in Symbolist allegory and sometimes appeared as Dionysian passion or diabolic fantasies, manic rather than depressive. But here, too, it was possible for the extremes to meet.

The present article focusses on Decadence in literature written in the Finnish language and on its four different variations. One of the most important works in this vein is *Antinous* (1903) by Volter Kilpi, in which the themes of illness and fatigue together with an aestheticism alien to life are staged in the decline of Ancient Rome. The other extreme is represented by the Dionysian decadence of Joel Lehtonen's early works, where the Finnish wilderness symbolises barbarian forces of destruction. Instead of resignation and withdrawal, this work proclaims abandoning oneself to life, wild pleasures and a reckless spending of vital forces – all done at the risk of melancholy, madness and disease. Moreover, an interesting feature of Decadence in Finnish is the fact that decadent eroticism, one of the main themes of French Decadence, is primarily represented by a woman author, *Mirdja* (1908). Here, the femme fatale figure originally corresponding to male fears and dreams is seen from a woman's point of view, with a radical transition of perspective. Other important themes of Decadence are equally prominent, but owing to the female perspective, are also partly problematised in *Mirdja*. Finnish Decadence is also associated with breaking down the idealised image of the common people as a symbol of the nation which was created by nationalist ideology in the 19th century to serve its own needs. In view of the approved image of Finnishness, the representation of the common people in a decadent and degenerate light, which had partly been made topical by contemporary political events and social unrest, marked a major collapse of illusions (among intellectuals).

Mortifying Aestheticism

Des Esseintes, the hero of Huysman's *A rebours* personifies the prototype of the Decadent aesthete. The main characteristics of this prototype are the tendency to create an aesthetically perfect environment solely for personal use, a quest for aesthetic pleasure instead of creative artistic work, and the separation of the aesthetic from the ethical.[7] *Antinous*, the most important depiction of Decadent aestheticism in Finnish literature, meets all these requirements, but represents a world totally different to Huysmans. Its author, the young Volter Kilpi (1874–1939), had already given offence with his debut novel *Bathseba* (1900), in which the Bible story of King David and Bathsheba was rewritten as a modern love story.[8] Despite the disapproval of conservative critics, he received a positive response among young writers.

Antinous remained completely misunderstood by Finnish-speaking critics (Finnish-Swedish critics were better able to place it in its European context). One reason for this was that it corresponded to Decadent ideals in structure and style in its fragmentary nature, its emphasis on detail at the expense of plot, and its representation of an internal rather than external world. It was also a "learned" work, i.e. based on cultural intertexts rather than on observation of the experiential world (realistic mimesis).[9] The unenthusiastic attitude of cultural circles in Finland towards Decadent experiments in style and aestheticism silenced Kilpi, who did not publish any other literary works until the 1930s, when he produced unique and unprecedented Modernist novels, which subsequently assured him an undisputed position in Finnish literature.

Kilpi's *Antinous* presents the eponymous character as an observer reacting to all things around him solely as an aesthete. The external framework is all that remains of the character's historical model. In Decadent literature, Antinous, a favourite of Hadrian, an emperor of the declining Roman Empire, makes fleeting appearances as a paradigmatic aesthetic and homoerotic ideal, while Kilpi mainly creates "a beautiful soul" out of him. Kilpi's book records Antinous' aesthetic experiences and his desire to merge into a vision of the world as a passive "world eye" (the *Weltauge* inspired by the aesthetic of Arthur Schopenhauer).[10] Landscapes as well as living beings within his horizons are turned into works of art to be admired, as contemplation is Antinous' only contact with the outside world. In the aesthetic vision, the outside world becomes part of the viewer's solipsistic self-reflection. The prominent Narcissus theme in the work demonstrates the nature of the aesthetic attitude as eschewing human interaction.[11] The Decadent aesthetic is the self-sufficient pleasure of an individual focussing on himself, which erodes the basis of communal life and morals alike.

Kilpi himself discussed this problem also in his writings on art,[12] noting the detriment of art and the aesthetic experience understood in Schopenhauer's terms to communal life, while still valuing art and internal experience above communal interaction. In *Antinous*, an aesthetic disorder results in the death of the protagonist, but the novel is above all a depiction of his enraptured aesthetic experiences. They are associated with restlessness about the transience of aesthetic merging and a premonition of the dark undercurrents of the self which threaten the peace of contemplation, but not with any concern for social interaction. For Antinous, other people exist only as objects of aesthetic experience. Voluntary death is his solution to his fear of life beyond the aesthetic sphere. According to Schopenhauer, death is the only certain cure for the suffering of life.

The only scene in Kilpi's novel where Antinous is faced with the challenge posed by another person is his encounter with a strange woman reclining on a tiger skin. Her open sexuality and gaze – a gaze that questions Antinous' monopoly on viewing – require both action and interaction. Antinous, however, for whom the woman is the incomprehensible Other, the Sphinx, whose mystery man cannot solve, chooses to flee.

The implicit homoeroticism linked to the figure of Antinous presents itself in Kilpi's novel only as the fear of life and the alienation from reality of an aesthetic narcissist. Real contacts are tempting yet impossible: for this Antinous, even Hadrian would have been abhorrent.

The woman on the tiger skin finds a parallel in the great sphinx which Antinous later meets. The most tangible connection between Kilpi's Antinous and the character's historical model is the fact that the novel occurs in the same places as the historical events themselves. From Bithynia, the town where he was born, Antinous moved to Athens, from there to Rome and finally to Egypt. For Kilpi, Egypt is the land of infinity and death and the scene of a "recognition" often repeated in the works of Decadence: (some) truth about life or himself is revealed to the protagonist. The scene is usually a variant of seeing oneself as described in the myth of Narcissus. In some works the mirror image is literal, while in others the reflection is represented by a double, a woman figure or a work of art. Kilpi's Antinous looks upon his life in the stone sphinx which seals his fate. The sphinx symbolises the harshness and sweetness of life which are inevitably intertwined. The aesthetic will ultimately only cloak suffering. Only death will remain an open possibility for the aesthete who cannot bear the suffering of life.

In keeping with Decadent narrational style, the pathology of Antinous recounted in Kilpi's work remains ambivalent. A focus on the internal world of the principal character largely obviates an external perspective or the narrator's voice that would place the subject of depiction in a certain valuing frame of reference. As is the case in Decadent literature in general, Kilpi's *Antinous* also provokes the reader, although it does not bring on to the scene the elements violence, sexual perversion or sacrilege typical of Decadence. For example, the homosexuality of the protagonist's historical model, often a provocative element in Decadence, remains solely on an implicit level. On the other hand, the novel contains a number of hints aimed at the knowledgeable reader. Allusions to Decadent themes are frequent: the enjoyment of violence and mass hysteria caused by it in the Colosseum of Rome, a brief description of a Roman orgy, and the presence of a seductive woman figure who is branded a predator. European Decadence is the context within which Kilpi writes, but he leaves it without further explication.

The Femme Fatale

Decadence deconstructed the pure, female ideal of Romanticism and Symbolism, in which woman was made into an Ideal, a mirror image of the man's ideal self and/or a symbol of a world of transcendental ideas. Decadence found its idols in femmes fatales, beautiful and mortifying at the same time, at once seducing and killing. Huysmans created one of the main prototypes of this character by analysing Gustave Moreau's Salomé paintings.[13] It was in these works that the principal character saw his dreams come true. As a seductive body, Salomé is able to break down the will and energy of a man. For des Esseintes, she was "the symbolic deity of unending pleasure, the goddess of undying Hysteria". Her transgressive beauty makes her the sacrilegious Madonna of Decadence appearing at the same time as an animal and as the Beast of Revelations foreboding destruction (*A rebours*, 144–145). Salomé is a creation of Decadence, but is also its symbol. Her name is, however, legion in the literature and art of Decadence: she is Eve and Lilith, Cleopatra, Mary Magdalene or Judith; she is characterized by the terms siren, vampire, mermaid, sphinx, and described as a feline beast, serpent or – in the Finnish context – a bottomless bog.

The femme fatale was threatening on the one hand, and the dream of the weak Decadent man on the other. The threat was to the spirituality of man: the attraction that women held for men was based only on the lower instincts which had survived in him – the animal in man. Intellect and reason were men's own capital of which woman could not partake and which she also sought to destroy in man.[14] The dream was linked to male masochism: the activity of the monster beauty of masculine overtones was sadistic, but this was enjoyable for the masochist, the creator of the fantasies.[15] The femme fatale was also associated with the dream of transgression. "The demon of perversion" worshipped by the Decadent leads one to see the possibility of the most tempting transgressions in the femme fatale. Emile Zola (in his novels *Nana* and *La Curée*) already associated this figure with prostitution and incest, underlining its specific nature of destroying all order and morality. While corrupting others, it was also the product of a more common corruption and degeneration. In Zola's description of femmes fatales, moralisation was linked to a masked allure which, in Decadence, turns into worship.

In Finnish literature the personifications of the femme fatale are as varied as in European Decadence, albeit often described in more alluding terms, for what was permitted in France would have been stopped by censorship in Finland. On the other hand, the biblical and Greco-Roman mythological or historical women figures also popular in Finnish Decadence were accompanied by certain figures from national mythology, which were then turned into incarnations of the femme fatale. Even in Finnish literature predatory seductresses were often made to function as metaphysical signs. In Baudelaire's poems, the cruel muse and loved one are also cruel life and cruel beauty which the artist masochistically worships. In Kilpi's *Antinous*, the stone sphinx, the image of the duality of life, which the leading character encounters in Egypt has the duality of the femme fatale. Yet the consciousness which reflects life and defines woman as both woman and symbol is exclusively a male consciousness.

The central role of an important woman writer in the context of Decadence is an exceptional feature of Finnish literature. With her novel *Mirdja* (1908), Onerva Lehtinen, who wrote under the pseudonym L. Onerva, generated attention and censure among the Finnish women's movement, which took a negative position on sexuality. Onerva's novel describes the urban life of the modern intelligentsia and the world of Decadent artists, and in this respect it is even exceptional in Decadence in the Finnish language. Most Finnish Decadent texts are located in far-off worlds, often of a purely mythical nature, or in an agrarian environment. Decadence situated in an agrarian or even wilderness milieu reflects the strange blend produced by the encounter of European currents and Finnish culture. The mixing of a society still in a highly pre-modern state and older Finnish literature depicting the countryside and the peasantry in an idealised light with an urban French mould reflecting completely different cultural values was a challenge to Finnish writers, and responses to this challenge produced strange hybrids.

In *Mirdja*, however, urban Decadence comes to the fore and Helsinki is given the role of an environment conducive to decadence in the manner of Paris or St. Petersburg (metropolises considered symbols of decadent life in Finland). As if by way of assurance also Paris becomes one of the scenes of events alongside Helsinki.[16] *Mirdja* is above all a novel depicting a woman as its principal character, in which possible roles for women are tested and in which the femme fatale is made into an acting and thinking subject. In the text of a woman writer, the femme fatale created by men, who is alluring and destructive, and is ultimately destroyed herself as the victim of male violence (or the sadistic imagination of a male writer), turns into a discussion on the conditions of being a woman and the deconstruction of a feminine narcissism seen from a male perspective. The eponymous Mirdja takes on the role of a femme fatale, because in a way it is the only role the society of men can offer a woman who desires freedom and the pleasures of life. At the same time, however, it is a problematic role and a dangerous one for the woman herself.

Mirdja carries on and transforms the narcissism central to Decadence, the worship of oneself and the quest for mirror images. Decadent narcissism, which drives men to seek their spiritual mirror image in woman or the world, was associated in a different way with women, who were thought to mirror their own bodies.[17] Mirdja, too, admires her own beauty, while yearning for a man to admire her. The objective is to exist for the male gaze, the admiration of others, which would also reinforce self-admiration. In *Mirdja*, man becomes the mirror of a female Narcissus, but in such a way that male admiration confirms the woman's self-image.

Mirdja emphasises the fact that women's self-admiration is produced in a male-defined culture. In concrete terms, a man engenders Mirdja's self-admiration in the plot of the novel. Mirdja has a decadent friend and "teacher", whose role in the novel is to fuel Mirdja's narcissistic tendencies and her role as femme fatale. The alcoholized master who has cast away his own abilities as an artist operates in the same way as Dorian's "patrons" who lead him on the path of decadence in *The Portrait of Dorian Gray* by Oscar Wilde.[18] Mirdja is also influenced by her mentor's decadent philosophy and Nietzschean worship of individuality (in its Decadent form). She seeks to be superhuman and a femme fatale in the same person. Both objectives fan her delusions of omnipotence, but in this manner she in fact combines in herself the male identity typical of Decadence and the role it offers women.

In *Mirdja*, the problem of the superhuman and the femme fatale is combined with a kind of performative identity game. In her relationships with men, Mirdja tests various roles belonging to the repertoire of models offered to women. At the same time, the reader is introduced to the alternatives available to women at the time. For example, Mirdja experiments with life as a "clinging vine" wrapping herself around a man seeking security and adapting to his will.[19] She enjoys her subordination and is intoxicated by the "fervour of feminine weakness", until the spell is broken and the man in question then appears in a banal, petit-bourgeois light for her. Mirdja carries on her experiments. She plays the role of a self-sacrificing nurse trying to arouse an incorrigible decadent to a new life. She is a sphinx to a man seeking the woman of all the clichés prevalent at the turn of the century: "you are complex, inexplicable, entangled in your own nets, contradictory, unnatural, rare, perhaps insane and criminal, and so you drive people mad with your wonderful dissonance..."[20] Finally, she offers an artist decadent eroticism at a distance,[21] in which he is allowed to look but not touch and which has the flavour of sadism. In all her relationships, Mirdja's thirst for power is emphasised; even as a nurse she is a destructive siren. She is unable to love, because she understands love to mean surrendering to someone stronger than her, and she is stronger than all the men she meets.[22]

Furthermore, the problem of being an artist is important in *Mirdja*. The Decadent idea that in the degeneration stage of culture even artists will only be dilettantes imitating the great masters gains an added tone in Onerva's novel from the then current concept that women as such were understood only to be creatures adept at imitation. Though not creative, a woman could be imitatively gifted.[23] It was therefore thought that only the performing arts were suited to women, and that as an actress or singer they could even be superior to men, but not as writers, composers or visual artists.

Bourget regarded dilettantism to be one of the characteristics of art and an attitude to life in a period of degeneration. He regarded it as the genius of intelligent and sensual free spirit, eschewing any kind of commitment and understanding all points of view.[24] In *Mirdja*, however, the dilettante remains quite an ambivalent figure, although Bourget's concept of the dilettante is part of the intertextual context of the novel. It is not easy for Mirdja to confess to being a dilettante. The distinction between genius and dilettante, the constructor of one's own self and the collector of mosaic sherds is maintained. However, Mirdja ultimately remains a dilettante making art only of her own life. In the context of Decadence, the decadent "new" woman, seeking to free herself from traditional women's roles as mother, wife and muse, becomes the victim of unresolved contradictions. At the end of the novel, Mirdja wanders about on a bog looking for her non-existent child. Here, the "child" can be understood as meaning any suitable goal in life or breaking out of the vicious circle of narcissism.

Dionysian Decadence

> And we want to be decadent, if everyone else flaunts their good health (Joel Lehtonen, *Mataleena*.)

In Finnish literature Decadence also took on a demonic or Dionysian form, in which resignation, weakness or refinement was replaced by defiance and destructive power. It inherited its demon hero from Romanticism. A demonic man with features borrowed from Satan in Milton's *Paradise Lost* was an important figure in the gallery of characters employed by Romanticism.[25] This type, known as the Byronian hero, undergoes a metamorphosis in Decadence and is mixed with the Nietzschean "superman". Even the demonic modern self in Goethe's Faust, with Mephistopheles, the devil himself, acting as his (Faust's) shadow and the perpetrator of his desires, carries on its life in the literature of the fin-de-siècle. On the other hand, Faust as a modern Prometheus came to be reassessed in the light of decadence and pessimism. Idealistic heroism degenerated, while sensuality and the power of instinct, which included greatness in crime and perversion, gained ground. The Don Juan figure, which focussed on boundless yearning in Romanticism, returned as an aesthete and Epicurean who had cast off his idealism.

For the Decadent man and male fantasy, the demonic man represents lost, archaic strength (and the reversal of masochistic fantasy into the sadistic). The demonic man is the yearned "strong man", a combination of spontaneous action, strong will and passion, which was thought to be a more genuine or authentic alternative to degenerate modern man. In Nietzsche's writings the ideal of authenticity is posed against the degradation and decadence of the modern. The Don Juan character of contemporary literature, with influences from Søren Kierkegaard, also approaches the Dionysian of Nietzsche: in literature, Don Juanism was combined with a Dionysian ideal. The devil and the demonic man represent a primal force and Schopenhauerian world will, and the tragic as analysed by Nietzsche. However, as opposed to Romanticism, the demonic hero of Decadence is always accompanied by the demon woman, the femme fatale.

Dionysian Decadence is the opposite of the aestheticism alien to life depicted in Kilpi's *Antinous*, in which the protagonist withdraws from life and the community of men to assume the role of the onlooker, for whom the only relationship with the world is an aesthetic one. Antinous is, however, also a narcissist seeking himself and a merging with the world, albeit only through contemplation. His only active deed is to drown himself in the Nile, and that too is described as an uncomplicated stepping into the embrace of death. Antinous is melancholy, but he lacks the manic face of melancholia, seeking fervent action. In Dionysian Decadence, on the contrary, passion and fury drive the principal characters to drown their melancholy in demonic action.

Dionysian Decadence presents a life in a world, of which the weak and tired Decadent, representing the other tendency, can only yearningly dream: a life in the chaos of barbaric power and orgiastic pleasure. Is this then still Decadence? Nietzsche at least sought to make the power springing from the Dionysian serve the affirmation of life as an antithesis to Schopenhauer's denial of life, and to achieve a liberation from decadence caused by weakness. In Decadence, the Dionysian aspect, as an instinct (transgressively) breaking down all order and boundaries, is in the service of destruction. Its affirmation of life passes through the destruction of all things old, and what is in fact affirmed is the principle of continuous movement and thus of continuous destruction. Nor are the demonic heroes true barbarians. They are simultaneously fervently active and fatigued, and their activities lack an objective and are without joy. Everything comes down to the idle actions of a melancholic and the raging of a madman. In the pessimistic atmosphere of decay and awaited destruction, the Dionysian only appeared as "creative" in a negative sense. There was an emphasis on manic destruction which failed to ask whether anything new would replace that which was destroyed.

The core of Decadent Dionysianism was in a sense crystallised in the poem "Alamäkeen" (Downhill) written in 1905 by the Finnish lyric poet Otto Manninen, a representative of Finnish Symbolism. The only consolation or pleasure of this world is free downhill movement, regardless of where it leads:

/../
Yks on riemu, muit' en tunne,
muitten murrunnan mi lientää,
liekin, myrskyn riemu: rientää,
kuolonkorska, sama kunne
/../
[A sole pleasure there is, others I know not,
That soothes the blows of others,
The flame, the raging of the storm: rushes on,
Throes of death, no matter where]

Dionysian Decadence did not present any visions of the future; there was merely the desire to escape everything that was old. The melancholy undercurrent denying the value of everything was distinct: since all things that exist are worthless to the melancholic, their only passion is to destroy everything. The depressed Decadent is even incapable of doing this, but the demonic Decadent capable of manic action will set out on the path of transgressions and gain pleasure from destruction.

The main works of Finnish Dionysian Decadence were written by Joel Lehtonen (1881–1934). Born in the outlying regions of Finland, Lehtonen experienced in his own life an immense gap between urban culture and the life of the common people in the countryside, which presented itself as primitive. He adopted Nietzscheanism, took new lyric prose as his model (particularly admiring the style of Volter Kilpi), but also sought influences from Selma Lagerlöf and Russian literature, especially Maxim Gorky's tales combining Romanticism with grotesque Naturalism. Through his early works, even Lehtonen failed to generate any great enthusiasm in a country which eschewed Naturalism, and he did not achieve the position of a respected and important writer until later, when he published works representing a new kind of realism, in which grotesque and decadent features were overlaid by a seemingly realistic and humoristic surface and in which aestheticism was channelled into depictions of everyday life.

Joel Lehtonen's novel *Mataleena* (1905) describes a poet's journey back to his roots, and is thus an allegory of a Decadent artist discovering his identity. The narrator is looking for his lost mother in a remote part of Finland. He finds her, a one-eyed human wreck, insane and wracked by a strange nervous disorder. This former beauty is condemned by her village community as a whore and the mother of illegitimate children. The poet-narrator, however, is not shocked by this grotesque figure but identifies with his mother, defiantly recognising in her his own fate, in which a blessing is mixed with a curse. His mother is the sinful Mary Magdalene (the mother's name Mataleena is a popular variant of Magdalene) and the holy Madonna of Decadence. The poet presents himself as the last of his kin, the most beautiful bloom of an accursed heritage. In him, the madness of the family has produced an artist. The artist is the "flower of the wilderness", drawing its strength from the mire of decadence to produce the new beauty desired by the modern era.

The artist's muse leaves the pale Ideals of Symbolism in her wake. In his visions the artist sees a wild, eroticised mother figure complementary to his actual mother. This female figure, known as the Wonder of the Forest, is nature and sexuality personified. The feeding mother, the woman desired and the destructive predator all come together in her. She flirts with swollen breasts, her nipples "shining bright red like the flowers of the maiden pink"; her hair is compared to the leaves of a birchtree, and her green eyes flash full of love and hate like the eyes of "a she-wolf in heat". She seduces the narrator, but is also said to have nursed him when he was a child.

The Wonder of the Forest is an emblem of Lehtonen's wilderness Decadence complemented by a manifesto of Dionysian Decadence placed at the end of the novel. In a vision, the narrator sees his whole mad family together with Satan, the patron saint of Decadence, and the Wonder of the Forest. The "feast of the insane" is celebrated under the mark of Bacchus and Eros; the poet praises the blessings of drink while the provocatively sexual presence of the Wonder of the Forest inspires the celebrants of the feast. The "song of the madmen" follows, in which the ancestors declare themselves to be decadent and entrust their descendants to follow the path marked out by them. This proclamation lists, one after another, all the transgressions which those who proudly identify themselves as decadent wish to commit: madness, immorality or the bypassing of morals, destruction instead of or taking precedence over constructive activity, disruption instead of preservation, joining the ranks of "criminals, harlots, thieves and prisoners" against society, proud and conceited individuality, self-indulgence and aestheticism, dilettantism, unbridled sexuality and paganism. Decadence was now the passion of transgression, a wild desire to cast oneself beyond the pale of all norms.

The theme of madness and illness, in which an inherited curse together with the negative effects of the environment leads to the ruin of the characters was already familiar from Naturalism, and Huysmans's *A rebours* also relies on this pattern. In Lehtonen's novel, the life of the narrator's mother follows this course of degeneration. A distinctive factor characteristic of Decadence is the active narrator-protagonist consciously adopting his genetic heritage as the guiding principle of his life. Madness and death are the price of a life worth living, the precondition of freedom for the artist. Being an artist also becomes a lifestyle rather than creative work. It includes a life of self-indulgence indifferent to morals and reckless extravagance.

The question of dilettantism associated with the Decadent artist also manifests itself in Lehtonen's writings. The narrator of *Mataleena* is clearly a creative artist, although for him, too, the artist's lifestyle is an integral part of his identity. In Lehtonen's other Decadent texts, however, the protagonists are only "artists of their own lives". The characters have artistic aims but no longer any creativity. Like other Decadents, they are thus weak and tired and incapable of creating works of art, but still full of transgressive energy in their personal lives. In pleasure and extravagance they neglect work inasmuch as they have work; they resort to fraud and crime, even defying death. The most important thing is ultimately to enjoy life to the very end, come when it may.

In the Decadent lifestyle, art loses all its sanctity, the aura of genius and chosenness given to it be Romanticism. Anyone can become an artist of his own life. In order words, we are here approaching the idea of man as a narcissistic maker of his own life, following his own desires and fantasies. "Post-modern" man was born in Decadence only to be reborn at the end of the 20th century.

Through Huysmans and Baudelaire, Decadence appeared as a challenge to all bourgeois values in which provoking the reader, moral scandal and making the reader an "accomplice" were given an important role. This questioning of all values in the Nietzschean sense was the emblem of Lehtonen's Decadence, and his works represent Finnish Decadence in its most provocative state. In Finland, however, the women's rights movement was, for example, more provoked by the Decadent female image represented by L. Onerva and Christian censure focussed on the modernisation of a Bible story in Kilpi's *Batsheba* rather than on Lehtonen's paganism. In the case of Lehtonen, the provocation was partly bypassed, because he appeared to be depicting the wild inhabitants of the Finnish wilderness and their descendants, and did not bring decadence to the halls and vestibules of the intelligentsia. At the same time the common people themselves generated a provocation which aroused the educated classes in a way that the literary and partly artificial provocations of Decadence had not been able to do. Social unrest, in which the working class began to demonstrate and wield its mass power, appeared as the real harbinger of decay and annihilation.

The Degeneracy of the Common People

The ideology of Decadence did not leave much room for nationalist sentiment. According to Paul Bourget, the Decadents were poor nation builders and only good at creating their own internalisations: "Although decadent citizens contribute poorly to building the greatness of the nation, are they not superior as the artists of the internal state of their souls? If lacking adeptness in private or public affairs, they are perhaps too skilled in private thought." (Bourget 1883/1895, 27.) Decadence signifies an emphasis on individualism and a cosmopolitan dilettantism, in which a life based on tradition and national values is no longer of any importance to the individual; only one's own desires and pleasures will dictate what a Decadent will set out to do. In Finland, this attitude ran counter to all the tendencies that Finnishness, existing under foreign rule and struggling for its national identity, had developed during the 19th century. It also had a specific role to play in undermining the image of the common people which began in the early 20th century.

During the National-Romantic period in the 19th century and especially in countries which had just begun to construct their national identity, such as Finland, nationalist ideological groups created idealised images of their own people to serve their own needs. In Finland, the patriotic pioneering farmer became the ideal, whose intellectual abilities were evinced by the rich folk poetry collected in the Finnish countryside during the 19th century and who were assumed to be loyal supporters of the nationalist objectives of the intelligentsia. The educated classes were to carry on their struggle in the domains of Finnish culture and the Finnish language to serve such a hard-working and respectable common people. Around the turn of the century, however, it became increasingly difficult to maintain such an idealised image of the common people. The autonomous social unrest of the "people" aroused the Finnish intelligentsia in 1905, when the political strike movement aimed against Russian rule also brought to the fore the differing interests of the working class and the intelligentsia. Even before that, Finnish literature began to reflect pan-European fears associated with the assumed decadence and degeneracy of the lower classes. As a literary current, Decadence led writers who had been brought up in the nationalist spirit to an internal conflict: the adoption of Decadence could not be combined with a nationalist commitment.

Decadence itself contains conflicting elements; the admirers of a degenerate life adopted aristocratic attitudes while admitting to their own wretchedness. Bourgeois life and popular phenomena were particularly despised: refined Decadence was kept apart from the utilitarian culture of the bourgeois public, which was branded as non-culture. On the other hand, the rising working class was seen as a potential new horde of barbarians threatening to deal a mortal blow to all civilisation. Whether this new barbarism was to be welcomed as a new, healthy phenomenon, or whether Decadent heroism is the last glimmer of civilisation, remained undecided in most situations. In any case, the Decadents presented themselves as great individuals, while suffering from the loss of their nationalist mission. In the National-Romantic conception, the artist was a leading figure of his people, while in Decadence he was at worst only the hero of his own life. There was nonetheless a tendency to hold on to heroism. In Finland, the spread of Nietzscheanism in particular led to an opposition between individualistic heroes and the "masses".[26]

The contradiction between nationalist objectives and individualistic ideologies questioning their worth preoccupied many of the leading figures of Finnish culture around the turn of the century. For Eino Leino (1878–1926), who had been raised in the spirit of national idealism and who sought the status of national poet, the contradiction became a personal problem reflected in many ways in his works. In the 1890s Leino adopted Symbolism and produced the first Symbolist texts in Finnish literature. In the manner of W. B. Yeats, he combined the national with the international by making Finnish folk poetry and mythology the sources of his symbols. However, in his early Symbolist plays, based on the Kalevala epic, the themes of decadence and reflections of contemporary discourse on decadence are conspicuous, even though the play distances the representation of degeneration into a mythical world. Leino's play *Sota valosta* (The War over Light) from 1900[27] is a depiction of the degeneracy of the common people and the relations between the people and the educated classes who lead them. This play makes distinct reference to its time of writing, although it appears to represent the disintegration of ancient Finnish society and its subjugation under foreign rule. The play also reveals contemporary Nietzschean impulses in dealing with the problems of the individual and the artist, themes which were important in Decadence, as well as the themes of fatigue and the depletion of vitality.

In Leino's play the people, spellbound by false promises, betray their leaders (the Kalevala heroes Väinämöinen, Ilmarinen and Lemminkäinen) after first suspecting them of similar treason. The people turn out to be fickle and of short memory, and they threaten to kill the heroes, who represent ideological, artistic and political leadership. They retreat before Väinämöinen who is bearing a sword of flames when he summons the people to war for light, but they are not inspired by a campaign whose only prize is "light" that is virtue, civilisation, the ideological happiness of the people. One cannot live on light; the people want material benefits. Väinämöinen in turn presents his own ideal of the superman and his contempt for the masses. Despite his pessimism and fatigue, he and the other heroes are nevertheless ready to fight, but the gap between the people and the heroes fighting on their behalf opens wide and the people turn their backs on their heroes. The play takes the side of the heroes – these superhuman figures are the bearing force of civilisation, while the people in their unreliability and gullibility are ready to further their own demise.

At the very turn of the century, the heroic era and the heroic people still existed as a dream or as the themes of patriotic poems written for special occasions. Perhaps it was this dream which made reality even more unbearable by fuelling the melancholia of the Decadents. Despite their melancholy, Nietzschean heroes seek to raise the people, but Leino's play paints quite a hopeless picture of both the aims of the people and the power of the heroes. The play, however, was only a prelude to the change which took place in the image of the people in Finnish literature. This change is generally dated to the period following the strike movement of 1905, and is particularly associated with the rise of the radical socialist workers' movement. The clashes which took place during the strike at least provided confirmation for the pessimistic views that had been adopted. From then on, it became justifiable to see the common people as a primitive horde of predators.

Leino also presented his most unbridled criticism of the people after 1905, particularly in his novels, in which the mythical landscape of his Symbolist plays was replaced by more contemporary settings. In 1907 he wrote an account of skirmishes between the civil guards and the red guards founded by the workers. In this work, a young woman who had moved to the city from the countryside and had joined the red side becomes a symbol of the whole corrupt nation. Raging in the skirmishes, she is described as a "Whore of Babylon". She represents the whole nation, now viewed as brutal and barbaric: "Was it not the spirit of the nation herself, dancing there, raw, red, wild, rejoicing in her release, trampling underfoot the forms, customs and moral laws of civilised society?" (*Kootut teokset* IX, 422). This depiction draws upon Decadent imagery continually present in Leino's oeuvre from the late 19th century onwards, albeit often symbolistically distanced. Now there is no distance and this reference to current affairs makes the novel a clear statement, in part promoting the deepening class divisions within Finnish society. Writers now began to take positions which led some of them into the joint right-wing front in the Finnish Civil War of 1918 between the socialist workers and the pro-independence political bourgeoisie. By that time, the aestheticism of Decadence and its provocations against bourgeois values had been left far behind.

Translated by Jüri Kokkonen

NOTES

1   For example Jean le Rond d'Alembert, *Mélanges de littérature, d'histoire et de philosophie*. Amsterdam 1767. Tome 1, 325.
2   The term *Decadence* has been used in different ways in research on literature. As the name of a literary current it meant, in its narrowest sense, a school that formed around Paul Verlaine in the 1880s, which published the short-lived journal "Le Décadent". At least outside France the term has gained an established usage in referring to a current that was influential in the late 19th and early 20th century and spread throughout Europe. Its starting points and course were marked by leading French masters, such as the poets Charles Baudelaire and Paul Verlaine, and

especially J. K. Huysmans with his novel *A rebours*. The present article seeks to define and characterise this broader trend primarily from the perspective of Finnish literature.

3   In *Naturalist Fiction. The Entropic Vision* (1990) David Baguley speaks of the entropic vision of naturalism. See also Riikka Rossi's article "Finnish Naturalisms" in the present anthology.

4   According to Wolfdietrich Rasch Decadence was specifically characterised by already recognising decay and death in florescence and full bloom of things: "Es gehört zur Inneren Verfassung der Décadence, zwanghaft im blühenden Leben den Verfall zu sehen." (Rasch 1986, 45.)

5   Bourget 1883/1895, 25–27.

6   In histories of Finnish literature and research on the fin-de-siècle, Decadence was almost completely bypassed. It is only in Rafael Koskimies's *Der nordische Dekadent* (1968) that Finnish Decadence of the 1910s is discussed. In my own study *Narkissos ja sfinksi* (1997), upon which this article is based, Decadence, however, proves to be an important feature of literature previously seen in the light of Neo-romanticism or Symbolism from 1900 at the latest, and the Decadence of the 1910s can primarily be seen as an echo of this earlier Decadence. This naturally calls for an acknowledgement of the fact that Decadence and Symbolism are partly intertwined, as for example in Baudelaire's poems.

7   In Théophile Gautier's novel *Mademoiselle de Maupin* (1835), ranked as one of the models of Decadence, an aesthetic of this kind extending beyond morality was already presented in provocative terms.

8   Although *Bathseba* was by no means as provocative in content as Oscar Wilde's *Salome*, which was banned in Britain for rewriting the events of the Bible, Kilpi's work provoked negative reactions specifically for "vilifying" the Bible.

9   The Decadent style was originally outlined by Désiré Nisard's work *Étude de moeurs et de critique sur les poètes latins de la décadence* from 1834, with an extensive discussion on "decadent" Roman authors, whose style was paralleled with that of 19th-century French writers. Nisard's ideas influenced e.g. Huysmans. According to Nisard, depiction predominated in Decadent style and the text was learned, i.e. based on references to earlier texts: research and literature are also used as an aid, which signifies precision and richness of details. According to Huysmans, Decadence replaces classical greyness with "tones" and "colour". His own style is in keeping with the ideal: the novel is full of learned depictions and it has hardly any plot. An important technique is also ekphrasism, the depiction of painting, the most impressive example being the detailed depiction of Moreau's Salomé paintings, which recorded the ideology of Decadence. In his *Essais de psychologie contemporaine*, Bourget, too, presents a description of Decadent style, which is known to have influenced for example Nietzsche. It underlines fragmentation and details at the cost of the whole.

10 Kilpi takes as his basis Schopenhauer's aesthetic, in which both subject and object liberate themselves from the bounds and norms of the everyday world to raise to universal status. In Kilpi's *Antinous* there is essentially an aesthetic subject of this kind, and hardly anything else. Moreover, Antinous is practically the only character in Kilpi's novel – even Hadrian is erased.

11 In the tradition of interpreting the story of Narcissus, this aspect is also significant. See Vinge, 182–183.

12 *Ihmisestä ja elämästä* 1902.

13 An important contribution is also provided by Baudelaire's prose poem "Double Room". This work juxtaposes a dreamed spiritual reality, an eternity dominated by a mystical yet sensuous Idol, mistress of dreams, with a mundane fallen world, governed by the demon of Time. The ideal presents itself in the light of eroticism; there is a shift from the heaven of Ideas to a sensuous earthly paradise and Decadent eroticism. The later Decadents eagerly took up Baudelaire's Decadent eroticism, in which sensual exoticism merges with sado-masochism and male fantasies of perversion. The Idol of Perversion is the new goddess and muse to which Decadence makes its obeisances.

14   Bram Dijkstra (1986, 210–234) thoroughly analyses these models of thought associated with Woman.
15   On the role of masochism in the culture of the turn of the century in general, see Stewart 1998.
16   In Finnish Naturalism, Helsinki as a locus of degeneracy is already present in earlier works, for example in Juhani Aho's novella *Helsinkiin* (1889), in which a young student's journey to Helsinki is also a voyage into ever deeper degeneracy.
17   Dijkstra, 144–146.
18   Another comparison could be Bourget's novel *Le disciple*.
19   See Dijkstra, 227–234.
20   L. Onerva, *Valitut teokset*, 74.
21   The intertext is Bourget's short story "The Flirting Club", telling of a gentlemen's club of this kind, and apparently certain works by the Swedish Decadent author Ola Hansson.
22   See also Viola Čapková "The Priestess of Desire. Decadent Woman's Dissonant Love Stories" in the present anthology.
23   For example, Cesare Lombroso's ideas along these lines in *La Donna delinquente* were well known in their day. See also Dijkstra, 120–123.
24   Bourget, 58–65.
25   See Praz, 57–59.
26   This was an international tendency in literature: see Carey 1992.
27   Leino: *Kootut teokset* V, 233–374.

BIBLIOGRAPHY

ADAMS, JAMES ELI 1995 *Dandies and Desert Saints. Styles of Victorian Manhood*. Ithaca and London: Cornell University Press.
AHLUND, CLAES 1994 *Medusas huvud. Dekadensens tematik i svensk sekelskiftesprosa*. Acta Universitatis Upsaliensis: Historia litterarum 18. Uppsala: Almqvist & Wiksell.
ANDERSEN, PER THOMAS 1992 *Dekadanse i nordisk litteratur 1880–1900*. Oslo: Aschehoug.
BAGULEY, DAVID 1990 *Naturalist Fiction. The Entropic Vision*. Cambridge: Cambridge University Press.
BAUDELAIRE, CHARLES 1855–1868/1972. *Le Spleen de Paris. Petits poèmes en prose*. Paris: Le Livre de poche.
BAUDELAIRE, CHARLES 1857–1861/1972 *Les Fleurs du mal*. Paris: Le livre de poche.
BORIE, JEAN 1981 *Mythologies de l'hérédité au XIXe siècle*. Paris: Galilée.
BORIE, JEAN 1991 *Huysmans. Le Diable, le célibataire et Dieu*. Paris: Bernard Grasset.
BOURGET, PAUL 1892 *Cosmopolis*. Paris: Alphonse Lemerre.
BOURGET, PAUL 1891 *Le Disciple*. Paris: Alphonse Lemerre.
BOURGET, PAUL 1883/1895 *Essais de psychologie contemporaine* Paris: Alphonse Lemerre.
CAREY, JOHN 1992 *The Intellectuals and the Masses. Pride and Prejudice among the Literary Intelligentsia 1880–1939*. London & Boston: Faber and Faber.
CARTER, A.E. 1958 *The Idea of Decadence in French Literature 1830–1900*. Toronto: University of Toronto Press.
CHAMBERS, ROSS 1987 *Mélancolie et opposition. Les débuts du modernisme en France*. Paris: José Corti.
DIJKSTRA, BRAM 1986 *Idols of Perversity. Fantasies of Feminine Evil in Fin-de-Siècle Culture*. New York & Oxford: Oxford University Press.
FISCHER, JENS MALTE 1977 "Dekadenz und Entartung – Max Nordau als Kritiker des Fin de Siècle", in *Fin de Siècle. Zu Literatur und Kunst der Jahrhundertwende*. Ed. by. Roger Bauer et alia. Frankfurt am Main: Vittorio Klostermann. 93–111

FOSTER, JOHN BURT JR. 1981 *Heirs to Dionysus. A Nietzschean Current in Literary Modernism*. Princeton University Press. Princeton.
FRITZ, HORST 1977 "Die Dämonisierung des Erotischen in der Literatur des Fin de Siècle", in *Fin de Siècle. Zu Literatur und Kunst der Jahrhundertwende*. Ed. by Roger Bauer et alia. Frankfurt am Main: Vittorio Klostermann. 442–464
GAUTIER, THÉOPHILE 1835/1994 *Mademoiselle de Maupin*. Paris: Le Livre de poche.
HOLLAND, EUGENE 1986 "On Narcissism from Baudelaire to Sartre: Ego-Psychology and Literary History", in *Narcissim and the Text. Studies in Literature and the Psychology of Self*. Ed. by Lynne Layton ja Barbara Ann Shapiro. New York & London: New York University Press. 149–169
HUYSMANS, J.-K. 1884/1977 *A rebours*. Paris: Gallimard.
JAY, MARTIN 1993 *Downcast Eyes. The Denigration of Vision in Twentieth-Century French Thought*. Berkeley, Los Angeles, London: University of California Press.
KIERKEGAARD, SOREN 1843/1987 *Either/Or*. Ed. and transl. by Howard V. Hong ja Edna H. Hong. Princeton, New Jersey: Princeton University Press.
KILPI, VOLTER 1900 *Bathseba. Davidin puheluja itsensä kanssa*. Helsinki: Otava.
KILPI, VOLTER 1902 *Parsifal*. Helsinki: Otava.
KILPI, VOLTER 1902 *Ihmisestä ja elämästä. Kirjoitelmia*. Helsinki: Otava.
KILPI, VOLTER 1903 *Antinous*. Helsinki: Otava.
KLIBANSKY, RAYMOND, PANOFSKY, ERWIN JA SAXL, FRITZ 1964 *Saturn and Melancholy. Studies in the History of Natural Philosophy, Religion, and Art*. New York: Basic Books.
KOSKIMIES, RAFAEL 1968 *Der Nordische Dekadent. Eine vergleichende Literaturstudie*. Helsinki: Suomalainen tiedeakatemia.
LEHTONEN, JOEL 1904 *Paholaisen viulu*. Porvoo: WSOY.
LEHTONEN, JOEL 1905 *Villi. Kuvitteluja*. Hämeenlinna: Arvi A. Karisto.
LEHTONEN, JOEL 1905 *Mataleena*. Helsinki: Otava.
LEINO, EINO 1931 *Kootut teokset*. Helsinki: Otava.
LLOYD, CHRISTOPHER 1990 *J-K. Huysmans and the Fin-de-siècle Novel*. Edinburgh: Edinburgh University Press.
LOMBROSO, C. & FERRERO, G. 1894 *Das Weib als Verbrecherin und Prostituirte*. Transl. by H. Kurela. Hamburg: A.-G.
LYYTIKÄINEN, PIRJO 1996a "Symbolismi ja dekadenssi", in *Katsomuksen ihanuus*. Ed. by Pirjo Lyytikäinen, Jyrki Kalliokoski ja Mervi Kantokorpi. Helsinki: SKS. 7–16
LYYTIKÄINEN, PIRJO 1996b "'Minun sydämeni oma kuva'. Volter Kilven Bathseba ja moderni minuus", in *Katsomuksen ihanuus*. Ed. by Pirjo Lyytikäinen, Jyrki Kalliokoski ja Mervi Kantokorpi. Helsinki: SKS. 40–64
LYYTIKÄINEN, PIRJO 1997 *Narkissos ja sfinksi*. Helsinki: SKS.
LYYTIKÄINEN, PIRJO (ed.) 1998 *Dekadenssi*. Helsinki: SKS.
MANNINEN, OTTO 1905 *Säkeitä I*. Porvoo: WSOY.
MAUGUE, ANNELISE 1987 *L'identité masculine en crise au tournant du siècle 1871–1914*. Paris & Marseille: Rivages.
MORT, FRANK 1987 *Dangerous Sexualities. Medico-Moral Politics in England since 1830*. London 6 New York: Routledge & Kegan, Paul.
MOSSE, GEORGE L. 1994 "Masculinity and the Decadence", in *Sexual Knowledge, Sexual Science. The History of Attitudes to Sexuality*. Ed. by Roy Porter ja Mikulás Teich. Cambridge: Cambridge University Press.
NIETZSCHE, FRIEDRICH 1980 *Sämtliche Werke. Kritische Studienausgabe in 15 Bänden*. Ed. by Giorgio Colli und Mazzino Montinari. München und Berlin: Deutscher Taschenbuch, de Gruyter.
NORDAU, MAX 1893 *Entartung. I–II*. Berlin: Carl Dunder.
ONERVA, L. 1908 *Mirdja*. Helsinki: Otava
PARENTE-ČAPKOVÁ, VIOLA 1998 "Decadent New Woman?Ó *NORA* 1, vol. 6.
PICK, DANIEL 1989 *Faces of Degeneration. A European Disorder, c. 1848 – c.1918*. Cambridge: Cambridge University Press.

PRAZ, MARIO 1933/1970 *The Romantic Agony*. Transl. by Angus Davidson. London & New York: Oxford University Press.
RASCH, WOLFDIETRICH 1986 *Die literarische Décadence um 1900*. München: C.H. Beck.
ROJOLA, LEA 1992 "Oman sielunsa hullu morsian. Mirdjan matka taiteen maailmassa", in *Pakeneva keskipiste*. Ed. by. Tarja-Liisa Hypén. Turun yliopisto, Taiteen tutkimuksen laitos A 26. 49-73
ROJOLA, LEA 1993 "Moderni elämä ja maskuliinisuuden kriisi", in *Nykyajan kynnyksellä*. Ed. by Minna Toikka. Turun yliopisto, Taiteen tutkimuksen laitos. 157–181
SARAJAS, ANNAMARI 1961 *Elämän meri. Tutkielmia uusromantiikan kirjallisista aatteista*. Helsinki: WSOY.
SARAJAS, ANNAMARI 1962 *Viimeiset romantikot. Kirjallisuuden aatteiden vaihtelua 1880-luvun jälkeen*. Helsinki: WSOY.
SARAJAS-KORTE, SALME 1966 *Suomen varhaissymbolismi ja sen lähteet. Tutkielmia Suomen maalaustaiteesta 1891–1895*. Helsinki: Otava.
SARAJAS-KORTE, SALME 1977/78 "Magnus Enckell ja kahlittu Prometheus". *Ateneum*-museojulkaisu.
SARAJAS-KORTE, SALME 1996 "Axel Gallénin joutsensymboliikasta", in *Akseli Gallen-Kallela. Ateneum 16.2.–26.5.1996/ Turun taidemuseo 26.6.–1.9.1996*. Helsinki: Ateneum. 48–59
SCHOPENHAUER, ARTHUR 1859/1988 *Die Welt als Wille und Vorstellung I–II*. Zürich: Haffmans Verlag.
SPACKMAN, BARBARA 1989 *Decadent Genealogies. The Rhetoric of Sickness from Baudelaire to D'Annunzio*. Ithaca & London: Cornell University Press.
STAROBINSKI, JEAN 1989 *La mélancolie au miroir. Trois lectures de Baudelaire*. Paris: Julliard.
STURGIS, MATTHEW 1995 *Passionate Attitudes. The English Decadence of the 1890s*. London: Macmillan.
SUOMI, VILHO 1952 *Nuori Volter Kilpi. Vuosisadan vaihteen romantikko*. Helsinki: Otava.
TARKKA, PEKKA 1977 *Putkinotkon tausta. Joel Lehtosen henkilöt 1901–1923*. Helsinki: Otava.
TARKIAINEN, VILJO 1954 *Eino Leinon runoudesta. Tutkielmia*. Helsinki: Otava.
THORNTON, LAWRENCE 1984 *Unbodied Hope. Narcissism and the Modern Novel*. Lewisburg: Bucknell University Press.
VINGE, LOUISE 1967 *The Narcissus Theme in Western European Literature up to the Early 19th Century*. Lund: Gleerups.
WHISSEN, THOMAS REED 1989 *The Devil's Advocates. Decadence in Modern Literature*. New York, West port, London: Greenwood Press.
WILDE, OSCAR 1948 *Complete Works*. London and Glasgow: Collins.
WIKANDER, ULLA 1994 "Sekelskiftet 1900. Konstruktion av en nygammal kvinnlighet", in *Det evigt kvinnliga. En historia om förändring*. Ed. by Ulla Wikander. Tidens förlag. 7–27
WIORA, WALTER 1977 "'Die Kultur kann sterben'. Reflexionen zwischen 1880 und 1914", in *Fin de Siècle. Zu Literatur und Kunst der Jahrhundertwende*. Ed. by Roger Bauer et alia. Frankfurt am Main: Vittorio Klostermann. 50–72
VIRTALA, IRENE 1994 *Narkissos i inre exil. En studie i begärets paradoxer i L. Onervas roman Mirdja*. Acta Universitatis Stockholmiensis; Studia Fennica Stockhomiensia 4. Stockholm: Almqvist & Wiksell.
ZWEIG, PAUL 1968 *The Heresy of Self-Love. A Study of Subversive Individualism*. New York & London: Basic Books.
ZOLA, ÉMILE 1880/1903 *Nana*. Paris: Eugène Fascelle.
ZOLA, ÉMILE 1872/1984 *La Curée*. Paris: Le Livre de poche.

RIIKKA ROSSI

Finnish Naturalisms
Entropy in Finnish Naturalism

Introduction

In the history of Finnish literature the 1880s and 1890s are known as the period of Realism. A critical attitude to society and a striving towards change were prominent concerns within it.[1] Naturalism, on the contrary, has not been recognised in Finnish literature, or it has been regarded as an auxiliary current of Realism.[2] Only few researchers have given a role to Naturalism in the literature of the "period of Realism".[3]

One reason for the rejection of Naturalism has been that it is conceived as an extreme phenomenon of documentation and scientific research as well as a garish depiction of ugliness and immorality, while Realism is understood to be more cautious and ethical. In the present article, however, I propose a new conception of Finnish Naturalism by "deconstructing" certain points of the traditional conception, such as the scientific nature and "ugliness" of Naturalism. I will also discuss the Finnish Naturalism at the close of the 19th century as a genre of its own. In my study a fruitful theoretical framework for the new conception of Naturalism is provided by David Baguley's work *Naturalist fiction. Entropic vision* (1990). I formulate my concept of genre according to the view of types of literature presented by Alastair Fowler in his *Kinds of Literature* (1982).[4]

I shall first study the background of research on Realism and the cultural context of the period. I shall then analyse Naturalist works using the concept of entropy, and on the other hand, I will present a genre model constructed on the basis of these works: I view late 19th century Finnish literature in terms of three distinct forms of Naturalism, displaying dynamic, tragic and static entropy. For my analysis I have selected the works which are of most interest for my reading.[5]

The vision of entropy

The interest of late 19th-century Finnish writers in French and Nordic Naturalism has been acknowledged by research and reviews ever since their works appeared. Ideas and inspiration were sought from abroad.

For example, Juhani Aho, Teuvo Pakkala and K. A. Tavaststjerna spent time in Paris studying Naturalism. The works of Émile Zola and Henrik Ibsen were discussed in the Finnish press, and the writings of Norwegian Naturalists, such as Alexander Kielland and Jonas Lie, were translated into Finnish. Nationalist-minded critics, however, sought to deny the existence of Naturalism in the works of Finnish authors. In the 19th century the pro-Finnish *fennoman* movement[6] sought to reinforce the national identity of Finland, at that time an autonomous Grand Duchy of the Russian Empire. *Fennoman* ideology especially subscribed to the ideals of the unadulterated purity and virtue of the nation, and the movement called for literature to support its aims. Accordingly, literature was expected to depict Finnishness in positive terms. Degenerate literature such as Naturalism was not accepted.[7]

Paris, a hotbed of eroticism and a city of dangerous liberties, enjoyed great popularity among these writers. Juhani Aho was criticised for drawing impulses for his novel *Yksin* (Alone, 1890) from "the sewers of Paris". Critics felt that Naturalism was a dangerous European contagion, which should not strike root in the soil of the "young" and "healthy" Finnish nation.[8] It was feared that Naturalism would upset the equilibrium of society. "For the most part, literature appears to mean the corruption of readers by mixing concepts and exciting passions with its lewd depictions," were the comments of the cultural journal *Valvoja* in an article on the problem of prostitution.[9] The fear of the polluting influence of Naturalist literature shows the fragility of the young nation and its social order. Even for the optimists, who believed in the future of the nation, the threat of disintegration was evident.

On the other hand, the fear of collapse and destruction was reflected in the comments of the Naturalist writers themselves: "From where does that disintegration come that prevails in cultural life, that state of illness in which all mankind is suffering?" asked the author Minna Canth in a letter.[10] Teuvo Pakkala, in turn, saw the problem as one of a lack of strength and of self-immersion and lamented: "Everywhere one comes across slackness, coldness and pessimism."[11] "The world is full of evil," Juhani dramatised his opinion of society.[12] The idea of man and the community balancing on the brink of disintegration was also present among European thinkers. For example in Hippolyte Taine's theories, a balanced, normal person was mainly presented as an exceptional case. Equilibrium meant victory over forces threatening the mind, such as insanity, illness and primitive impulses. Taine compared the mind of man to a slave that must survive in a circus arena full of bloodthirsty wild beasts.[13]

This vision of cultural disintegration offers an interesting viewpoint on literary texts too. Research has associated the concept of entropy, disintegration, with Naturalist works: an entropic process leading to destruction and decay is played out in the world of these works.[14] Borrowed from the natural sciences but metaphorically understood in literary research, entropy essentially means disintegration, increased disorder in a system, and the decaying of matter and energy. The idea of entropy is associated with the dynamics of balance and imbalance which had already been discussed by Zola in his theory of Naturalism, particularly in his treatise *Le Roman experimental* (1880). Zola regarded society as a circular organism similar to the human body, in which damage to one organ would make the whole body of society ill and upset the balance of the community.[15] According to Michel Serres, Zola's *Les Rougon-Macquart* series of novels is organised as a circular system in imitation of the principles of thermodynamics. Zola's texts manifest the poetics of entropy: movement between entropy and balance, between ever faster disintegration and static order.[16]

A genre model which I have developed to describe late 19th-century literature in Finland, presents the variations of entropy appearing in Naturalist literature. The model consists of three modes of decay: dynamic, tragic and static entropy. These entropies are not mutually exclusive but can also describe different aspects of one individual work. They will also mix in chronological terms. The order of presentation – dynamic, tragic and static – does not signify any historical order of appearance.[17] The purpose of my genre types is thus to characterise the features of Naturalist literature and not to classify works in fixed categories.

By using this scheme of different entropies I outline the family resemblances between works. Of interest here are the relationships of the individual works with the thematics of the genre. How do individual motifs contribute to constructing the entropic vision characteristic of the genre? How do texts transform, vary, parody or challenge the themes of the genre and discuss the poetics of disintegration? The family resemblances shared within the genre serve as a means of communication – for writers this genre is the repertoire of variations and for readers a code of interpretation. The genre has a historical dimension, for the phenomena articulated within it can be understood in relation to other cultural discourses of the period. When making up a Naturalist family of texts, however, it is the literary works themselves which are of most importance.

Dynamic entropy

In dynamic entropy emphasis is placed on the character's own degenerate and immoral activity, which furthers the process of destruction. The works of Kauppis-Heikki[18] (1862–1920) are good examples of dynamic entropy. Originally a farmhand and later a schoolteacher, Kauppis-Heikki depicted a rural milieu, but he did not paint a flattering picture of the peasantry. The eponymous protagonist of his novel *Laara* (1893) is a poor cottager's daughter of unscrupulous nature. During a famine she leaves her home with the intention of marrying a rich man. Laara marries an old widower, but at the same time enters into relationships with the farmhand of the property and the neighbouring farmer. Children are born in and out of wedlock. Her sexuality helps Laara to become a rich farm owner. With her deceitful acts she spreads suffering throughout her environment: the men with whom she is involved always have to pay for it.

The principal character in Ina Lange's (1846–1930) novel *"Sämre folk". En Berättelse* ("Rabble". A Story) from 1885 is a destructive seductress along the lines of Laara. Ina Lange, a woman author, who wrote in Swedish and published her works under male pseudonyms, came from a completely different cultural background to Kauppis-Heikki, but what the works of both have in common is that they depict the decadence of the common people. The principal character of *"Sämre folk"* is propelled by her "low nature". Raised in a poor home in Helsinki, Nadja becomes a chorus girl in Helsinki who seduces upper-class men. She goes on to become a "wildcat" who casts her spell on men in St. Petersburg. She finally ends up as a bar singer in Moscow. While seducing men and leading them to ruin, Nadja functions as the dynamo in processes of destruction taking place in the novel.

Dynamic entropy underlines the biological nature of disintegration, destructive drives and instincts. A central motif in it is stressing the catastrophic influence of the female body, a theme already familiar from the literature of Antiquity. The mythical femme fatale interested contemporary physiologists and physicians, whose theories of hysteria, prostitution and heredity inspired the Naturalists. In *Laara* and *"Sämre folk"* the female body is the starting point of the entropic process. The principal characters of both works use their bodies in order to rise in society, but the body also becomes a factor threatening the order of the community. Jealousy among Laara's men leads to a knifing scandal in the village. Nadja, the Finnish "Nana", in turn poisons the upper class with her body. Threatening public scandal, she extorts money from her lover, an officer in Helsinki, and in St. Petersburg her affair results in wrecking a bourgeois marriage.

Characteristic of dynamic entropy are the quick peripetias of the plot, such as sexual fall leading from innocence to decadence. The rhythm of the narrative is marked by the protagonist´s fall into misfortune, a momentary raising of hopes and a new fall. Nadja's career in the theatre ends in catastrophe when she comes on stage drunk, but this is set right by a new life in Russia. Laara, on the other hand, is almost killed in the middle of the novel when she is knifed by mistake. Patrick O'Donovan, who has studied Goncourt's novels, notes that the body as the focus of the texts is reflected in the narrative structure of the works.[19] This is what David Baguley points out, too. In the texts, which he assigns to the Goncourtian type, the plot is given rhythm by a series of falls, either as sexual falls in concrete terms or metaphorical "falls" into misfortune.[20]

Finnish nationalism in the 19th century took the Finnish peasant as its ideal, a person who was supposed to be a pure and unspoilt child of nature. The educated classes wanted to see their ideal of the common people as humble, hard-working, God-fearing and loyal to the national intelligentsia. But in Naturalist works, the dynamic entropy of the forces of decay break down these national ideals of the 19th century.[21] Among the common people depicted by Kauppis-Heikki, drunkenness, premarital sex and adultery predominate, and the marriages presented in his works are transactions for the purpose of financial gain. Kauppis-Heikki's

Kirottua työtä (Accursed Labour) from 1891, in particular, reveals the fragility of nationalist ideals with its criticism of the ideology of popular education and literacy. In this book, a farmer teaches his daughter Anna-Liisa to read and write. She soon begins to correspond with a hired hand of the farm, which results in an affair. She becomes pregnant and gives birth to a child out of wedlock. Her fall ultimately leads to the ruin of the whole family. The "accursed work" of the novel was literacy leading to promiscuity and unwanted pregnancy. –"That work was accursed, and may it be so, "[22] ranted her father in anger.

The common people of dynamic entropy are represented as a homogenous mass driven by shared biological instincts. Even though a story may be told via an individual, its commonplace nature is also often alluded to. Anna Liisa of *Kirottua työtä* is not the only fallen one in her village, but the danger of sexuality is always present in her community. At the beginning of *Kirottua työtä*, the farmer sacks foul-mouthed hired hands trying to lure girls to the hay barn. "Girls, in want of men, flirting where even boys are to be found, and the boys doing likewise," says a matchmaker, expert in marital transactions, while telling of his own son, whose daughter was conceived before the wedding.[23] People driven by instinct react to each other like chemical substances. In *"Sämre folk"* a young student cannot resist the attraction of Nadja and her "southern" and "warm-blooded" nature. His will is powerless against his lower instincts.[24] This mechanistic aspect of decadence had already expressed in the theories of Naturalism. In his breakthrough novel *Thérèse Raquin* (1869), Zola wanted to create "soulless" people whose actions are dictated by their blood and instincts. The adultery which took place between Thérèse and Laurent was like a chemical reaction – they hardly spoke to each other before making love for the first time.

The "soullessness" of decadence is also underscored by comparing man to an inhuman machine. The young student is fascinated by Nadja's "magnetic" and "electrifying" nature.[25] On the other hand society as a whole can be represented as a mechanism with a chain of disintegration taking place. An example is Minna Canth's *Köyhää kansaa. Kuvaus työväen elämästä* (Poor Folk. A Description of Workers' Lives) from 1886, a depiction of the urban working class. This novel contains intertextual connections with Zola's *Germinal*. Canth was the leading Finnish woman author of the period and the only woman Naturalist to write in the Finnish language. *Köyhää kansaa* is a typical work in the oeuvre of Canth, who gained her reputation by her depictions of women's tragic fates; it describes the gradual descent into insanity of Mari, the mother of a working-class family. Even though the work describes Mari's tragedy, the community of the poor is like a machine producing destruction. In walking the streets, Mari meets a woman whose distress is even greater than hers, and at the end of the novel Mari is committed to an asylum only to take the place of an inmate who has just died. The decadence in Canth's work progresses in a circular manner, adopting Zola's idea of society as an organism, in which the decay of one part will ultimately destroy the rest. After Mari descends into madness, the symptoms of mental disintegration pass on to her daughter and husband: the daughter suffers from phobias and the husband tries to avoid losing his sanity by sleeping.

The narrative structures used in dynamic entropy emphasise its "mechanical" entropy. External focalisation dominates the narrative, thus avoiding a depiction of the internal processes of the individual. "Her own small child died from lack from care in the house of a 'child-loving madame' in Punavuori," is all that is said in "*Sämre folk*" of Nadja's illegitimate child – what Nadja thinks of all this is not told.[26] Likewise, Kauppis-Heikki's characters are sketched in sparse terms, as if they were only half-persons. *Kirottua työtä* does not give Anna Liisa's appearance in concrete terms, not even her face. In fiction a character generally has a structuring element to it; the objects and events of fiction exist in one way or another because of the character.[27] However, things are partly different in dynamic entropy, where the most important thing is to present the process of degeneration, which "uses" the character in order to be realised. The decay emphasised in the narrative is complemented by accurate descriptions of ugliness, for example Nadja's unclean, cockroach-ridden stepfather in "*Sämre folk*" or the stinking, filthy asylum cell at the end of *Köyhää kansaa*.

Despite their pessimistic world view, Naturalistic works often contain in masked form the conventions of romantic and idyllic literature. Kauppis-Heikki, for example, employs the repertoire of the folk tale in *Kirottua työtä*. Anna Liisa is the ideal woman of the fairy-tale, the beautiful, only daughter of the rich "king". The father-king has to wield his whip to fend off suitors, coming from near and far, from entering Anna Liisa's room in the night like the princes climbing into the princess's tower. Then Anna Liisa rejects the role of the passive princess, runs away from home to a dance, begins to correspond with the hired hand of the farm and becomes pregnant. Instead of a prince and half the kingdom, Anna Liisa is given a drunkard of a husband who leads the farm to ruin. The story turns the fairy tale upside down: in this manner Naturalism takes the form of an antigenre to romantic literature, deconstructing the values of romantic literature.[28] The world of idyllic literature can, however, live on in the beliefs of the characters – in Laara's fantasy the world beyond her immediate home region is a fairy-tale land of happiness. Yet in the reality of the novel it proves to be a community dominated by envy, greed and the pursuit of personal gain, and Laara herself is an integral part of the corruption of this world.

A different caricature of romantic love is presented in Minna Canth's 1887 novel *Salakari* (Pitfall), describing a bourgeois housewife committing adultery. Her adultery lacks all the noble and heroic qualities attached to it as a motif of romantic literature, such as the idea of lovers as kindred spirits or descriptions of the illicit act as an exciting and fascinating adventure. The location of the act, a counter-topos of the *locus amoenus*, is a dark, cold, wintry forest by an ice-covered lake, with the cold, frozen ground as the lovers' bed. The consequences of the act are disastrous. As if to punish the adulterous mother of the novel, her son dies, and before long she too loses her life.

Antigenres are often thought to parody, mock and ridicule the noble values of the opposite genre.[29] The reversal of the conventions of idyllic and romantic literature in dynamic entropy does not, however, produce a comic effect, but rather demonstrates the decay and suffering of man and society. The conventions of fairy-tale are only used to demonstrate the entropic nature of the world: in the reality of Naturalism, the world of romantic and idyllic literature cannot survive and its dreams are an empty illusion. The conventions of fairy-tale thus do not seek to mock its idyll or to bring down the lofty as in parody[30], but are used to criticise the world of the Naturalist work itself. Accordingly, the idyllic genre serves rather as the means of bringing down the lowly. The rabble, already miserable and poor, is cast further into misfortune, and the foundations of life, already rotten and shaky, collapse. In *"Sämre folk"* Nadja and the student reminisce about playing princes and princesses as children. Nadja's fantasies of a "royal kingdom" come to an ironic end. She makes her way to the Russia of the tsars, where the opulence of the Kremlin palaces can be seen from outside, but her own realm proves to be a dark, smoke-filled bar, inhabited by a rabble in Moscow. In this kingdom the last will not be the first, as promised in the Gospel, but as noted by the narrator of *"Sämre folk"*: "He who has a great deal will receive more, and those who want will lose what little they have".[31]

Tragic entropy

In dynamic entropy, the characters themselves contribute to the process of destruction. But there are also characters in Naturalism who seek to anticipate and prevent possible ruin and decay through their own acts. Such characters are Elsa in Teuvo Pakkala's (1862–1925) novel *Elsa*, and Junnu, the principal character of Juhani Aho's (1861–1921) *Maailman murjoma* (The Outcast) from 1894. Pakkala was a teacher of French and Finnish who is particularly known for his short stories about children. Like most of Pakkala's works *Elsa* is set in his home town, a port in the north of Finland. In *Maailman murjoma*, Aho – like his friend Kauppis-Heikki – describes the Eastern-Finnish countryside. Accorded the status of national author, Aho was professionally active as a journalist and involved in the *Fennoman* movement.[32]

These works by Pakkala and Aho offer an interesting perspective on the connections between Naturalism and tragedy. In late 19th-century Finland, tragedy was already a well-known literary genre. Shakespeare's plays were translated into Finnish and performed at the Finnish Theatre in Helsinki, and Aeschylus and Sophocles, among other classics, were translated into Finnish too. In terms of genre theory, the relationships of tragedy and Naturalism can be described by using Alastair Fowler's concept of mode. In Fowler's theory, modes are linked with some themes and motifs typical of kinds, and they always have an incomplete repertoire, a mere selection of the corresponding kind's features, from which overall external structure is absent.[33] Likewise, although Naturalist works cannot be called tragedies, they can be linked to some key themes of tragedy.

Tragic entropy plays out the peripetia of tragedy. Peripetia, which can be regarded as the core of tragedy, means that a person with good intentions ultimately "scores" negative results. This kind of peripetia plays an essential role in Aho's *Maailman murjoma* and Pakkala's *Elsa*. The protagonists seek to do what is good and right, but they are ultimately drawn into doing bad and evil things and ultimately into ruin. Junnu in *Maailman murjoma* is an orphaned farmhand who is mocked and harassed by those around him, but despite this mockery he seeks to show consideration for his fellow man, even those who torment him. He is conciliatory and appeasing, and finally moves away to live in the wilderness. Elsa, in turn, is an angelic girl, hard-working, virtuous and God-fearing. She goes to religious meetings and tries to keep on the straight and narrow in all that she does, to avoid sin and follow the Christian commandments. At the beginning of Pakkala's novel Elsa's mother meets a dying man who predicts that things will go badly for Elsa. The prediction of "Teiresias" is borne out: Elsa is seduced, gives birth to an illegitimate child and, despised by her community, finally dies. The upper-class father of the child survives untarnished, marries respectably and even serves as an official in the auction in which his son by Elsa is sold into service. Junnu is also doomed. He loses his home because of a railway line built into the wilderness and becomes a violent, deranged avenger, who tries to derail a train on the new line and dies as a result of his own act of vengeance.[34]

What is typical of tragedy is that life has actually ended before death, with the loss of both dreams and self. Elsa and Junnu experience a death of this kind. At her hour of death, Elsa, a fallen woman, is an outcast from her community and the object of its derision. She no longer has any hope of happiness in love. Junnu is also dispossessed of everything. His landlord sold Junnu's croft and its fields to the state, which tears down the house that Junnu built with his own hands. A railway engine has killed his cow, and the other hired hand of the farm has almost tortured Junnu's horse to death. People have teased and betrayed him. By the end of his life, Junnu has actually lost his reason as well – he wanders in the forest seeing invisible spirits.

At the end of *Maailman murjoma*, Junnu is walking through the forest into the wilderness. For a moment, he forgets his plan of revenge and asks:

> What has he done to make people so merciless to him, and for the world to mistreat him so? Did he not always try to serve it, and to be conciliatory with those against whom he may have transgressed? Did he not always leave them in peace and run away from them? Did he not step aside to let them drive by? Why did they chase him away even from there? (Aho 1894/1951:327).

Junnu hopes that the truth will come out. What merciless fate is it that drives him to ruin? Junnu tries in many ways to understand the senseless mystery of fate. For example, he thinks of his mother, a fallen woman who – like Junnu – was mocked by others and jailed. Elsa also ponders the reasons for the conflict between her acts and her fate. She feels that she "had not transgressed against anyone, no one at all", but had come to ruin. In tragic entropy, of paramount interest is the question of anagnorisis – "recognition" associated with tragedy.[35] In *Poetics* Aristotle defines anagnorisis as the dawning of the truth – as the recognition of a person, event or state of affairs.[36] At the moment of his ultimate doom, the hero of a tragedy nevertheless becomes aware of the factors that contributed to his fate. Regardless of his doom, the hero becomes aware of his own humanity and life, and achieves a whole identity.[37]

For Elsa and Junnu, however, it proves difficult to comprehend the reasons for their ruin, because all reality appears to be working against them. Not only poor and oppressed by society, they also encounter the meanness and mockery of other people, in particular the people of their own class – Junnu's worst tormentor is a farmhand like him. "A cat will not torture a mouse like people torment each other," ponders Elsa.[38] Even God is of no avail. In his zeal, a clergyman preaching to Elsa about sin and fornication appears like a representative of the devil. Through their anagnoristic questions, no truth dawns, rather everything becomes more blurred rather than clarified. Junnu loses his sense of reality. He begins to have visions and imagines that the trolls of the forest are throwing stones at his cabin. Elsa falls ill, withers and dies. Roland Barthes has pointed out that in Naturalism the healing effect of anagnorisis often remains unrealised. According to him, Zola's Nana, for instance, operates only as a means, a destructive mechanism. The characters lack the power of understanding, which they have in classical tragedy.[39] In moving to modern drama, anagnorisis changes character: the characters gradually cease to know who they are, or what is truth, reality, right or wrong.[40] In tragic entropy, anagnorisis dissolves into non-identification and the loss of self – the disintegration of identity instead of becoming whole.

However, some researchers have questioned the existence of tragedy in the 19th century. George Steiner, for example, suggested that the 19th century marked the death of tragedy. According to Steiner, modern ideologies appealed to the perfection of man and believed in the possibility of social progress. With the introduction of a modern and scientific world view the mythical conceptions of the world view of tragedy, such as the revenge of the gods, could no longer be cited as the reason for human misfortune.[41] One of the prime conditions of tragedy was that the universe is not completely rational, but contains uncontrolled forces which make people commit senseless acts.

The scientific world view attendant to Naturalism, however, was not very modern or scientific in the present sense of these terms. Nature was seen to be the domain of spiritual and vital forces. An article in the Finnish cultural journal *Valvoja* in 1885 noted that in the "chaos of atoms, each of the atoms, unbeknowns to one another, only follows its own nature, developing its internal force".[42] Moreover, many scientific theories sought to reinforce existing cultural preconceptions and beliefs, as demonstrated for example by Cesare Lombroso's claim that all women were prostitutes in primitive cultures, and woman was therefore in danger of falling into atavistic regression, her original state.[43] Hereditary degeneration, of which Naturalism gained reputation, can also be seen as a variant of old myths. The inheritance of the forms of degeneration resembles a motif found in Greek tragedy and the Old Testament: curses cast on families and the depiction of a vengeful God who makes posterity pay for the sins of the forefathers.[44] Even Zola noted in his theory of Naturalism that many phenomena in the world remain to be unknown and that scientific observation of the outside world always includes interpretation and assumptions.[45] In his experimental novel, Zola did not primarily put emphasis on the original cause of things, but on how different phenomena were associated with each other. According to Zola, the novelist's task was to establish the "comment des choses" while the "pourquoi des choses" – the reason for things – was the task of philosophers.[46]

More importantly, the tendency to explain reality in rational terms was not evident in the depictions of literature. The motif of the railway in *Maailman murjoma* serves as an example. In the story of Junnu, the author Juhani Aho was inspired by Zola's novel *La Bête humaine* (1890), in which a train is given human and animal traits. For Junnu, the train is a magical phenomenon, drawing him "irresistibly to the track".[47] The train is identified with Junnu's human tormentors and it appears personified in his dreams, "tearing the roof off his cabin and pressing him face down on the ground".[48] The train sets in motion Junnu's final collapse. The "shining, taunting, meanly hissing locomotive" launches a reaction of fear in Junnu and he loses his mind.

> He felt as if he were being ambushed by invisible spirits of hatred, watching him from the woods, reaching out to grab him by the feet, whistling and hissing around him. (Aho 1894/1951:329)

The features of the train are spread into the surroundings. All of a sudden, the environment contains living spirits and uncontrolled organic energies. Man is no longer superior to the reality that he encounters, a viewer in possession of phenomena. The depiction of tragic entropy shows that Naturalism is not restricted solely to the minute documentation of everyday reality that is observed with the senses. Christophe den Tandt, who has studied American Naturalism notes that Naturalistic writing "exceeds" the strategies of the Realistic representation of everyday reality. There are unobservable levels in the world. Reality is not the totality of Lukácsian Realism[49], a "knowable community", a familiar and delimited entity the factors of which can be known and understood.[50]

The uncontrollable forces depicted in *Maailman murjoma* are present not only in the train and the forest peopled by Junnu's imagined spirits but also in Junnu himself. He suffers from violent fits in which he loses his sense of reality. Like Jacques Lantier, the principal character of Zola's *La Bête humaine*, Junnu is also a human beast combining the traits of a human being and an animal of instinct. The motif of the human beast is also brought forth in Lange's "*Sämre folk*", in the character of a deranged man who murders his brother. Like Junnu, he is a large ugly man. Junnu is described as a lanky, swarthy man of deformed proportions.

Maailman murjoma begins with a scene in which Junnu tries to kill his tormentor by throwing a large rock at him. When committing this act, Junnu loses his sense of reality, "the world turns red and yellow", and the contours of the earth and the forest are blurred. Only after setting out into the wilderness, he realises that he almost killed a man, and is shocked. His actions are not conscious, premeditated or evil. Instead, he becomes aware of himself only afterwards. The characters in Naturalistic writing often have a strong feeling of an all-powering second self which disappears at times, but will time to time return to disturb normal activities.[51] Junnu has to struggle with himself in his fits. After being irritated by people, Junnu usually grabs "some object his own size", throwing it away "to calm his spirit" as if ridding himself of his double.[52] The theme of the second self, the double, appears in the novel in that Junnu is associated with a tragic avenging figure in Finnish mythology, Kullervo of the *Kalevala*.[53] Junnu's actions are thus steered by a mythical self, an inherited avenger role, "Kullervo" forcing himself into the events of the novel. The "heritage" of Kullervo in the guise of Junnu manifests itself, however, only as defiance and a desire for vengeance and not in the form of heroism. Kullervo kills his enemies, succeeding in his revenge and fulfilling the role of the hero, while Junnu only manages to destroy himself.

Naturalism thus has relations with many genres – such as fable, tragedy and folk tales. On the other hand, Finnish Naturalism clearly communicates with other European literature. Dialogues with different genres and the search for models from abroad are partly explained by the specific culture-historical situation of texts. At the time, literature in the Finnish language was only developing and there was only a minor domestic literary tradition. On the one hand the multigeneric character of Naturalism puts Zola's claims of the non-literary and "scientific" nature of Naturalism in a critical light, and demonstrates that Naturalism as a genre is highly aware and conscious of other genres.[54] On the other hand, the heterogeneous nature of Naturalism[55], its "bastard nature" conforms in a sense with the overall poetic of entropy in the works. The requirements of classical poetics are not respected: the boundaries of genres are disrupted and broken down.[56]

Static entropy

In *Laara* and in *Köyhää kansaa*, degeneration proceeds at a dynamic pace. At the end of *Laara* by Kauppis-Heikki, Laara's beautiful face becomes ravaged by illness. The character Mari in Minna Canth's *Köyhää kansaa* evolves from a self-sacrificing mother into a screaming human animal. On the contrary, Juhani Aho's novel *Papin rouva* (The Wife of a Clergyman) from 1893 describes in a slow tempo the unhappy marriage of Elli, the wife of a rural clergyman, and her summer-long relationship with the pastor's old schoolmate. The reader is motivated to expect and wait for a scene of infidelity, but this never takes place; the student Elli loves eventually leaves the vicarage and the novel ends in the disillusionment of love, repeating a disappointment that she had experienced in her youth. *Papin rouva* is characterised by the repetition of events – Elli's life repeats the fate of her mother. The stagnant nature of the story is emphasised by intertextual repetition. The combination of characters show that Aho reiterates the events of Gustave Flaubert's *Madame Bovary* (1857) and Victoria Benedictsson's Bovary version, *Fru Marianne* (Madame Marianne) from 1887.[57]

From a dynamic process we have moved into a world of static repetition. The difference in the plots of the Naturalist works can also be described with reference to Tzvetan Todorov's concept of the mythological (mythologique) and the gnoseological or epistemic (gnoséologique, épistemique). The works by Kauppis-Heikki and Canth clearly implement a mythological type of plot in which the narrative seeks to represent a change of events in relation to the conditions prevailing at the beginning of the story, a transition from one space to another – from A to non-A.[58] As in the gnoseological plot type as defined by Todorov, such progress in the plot, changes and activity are not important in *Papin rouva*. What is primary in this type of plot is the understanding of phenomena and apprehension of the events, an orientation towards knowledge, gnosis. What is the meaning of life amidst Naturalistic suffering? *Papin rouva* gives a nihilistic answer to this important question: Elli's existence is one of atrophying to the state of life being nothing.

Moving with her husband from her childhood home to the vicarage of Tyynelä, Elli enters her new bedroom for the first time and thinks:

> But entering this room with its two beds in a row and seeing the windowpanes half covered with snow on the outside, she felt as if she were buried alive. (Aho 1893/1951: 233–234.)

The mental vista on to which Elli's window opens is a desolate one, for the outside world can barely be seen through the snow-covered windowpanes. In Elli's words, life is the experience of being buried alive, dying alive. In the silence of the vicarage Elli forgets the passing of time. "Weeks and months have passed leaving hardly a trace, like raindrops one after another on a rainy day, falling into the sand so slowly and with such annoying boredom."[59] Life is running into the sand, crumbling slowly like a process of erosion. *Papin rouva* is a prototypical example of what I would call static entropy: its undercurrent is negation, it is a non-novel, non-progress, non-happening and non-development, a paradoxical non-existence.

Besides a static plot, *Papin rouva* takes a distance from the historical context in which the work is inscribed. The events of the novel are connected in only a loose manner to the world. The distant scene of events of the story is far from the rest of the world – far from other settlements and a day's journey from the nearest town. Connections with the world at large and contemporary issues, touch it only through Olavi, the former schoolmate of the vicar and Elli's beloved never-forgotten, a student who arrives in Tyynelä almost directly from Paris. The depiction of concrete events is secondary. More importantly, *Papin rouva* is an account of the inner process of a person, Elli's subjective world with its fantasies. Georg Lukács pointed to the privatisation of history in Naturalism. Instead of a common, shared reality, Naturalism undertakes the subjective depiction of the individual. Lukács maintains that Naturalism launched an "antihistorical" tendency: the human condition has no social benchmarks, instead, existence is characterised by a Heideggerian *Geworfenheit ins Dasein*.[60]

Presented through internal focalisation, Elli's fantasies open up a completely different world to that of her static everyday reality. In fantasy everything is possible: the ship that Elli awaits in her dreams will come to the vicarage pier and its captain will save her and take her to Helsinki. In her fantasies, the pastor drowns in the lake while Elli and Olavi are both rescued. The illusions free her from melancholy, but are nonetheless doomed to die amidst the middle-class everyday life of the vicarage. In static entropy life entwines chiasmatically completely opposite elements: the mercilessness of the outside world and dreams, an intact bourgeois façade and disintegration within the mind. Having collapsed, these fantasies only generate the torment of dying alive. "But she will always remember him, always letting the wound bleed until the blood has run dry,"[61] Elli thinks when the student has left the vicarage. The character in static entropy has to be aware of his own suffering, bearing in a sense a double load of pain in comparison with the characters of dynamic or tragic entropy who have the "easy way" of physical death.

The change that takes place in static entropy in the depiction of overall historical reality is also underscored by the fact that *Papin rouva*, like *Maailman murjoma*, is linked with intertextual references to Finnish mythology, a mythical, fictive history of the Finns passed on in oral tradition: the *Kalevala* and the *Kanteletar*.[62] In *Papin rouva*, the most distinct reference to myth is in a fantasy passage set in church at the beginning of the text, in which Elli is compared to the maiden *Aino* in the Kalevala.[63] Her habit of sitting on a rock on the shore of a lake and waiting for her rescuer to come by water, also has parallels with many other women figures of Finnish folk poetry: the character of a woman waiting for a man to come from the sea is a familiar motif both in the *Kalevala* and the *Kanteletar*. The introduction of myth into *Papin rouva* and *Maailman murjoma* is a way of participating in a debate on knowledge and the nature of reality. The theories of Naturalism proceeded from the positivist idea that reality could be grasped by investigating it scientifically. The objective was the demythologisation of reality, the investigation of reality with the aid of scientific knowledge. It can be presumed that rational knowledge of reality runs counter to the mythical representation of reality: science emerges as the opposite of myth, as a result of the loss of the enchantment of myth.[64] Static entropy, however, paradoxically seeks to restore the legendary allure of reality, which was denuded and made ugly by Naturalism. Myth offers an alternative for the bourgeois everyday world. In the *Kalevala*, Aino avoids a repugnant marriage by drowning herself in the lake. In Elli's fantasies things are even better: Elli is only believed to have drowned, but "in reality" she was rescued from the lake shore by a man who takes her far away. Of course, the opportunity provided by myth is realised only in fantasy. In the real world, fantasy remains fantasy.

Even the internal analepsis, which depicts Elli's honeymoon, her crying in her mother's arms, the sledge taking her brutally from home, her journey on a cold, bleak winter's day, alludes to a mythical world. This analepsis refers to the many poems of the *Kanteletar* that were meant for the bride leaving home to be married. In these poems the descriptions of the future home of the bride are tinged by melancholy and fear. The separation from the old home is like banishment from Paradise. Moving into the bridegroom's home is a step towards death, as described in a folk poem on the lifespan of a woman:

> So is she made,
> even as cradled girl,
> to go from father's home to marital stead,
> from there to the realm of the dead.[65]

In the frame of reference of folk poetry, the scene of *Papin rouva*, a vicarage named Tyynelä is associated with the phonetically parallel Tuonela, the Hades in Finnish mythology. The journey to Tuonela is also underlined by the scene of arrival in Tyynelä: as Elli looks out of the snow-covered windows and she feels that she is buried alive.

Naturalism has traditionally been associated with an unvarnished depiction of reality, which does not eschew dirt and filth and ugliness. "You deliberately tread on the laws of beauty, drawing out ugliness of all kinds," wrote a Fennoman poet offended by Minna Canth's Naturalism in a poem dedicated to Canth.[66] But beauty instead of ugliness dominates the description of static entropy.[67] *Papin rouva* is famous for its depiction of nature. The lyrical beauty of nature culminates in a scene in which Elli and the student climb to a lookout and the "adultery" takes place – a passionate kiss. The journey to the lookout passes through an idyllic forest. The beauty intoxicates Elli and kindles her old dream of climbing ever higher away from her existing reality.

> They walked through a dense-grown thicket, rising for a long while along a path where they could not see anything around them. But the forest was like an illuminated place, full of light coming from all directions. Far-off waters and open reaches glimmered between the trees to the left and the right. They would have liked to go faster, to leave the winding path, and run straight ahead or stand on their toes and jump to see over the tops of the trees. (Aho 1893/1951:346)

The journey of Elli and the student to the hill which Elli has named as the Pinnacle of the Temple passes in an almost sacral mood. Aho uses religious rhetoric in his depiction of the journey. The stand of pines is a "sacred grove", while the forest is a "church vault". In 1893, in an article on Finnish landscapes Aho compared the experience of natural beauty to the religious experience of a pilgrim. At the Pinnacle of the Temple Elli and the student are blinded by the ecstasy of paradisiacal nature: the rest of the world below seems distant and forgotten. For a moment, Elli becomes the active heroine of her dreams and kisses the student with fervent passion. The kiss under a tall birch, however, becomes like the picking of the fruit from the tree of the knowledge of good and evil. The idyll is shattered and Elli says that the kiss was "the first and last time". Her return to the normal world is bitter.

Thus underlying the lyrical beauty of nature looms disintegration. This conflicting combination of beautiful and horrible shows resemblance to what Philippe Bonnefis points out about depictions of nature in *La Faute de l'abbé Mouret*: they express not only fascination but a discourse of perversion and death.[68] The beauty of paradise produces a nauseous overdose, *nausée*. The same impression is given in K. A. Tavaststjerna's novel *Hårda tider* (Hard times) from 1891, when the depiction of the arrival of famine-causing summer night frost emphasises the exceptionally beauty of the evening. Miss Louise is playing the piano with the soft, silvery tones accompanying the frost descending on the fields. It is as if fairies dressed in mist were dancing enchantingly in the moonlight. But it is a danse macabre that spells famine. By morning, the grain crop, the mainstay of the coming winter, has been lost.

On the other hand, colour symbolism betrays unexpected depths under a beautiful surface. In *Papin rouva*, Elli and the landscapes of the novel are continuously and markedly in blue.[69] This motif is made evident from the first pages of the book, when Elli, dressed in blue and grey arranges a bouquet of flowers in these colours. Panoramic depictions of the landscape mention "bluish fells" off in the distance, or the setting sun and the landscape covered in a gauze-like haze. According to the student, Elli's blue eyes are marked by melancholy and sadness. The calm blue waters of a lake in the summer invite Elli to cast herself in and commit suicide. Death and grief as the signification of blue in *Papin rouva* are also reinforced by the intertexts of the work. As pointed out by Mouchard and Neefs, blue (*bleu*) and bluish (*bleuâtre*) are repeated in *Madame Bovary*,[70] where blue appears in the negative connotation of the hereafter and death. The blue discourse of melancholy in *Papin rouva* refers to the entropy taking place amidst the lyrical landscape.

The negative force of entropy erodes the meanings of beautiful phenomena. At the end of *Papin rouva*, Elli's life is characterised by an experience of emptiness and meaninglessness. "For ever, boats will pass by here, and for ever the waves will splash to tell her of gloomy hopelessness and the emptiness of life."[71] Emptiness, the terminus of the suffering of static entropy is the end result of entropy, inertia. The tendency of different entropies to erase differences culminates in the static experience of emptiness.

Towards reconciliation

Man and nature imitate each other in Naturalistic literature. Kauppis-Heikki's *Laara* begins with a description of a rotting crop destroyed by frost and ends in a scene in which Laara's body undergoes the same process of destruction. The human life-span follows the biological model of the cycles of nature: birth, life, degeneration and death.[72] On the other hand, nature, like landscape, is given human features. In *Maailman murjoma* for instance the forest is full of vital energies. Man takes on animal features: Junnu of *Maailman murjoma* is a human beast and, the character Mari in *Köyhää kansaa* becomes a suffering, non-rational animal. The train in *Maailman murjoma*, in turn, combines mechanical and organic features. Man, animal, machines and even plants imitate each other. Baguley points out that the usual function of mimesis is to produce differences and to diversify the world.[73] In Naturalism mimesis, however, functions as a force producing sameness instead of difference, as repetitive copying that erases difference. Becoming the same is a trait common to all entropies. individuals are dissolved in the entropic process, which merges them into one and the same universe.

The relationship between disintegration and mimesis has also been discussed by René Girard in his work *La Violence et le sacré* (1971). In his analysis of tragedy, Girard presents the connection between the destruction that takes place in it and replicating mimesis. Girard maintains that order, peace and fertility are based on differences prevailing in culture. Differences are also a precondition for achieving individual identity: the individual can define his relationship with others and thus his own place in culture. Tragedy, destruction and violence, in turn, begin with the disappearance of differences.[74] As a result of the disappearance of differences, nothing will be stable any more in society.[75] As pointed out by Michel Serres, the chaos and disorder of entropy signify the termination of difference.[76]

On the other hand, the extreme nature of suffering makes Naturalistic characters hope for death and destruction. Mari in *Köyhää kansaa* wants to kill first her family and then herself, for "it would have been better not to have been born than to come here to suffer the sorrows of the world. He who is non-existent will not feel pain or go hungry" is Mari's train of thought.[77] On the other hand, there is also a cathartic element to the ruin of Mari and her family. At the end of the book Mari´s deranged scream of pain echoes through the city to comfort others who are suffering. Despite its pain, this scream, resounding over the fields and along the highway, is like the first bud of hope rising from a soil destroyed by entropy. The way in which Canth describes the progress of the scream through the city resembles the final passage of Zola's *Germinal*. At the end of *Germinal*, after the uprising has been quelled, the mine has collapsed and everything has been destroyed, Zola paints the image of a landscape sprouting and putting forth buds. In addition to this biological process, another *germination* also takes place at the end of *Germinal*.[78] The closing remarks point to the generations of the future who will rally for revenge. Naturalistic entropy is in a circular relation with cohesion, as Michel Serres points out: the difference which maintains harmony is reborn from the sameness caused by the entropic process.[79] The hope of better things resides in complete destruction.

The pessimistic philosophy of Arthur Schopenhauer with its conception of man locked in the endless circle of Will and desire influenced the thinking of Naturalistic writers. But Schopenhauer's philosophy also contains features of reconciliation and optimism associated with the terminus of entropy, the merging to become the same. Schopenhauer's ethic presents the opportunity to overcome Will and desire specifically by becoming the same: it is possible to transcend suffering if man exceeds the boundaries of the subjective self, removing the border between self and other to see the world as one and the same Will and to see in other creatures oneself and one's own suffering.[80] The ending of suffering is realised by a process of becoming the same, thus by a kind of entropic disintegration. The Schopenhauerian solution appears in Zola's novel *La Joie de vivre* (1884), in which the principal character Pauline is able to rise above all the suffering that she has encountered, accepting the sufferings of life as belonging to it and concentrating her efforts on love for her fellow man.

Static entropy ends in a chaotic void, but paradoxically rising above suffering and optimism are possible in this entropy. An example of a person who despite her own suffering is able to feel compassion for others and to understand their disruption and pain is Elsa's mother in Pakkala's novel *Elsa*. The mother is an onlooker of the tragic and dynamic suffering played out in the work and herself experiences static suffering. Her daughter, who has given birth to an illegitimate child, dies and her grandson is sold into service. At the end of *Elsa*, the mother is surrounded by the lifelessness, emptiness, vacuity and lonesome suffering of static entropy. Nonetheless, she tries to pray for Elsa's friend, a prostitute: "God help her if she lacks strength, and we people are weak in our strength."[81] The mother also stands up for the ridiculed prostitute, asking the one who mocks her: "Where is your pity and compassion?"[82]

Elsa's mother is able to cross the boundary between self and other, and in a way she also receives a prize for her compassion. The novel ends on an optimistic note, when Elsa's son is brought back to his grandmother. The child is a kind of pardon, an inkling of reconciliation, a spark of hope for the future amidst continuous disintegration. In dynamic entropy a child often signifies only the eternal continuation of degeneration. Children are incarnations of degenerating biological nature: the child will suffer from the consequences of its mother's sins, as in Kauppis-Heikki's *Kirottua työtä*, where Anna Liisa's child is a sickly dying weakling, or in Canth's *Salakari*, where the adulterous mother's son dies. In static entropy, however, the child is presented as an atonement, a sign that the chain of degeneration will not continue endlessly. Through her grandson, Elsa's mother receives at least something good to replace all the bad things that have happened. The child raises hope of the possibility of justice. A generation of suffering may be only one stage in the grand passage of history – things may be different in the future.

Conclusions

Finally, I would like to underline certain points mentioned above. First of all, although the discussion of the various entropies focuses on certain works of literature, I would emphasise that the models I have presented are realised only in part in the individual works. The entropies are not mutually exclusive. Teuvo Pakkala's *Elsa* is a good example of a work of literature with all the entropies. In addition to tragic and static entropy mentioned above, the features of dynamic entropy are brought out in Pakkala's novel – Elsa's death underlines dynamic physical disintegration.

The family resemblance – entropy – which gives the three genres cohesion is another matter of great importance. What does it ultimately mean? Based on my analyses, it can be said that the relationship of the texts to the entropic vision shared by the genre do not necessarily mean simply the acknowledgement of disintegration and degeneration. The texts can also express a critical attitude towards the entropy played out in the works, a tendency towards the reconciliation of suffering and degeneration, as noted at the end of my article. In this way the poetics of disintegration will – paradoxically – also produce continuity.

Translated by Jüri Kokkonen

NOTES

1. By "Realism" I refer here to a period associated with a certain historical era. Further information in English on the literature and writing of the period can be found, for example, in George C. Schoolfield's *A History of Finnish Literature* (1998). Lincoln: University of Nebraska Press.
2. Among literary historians Rafael Koskimies and Kai Laitinen, for example, do not recognise Naturalism in Finnish literature. Koskimies 1965:12 and Laitinen 1991: 218.
3. Päivi Lappalainen's *Koti, kansa ja maailman tahraava lika* (2000) deals with Naturalism in Finnish literature. Pekka Lappalainen's study *Realistisen valtavirtauksen aatteet* (1967) also recognises the natural-scientific factors of Naturalism, such as Darwinism, as one of the background factors of "the period of Realism". Naturalistic features in Finnish literature have also been noted by Mikko Saarenheimo (1924), but he chose to regard it as a by-product of the Realist School. Saarenheimo 1924: 194.
4. Central to Fowler's research is the rejection of a classifying and categorising concept of genres. According to Fowler, the individual works of a genre are linked by family resemblance. According to him, even genres are not eternal and unchanging, but rather in a continuous state of change. "It is by their modification, primarily, that individual works convey literary meaning", notes Fowler. 1982:24.
5. This material is a selection, but it includes works by the best-known Finnish authors of the period (Juhani Aho, Minna Canth, Teuvo Pakkala), works by Finland-Swedish writers (Ina Lange and K. A. Tavaststjerna), and works that have received less attention in earlier studies (the writings of Kauppis-Heikki and Ina Lange).
6. The term *fennomania* was applied in the 19th century to a political orientation that had formed around the so-called Finnish Party and called for reinforcing the

national status of Finland and Finnish culture and its supporters were known as *fennomans*. During the 1870s the fennoman movement split in two. These young fennomans wanted separation from the conservative ecclesiastical-agrarian thinking of the older generation. Young fennomans were supposedly liberal, yet they opposed Naturalism. The cultural journal *Valvoja*, in which anti-naturalist criticism was published, was an organ of the young fennomans. The author Juhani Aho, discussed below, and Th. Rein and O. E. Tudeer, contributors to *Valvoja* quoted here, were all young fennomans.

7   This is pointed out in Mervi Kantokorpi's article "Naturalismin kuvotus" (1998), in which she discusses the reception of Naturalism in the *Valvoja* journal. – Opposition to Naturalism as an "un-Finnish" tendency lived on in literary histories in the 20th century, which continued to be written in a nationalist tone for a long while. On the other hand, Marxist literary studies of the 1970s established the concept of Realism at the cost of Naturalism, as the latter did not carry out the requirement of social change posed by Marxist research.

8   "The Finnish people are young and healthy; they know that the future lies before them, but it is a future that must be earned with hard concerted effort," wrote O.E. Tudeer in his review of Juhani Aho's *Papin rouva* in *Valvoja* in 1894. Tudeer was not satisfied with the French influences of Aho's novel, which he regarded as unnational. Tudeer 1894: 35. See also the article by Kantokorpi.

9   Article by Th. Rein in *Valvoja*. Rein 1888: 548.

10 Letter to Kaarlo Brofeldt 1884. Canth 1973:142.

11 Pakkala wrote thus to his wife in 1888. Pakkala 1982: 75.

12 Aho 1885/1964: 11.

13 Weinstein 1972: 48.

14 Entropy is associated with Naturalism not only by David Baguley but also by Michel Serres in his study *Feux et signaux de brume. Zola.* (1975). Baguley discusses two forms of entropy, the Goncourtian and the Flaubertian in French Naturalism. The Goncourtian type represents a more Darwinistic Naturalism "that takes up the tragic model of the fall, presenting it as a process of deterioration, prolonged in time and deriving its causality from particular determinig factors (hereditary taints, neurotic dispositions, adeverse social conditions)". The Flaubertian type, in turn, is a more Schopenhauerian Naturalism, in which "the determining factor is more generalised, a fundamental inadequacy in the human condition which traps the individual in the inextricable dilemmas, frustrations and disillusionment of daily existence". Baguley 1990: 95–96.

15 Zola 1880/1909: 26–27.

16 Serres 1975: 63.

17 Here my conception of the variations of the genre differ from Alastair Fowler's theory, in which they are chronologically consecutive, periodically arranged "stages". Fowler, for example, sees the development of the Gothic novel as a process of primary, secondary and tertiary stages. Fowler 1982: 163. This model of entropy, however, is not such an evolutionary theory of Naturalism or a chronological continuum.

18 "Kauppis-Heikki" was a pseudonym, The author's real name was Heikki Kauppinen.

19 O'Donovan 1995: 220.

20 Baguley 1990: 102.

21 On the common people as a threat to the educated classes in literature at the turn of the century, see Pirjo Lyytikäinen's article in the present volume.

22 Kauppis-Heikki 1891/1921: 62.

23 Kauppis-Heikki 1891/1921: 51.

24 Lange 1885: 71.

25 Lange 1885: 77.

26 Lange 1885: 101.

27 Ferrera, quoted in Rimmon-Kenan 1983/1991: 48.

28 In his theory of genres Alastair Fowler speaks of the concept of the antigenre. New genre can develop as antitheses and counterstatements to existing genres. Fowler 1982:174.
29 In antigenre theories, comic texts are specifically regarded as examples of antigenre. Fowler's example of an antigenre is *Don Quijote* as the antigenre of the romance. Fowler 1982: 174. *Don Quijote* is also analysed by Gerard Genette in his section on the antinovel in *Palimpsestes* (1978). Genette 1978: 164–175.
30 Parody can be understood in a limited sense to be a comic version of a work, seeking to mock and ridicule the heroic figures and events of the antiwork. For example The Battle of the Frogs and Rats is a parody of Homer's *Iliad*. See Genette 1978: 147.
31 Lange 1885: 13.
32 Aho's naturalistic works, however, are not in agreement with his idealisation of Finnishness. On the other hand, the enthusiasm of the fennomans, including Aho, waned towards the turn of the century, and many of the fennomans who believed in the sanctity of the Finnish nation (Aho included) noted their disappointment in the Finnish people and in their own ideals.
33 Fowler 1984: 106–107.
34 The end of *Maailman murjoma* is somewhat open to interpretation, as pointed out by Kai Laitinen (1984: 84): does Junnu die or is he only imprisoned? I would tend to support the interpretation that Junnu dies, because the text notes that he went on his "eternal way". In any case the end of the story also signifies the end of Junnu's life.
35 Baguley also refers to anagnorisis in Naturalism. Baguley 1990:80.
36 Aristoteles 1967/1977: 34.
37 Barthes 1955/1986: 90–91.
38 Pakkala 1894/1958: 141.
39 Barthes 1955/1986: 90.
40 Kinnunen 1985: 191.
41 Steiner 1961: 291.
42 Ruin 1885: 144.
43 Bernheimer 1989: 783.
44 For example in Zola's *La Bête humaine* hereditary degeneracy is compared to paying the debts of one's forefathers. Suffering from his inexplicable homicidal lust, Jacques Lantier thinks that "he paid for others, fathers, grandfathers, drunken generations…" Zola 1890/1997: 99.
45 Zola observes for example that the constituent factors of passions are not precisely known.Zola 1880/1909: 8.
46 Zola 1880/1909: 37.
47 Aho 1893/1951: 337.
48 Aho 1894/1951: 309.
49 Lukács's concept of Realism proceeds from the idea that one can know from reality what it is. A realistic work will thus crystallise, as it were, for the reader the ultimate nature of reality. Art binds phenomena that appear fragmented and alienated to man.
50 Den Tandt 1998: 17.
51 Baguley 1990: 213.
52 Aho 1894/1951: 291.
53 The *Kalevala*, Finland's national epic, was compiled and prepared by Elias Lönnrot on the basis of folk poetry that he had collected. It appeared in its present scope in 1849, a more limited version having already appeared in 1835–1836. The motto of *Maailman murjoma* is a verse from the Kullervo poem of the *Kalevala*. Kullervo is a figure of vengeance sold into slavery and avenging the wrongs that he has suffered. Among those he kills are the members of his own family. The tragedy of Kullervo includes incest – he sleeps, unwittingly, with his sister. There is no incest motive in *Maailman murjoma*.

54 Zola maintained that Naturalism is not really literature, because it was associated with natural-scientific research and marked a return to nature and reality. The word 'literature' was pejorative for Zola, for whom it meant idealistic and romantic literature, such as the works of Victor Hugo.
55 The heterogeneous nature of Naturalism is underlined by Baguley. Baguley 1990: 73.
56 The requirement of strict boundaries and the purity of genres derives from Antiquity. "Versibus exponi tragicis res comica non vult – a comic theme should not be presented in tragic verse, wrote Horace in *Ars Poetica*. Horatius: 31.
57 Ernst Ahlgren is the pseudonym of the Swedish author Victoria Benedictsson. In *Fru Marianne* (Madame Marianne) the bourgeois girl Marianne marries a man with a farm in an outlying region, but falls in love with a decadent student who comes to spend the summer with his friend the farmer.
58 Todorov 1978: 67–68.
59 Aho 1893/1951: 155.
60 Lukács 1955/1958: 17. In *Wider den Missverstandenen Realismus* (1955) Lukács analyses decadent/avant-garde literature stemming from the Naturalism of the 19th century yet living on the modernism of the 20th century. In Lukács' theory decadent literature is the opposite of Realism. In Realism the being of man is linked to social reality and man is an Aristotelian "political animal". In Decadence, in turn, such ties do not exist, and the basis of being lies in existential loneliness.
61 Aho 1893/1951: 295.
62 Elias Lönnrot also compiled the *Kanteletar* (1840–1841) on the basis of the folk poetry he had collected. The *Kanteletar* contains lyric folk poems, ballads and legends.
63 Lyytikäinen 1991: 175. Aino of the *Kalevala* is a beautiful young woman whom the old rune-singer tries to woo to be his wife. She chooses to drown herself in a lake rather than to marry the old man.
64 Vattimo 1989: 41.
65 *Kanteletar*, First book, poem 145.
66 This is a poem by Arvi Jännes from 1889.
67 The "beauty" of Naturalism has also been discussed in French studies. Pierre Martino describes novels by Zola such as *La Faute de l'abbé Mouret* (1875), *Une Page d'amour* (1878) and *La Joie de vivre* (1884) as "works of repose and re-creation", marked by linguistic freedom, lyrical presentation and a kind of new beauty. Martino 1969:85.
68 Bonnefis 1978/1982: 129; 143.
69 The blue theme in *Papin rouva* has previously been interpreted as a Finnish-national symbol (e.g. Niemi 1985: 107). This interpretation is relevant in itself, but I want to present a different perspective.
70 Mouchard & Neefs 1986: 162–163.
71 Aho 1893/1951: 395.
72 Baguley 1990: 216.
73 Baguley 1990: 219.
74 Girard 1971: 76–77.
75 Girard 1971: 220
76 Serres 1975: 76.
77 Canth 1886/1974: 253.
78 germination= sprouting, coming into being
79 Serres 1975: 77.
80 Salomaa 1944: 286–287.
81 Pakkala 1894/1958: 182.
82 Pakkala 1894/1958: 183.

BIBLIOGRAPHY
Primary sources

AHO, JUHANI 1951: *Kootut teokset 2*. (Papin rouva, Maailman murjoma). Helsinki: WSOY.
AHO, JUHANI 1893: "Kauniita näköaloja Suomessa. Kolivaara." *Uusi Kuvalehti*, toukokuu 1893.
AHO, JUHANI 1885/1964: "Realistisesta kirjallisuudesta sananen." *Suomen kirjallisuuden antologia 3*. Ed. Kai Laitinen & Matti Suurpää. Helsinki: Otava.
CANTH, MINNA 1974: *Valitut teokset* (Köyhää kansaa, Salakari). Hämeenlinna: Karisto.
CANTH, MINNA 1973: *Minna Canthin kirjeet*. Ed. Helle Kannila. Helsinki: SKS.
JÄNNES, ARVI 1918: *Muistoja ja toiveita*. Helsinki: SKS.
KALEVALA 1849/1963. Helsinki: WSOY.
KANTELETAR 1840/1954. Helsinki: SKS.
KAUPPIS-HEIKKI 1891/1921: *Kirottua työtä*. Helsinki: WSOY.
KAUPPIS-HEIKKI 1953: *Valitut teokset*. (Laara). Helsinki: WSOY.
PAKKALA, TEUVO 1958: *Valitut teokset*. (Elsa). Helsinki: Otava.
PAKKALA, TEUVO 1982: *Kirjeet 1882–1925*. Ed. Maija-Liisa Bäckström. Helsinki: SKS.
STEN, DANIEL (INA LANGE) 1885: *"Sämre folk". En Berättelse*. Stockholm: Albert Bonniers Förlag.
TAVASTSTJERNA, K. A. 1924: *Samlade skrifter 5* (Hårda tider). Helsingfors: Holger Schildts Förlagsaktiebolag.
ZOLA, ÉMILE 1890/1997: *La Bête humaine*. Paris: Livre de poche.
ZOLA, ÉMILE 1880/1909: *Le Roman Expérimental*. Paris: Fasquelle.

Secondary sources

ARISTOTELES: *Runousoppi*. Tr. Pentti Saarikoski. 1967/1982. Helsinki: SKS.
BAGULEY, DAVID 1990: *Naturalist Fiction. The Entropic vision*. Cambridge: Cambridge University press.
BARTHES, ROLAND 1955/1986: The Man-eater. *Critical Essays on Emile Zola*, toim. David Baguley. Boston: C.K. Hall. & Co, 90–93.
BERNHEIMER, CHARLES 1989: Prostitution in the Novel. *A New History of French Literature*, ed. Denis Hollier. Cambridge: Harvard University Press, 780–785.
BONNEFIS, PHILIPPE 1978/1982: *Trois figures de l'amateur propre. Zola, Maupassant, Vallès*. Lille: Université de Lille 3.
DEN TANDT, CHRISTOPHE 1998: *The Urban Sublime in American Literary Naturalism.*Urbana And Chicago: University of Illinois Press.
FOWLER, ALASTAIR 1982: *Kinds of Literature*. An Introduction to the Theory of Genres and Modes. Cambridge: Harvard University Press.
GENETTE, GERARD 1982: *Palimpsestes. Littérature au second degré*. Editions du Seuil: Paris.
GIRARD, RENÉ 1971: *La Violence et le sacré*. Paris: Grasset.
HORATIUS 1978: *Ars poetica – runotaide*. Teivas Oksala ja Erkki Palmén (ed). Helsinki: Gaudeamus.
KANTOKORPI, MERVI 1998: Naturalismin kuvotus. Pirjo Lyytikäinen, (ed), *Dekadenssi*. Helsinki: SKS, 16–31.
KINNUNEN, AARNE 1985: *Draaman maailma. Villiintynyt puutarha*. Helsinki: WSOY.
KOSKIMIES, RAFAEL 1965: *Suomen kirjallisuuden historia 4*. Helsinki: Otava.
LAITINEN, KAI 1984: "Juhani Ahon pienoisromaanit". Kai Laitinen, *Metsästä kaupunkiin. Esseitä ja tutkielmia kirjallisuudesta*. Helsinki:Otava, 81–96.
LAITINEN, KAI 1991: *Suomen kirjallisuuden historia*. Helsinki: SKS.

LAPPALAINEN, PEKKA 1967: *Realistisen valtavirtauksen aatteet ja niiden kontinuitiivisuus Suomen kirjallisuudessa vuosisadan alkuun saakka. Kaunokirjallisuuden ja sen arvostelun aatehistoriallinen tutkimus.* Jyväskylä: Jyväskylän yliopisto.

LAPPALAINEN, PÄIVI 2000: *Koti, kansa ja maailman tahraava lika. Näkökulmia 1880- ja 1890-luvun kirjallisuuteen.* Helsinki: SKS.

LUKÁCS, GEORG 1955/1958: *Wider den missverstandenen Realismus.* Hamburg: Claassen.

LYYTIKÄINEN, PIRJO 1991: Palimpsestit ja kynnystekstit. Tekstien välisiä suhteita Gerald Genetten mukaan ja Ahon Papin rouvan intertekstuaalisuus. Auli Viikari (ed), *Intertekstuaalisuus.* Helsinki: SKS, 145–179.

MARTINO, PIERRE 1969: *Le Naturalisme français* (1870–1895). Paris: Armand Collin.

MOUCHARD, CLAUDE & NEEFS, JACQUES 1986: *Flaubert. Une vie, une oeuvre, une époque.* Poitiers: Balland.

NIEMI, JUHANI 1985: *Juhani Aho.* Helsinki: SKS.

O'DONOVAN, PATRICK 1995: The Body and the Body Politic in the Novels of the Goncourts. Margaret Cohen & Christoper Prendergast (ed), *Spectacles of Realism.* Minneapolis: University of Minnesota Press, 214–230.

REIN, TH. 1888: "Prostitutsioonikysymys." *Valvoja* 1888.

RUIN, W. 1885: "Taistelu naturalismia vastaan." *Valvoja* 1885.

RIMMON-KENAN, SLOMITH 1983/1991: *Kertomuksen poetiikka.* Tr. Auli Viikari. Helsinki: SKS.

SAARENHEIMO, MIKKO 1924: *Suomalainen 1880-luvun realismi. Kirjallinen tutkimus.* Helsinki: WSOY.

SALOMAA, J. E. 1944: *Arthur Schopenhauer. Elämä ja filosofia.* Helsinki: WSOY.

SERRES, MICHEL 1975: *Feux et signaux de brume. Zola.* Paris: Grasset.

STEINER, GEORGE 1961: *The Death of the Tragedy.* London: Faber and Faber.

VATTIMO, GIANNI 1989: *Läpinäkyvä yhteiskunta.* Tr. Jussi Vähämäki. Helsinki: Gaudeamus.

VIOLA PARENTE-ČAPCOVÁ

Free love, mystical union or prostitution?
The dissonant love stories of L. Onerva

"How beautiful is to carry the drowning moment in one's heart! There is no morning, no evening, only love, only love!" (Onerva, 1910)

"Where is now the healthy, subconscious difference between man and woman, that source of all love and beauty?" (Onerva 1908/1982, 194)

The issue of love, mostly its romantic mutation with its traditionally heterosexual connotations, has been a complicated one for all women writers, artists and thinkers concerned with women's emancipation. On the one hand, the emancipationalist feminist movement – from the nineteenth century to the present day – has traditionally viewed the heterosexual discourse of love with suspicion, emphasising a relationship between the traditional figurations of love and the reproduction of patriarchal power.[1] On the other hand, other currents within feminist and gender-conscious thought sought to appropriate the idea of love and develop various, mostly more or less utopian, theories of "new love", "new Eros", purified from the relations of domination and subordination, considered typical of the traditionally perceived heterosexual union.[2] The approach to the issue of love, however, has almost always been an important aspect of the feminist approach to the issue of woman's identity formation. Recently, emphasis has been placed on textuality, narrativity and the performance of love and romance, on the concept that love stories are "already written" and that their actors, in a way, "write themselves into these narratives", and they can also "rewrite" or "rescript" them.[3]

*

In the early poetry of the Finnish writer L. Onerva (Hilja Onerva Lehtinen, 1882–1972), love is, in line with the *fin-de-siècle* poetics, often depicted in an ecstatic, vital manner, at times as an essential basis for new concepts of humanity. At the same time, it is imbued with transient qualities, and romantic clichés mingle with tragic and ironic overtones. Falling in love with the idea of love, longing for an unattainable ideal, and the cosmic and mystic dimensions of love merge with jaded and analytical *fin-de-siècle* scepticism. Some poems, however, as is true of most of Onerva's early works, explicitly adopt the woman's point of view when discussing love: thus they foreground the tension between aesthetic concerns, in Onerva's case represented primarily by Symbolism and Decadence, and political ones, which, in this case, means Onerva's concern for the "women's question" in the broadest sense of the term. The dissonances created by Onerva's way of employing various discourses on love in her writings can help us to analyse her strategies for constructing a female subjectivity, the so-called New Woman[4].

By employing the feminist theory of sexual difference, I will concentrate on the ways various discourses, cultural myths, archetypes, ideologies and dichotomies of love and sexuality are negotiated in Onerva's early work. Sexual difference can be analysed on a number of levels suggested by feminist scholarship: as the difference between man and woman, the difference between woman as a cultural image and real, physical, historical women, as differences among women, and as differences within a single woman, who is conceived as a split, multiple subject (cf. De Lauretis 1986, 1987, Braidotti 1991, 1994). The approach to the theme of love of women at the turn of the 19th and the 20th century can be fruitfully explored from all these perspectives, as recent scholarship on Onerva has shown.[5] In the present article, I will concentrate on Onerva's treatment of the relationship between woman and man, which is one of the major concerns in her early texts. Indeed, this can be seen in the title of a collection of short stories and drama pieces from 1912 entitled *Mies ja Nainen* (Man and Woman). Looking at the ways Onerva's early work negotiates the relationship with the heterosexual other, I will also tackle the question as to what extent the heterosexual character of the lovers, the heterosexual essence of the other is absolutised and to what it is questioned. Exploring the discursive structures that informed Onerva's figurations of both the institutionalised form of heterosexual relationships in the form of marriage, and the various possibilities of "new", "free" relationships, I will also deal with the ways in which Onerva's texts treat the societal constraints faced by real, historical women of different social classes at the beginning of the 20th century.

Comparing the texts strongly influenced by Decadence and Symbolism with those less so, I will address Onerva's treatment of heterosexual love, focusing on the novel *Mirdja* (1908), in which this concept is strongly intertwined with that of creativity. *Mirdja* can be characterised as a Decadent *Bildungs/Künstlerroman* with a female protagonist, dealing with the development and the quest for identity of an aspiring woman artist, seemingly free from the constraints of society, due to her education by Decadent dilettantes. The novel *Inari* (1913), the story of an aspiring woman intellectual and her wavering between two lovers, also bears strong traces of Symbolist and Decadent mode, though less so than *Mirdja*. Apart from these two works, I will refer to other Onerva's texts (mainly short stories) from the beginning of the century until 1915, labelled by early 20th century critics as "more realist", but also employing elements ascribable to Symbolism, Decadence and Naturalism. I shall also point to several of Onerva's early poems, but on the whole shall leave her poetry outside my analysis.

*

Due to women's confinement to the private sphere, human relationships, including love, have been seen as a matter of women writers' concern since their entry to literature, emotionality and love being associated with the feminine domain. The more philosophical, 'transcendent' treatment of love, divorced from everyday reality, namely the Romantic and Neo-Romantic discussion of love in conjunction with creative genius and aesthetics, was, of course, considered more of a male domain. Women writers and thinkers had to fight for their place in this debate by showing their competence in philosophy and aesthetics, which Onerva, as a member of the first generation of women who could study at the university without a special permit, did by means of her university essays, newspaper articles and reviews, translations of important works of European literature and philosophy of art, and, of course, her own literary works. Thanks to her university degree, her interest in philosophy and her versatile talents, Onerva is an example *par excellence* of a New Woman writer who made abundant use of the existing discourses on femininity and love and developed various strategies for commenting on them and using them.

The (inter)textuality of the discourses on love employed in Onerva's works is highlighted in her university thesis from 1905 on Alfred de Musset's female characters, in which she assessed love as the key notion of Musset's work as a whole, the most powerful force to lead his characters. What she particularly emphasises is the huge difference between male and female approaches to love in Musset's texts: "Man can be torn between the most painful contradictions, with his heart jaded with doubts and uncertainties, but woman exists only for love, only for man."[6] It is precisely in this dependence that lies woman's condition of existence, its meaning; and this dependence is the essence of femininity, of woman's being, it is a "natural instinct". For woman, the refusal of this inclination means to "strive to liberate herself from her sex", in other words, to deny her "nature". Musset's women never use intelligence and spiritual strength to gain emancipation from men, but only to enchant them. (Onerva 1905.)

Onerva's interpretation of Musset's female characters brings to mind the famous statement of the late 19th century thinker and writer Laura Marholm that "man is the content of woman's life". It is through love, through man, that woman can find her self, her "true womanhood", and become "truly free", without imitating or pleasing men. (Marholm 1895/1897.) If we compare these observations with the approach to love in Onerva's early literary works, we can see, on the one hand, a fascination with such approaches to woman's "nature", fed also by Onerva's Rousseauan and Spencerean inspirations on the essential difference and complementarity of the sexes, and, on the other hand, a cautious consideration of the implications these ideas might have for the development of the New Woman.

Aging muse – a symbol of her own self

In her study subtitled "Watteau, the dreamer-creator of the Rococo", apparently meant as a sketch for her doctoral dissertation on Rococo painting, Onerva sees love as Watteau's only great, eternal dream; it is "unreal to the point of disease" and, in the form of a dream, is always "a hundred times better than reality". Though Onerva repeatedly emphasises that Watteau's concept of love is "demonic, but not poisonous", unlike that of contemporary, *fin-de-siècle* artists, her assessment of Watteau's art is informed namely by the *fin-de-siècle* itself and predominantly by Decadent ideas about love. These ideas constitute the core of the discourse of love in the novels *Mirdja* and *Inari*. The heroines understand their identity as shaped by their male "educators"/lovers, artists and aesthetes, "Decadent Pygmalions" (cf. Lyytikäinen 1997, 119–122) and they thoroughly contemplate the role offered to woman within the Symbolist-Decadent concept of love, into which they are styled by their male counterparts.

The beloved woman is figured as a dream-like being whose only value is to function on an abstract level, in accordance with the Symbolist and Decadent concept which emerges from the ancient way of idealising a beloved object, by making it either an abstraction or a symbol, or by choosing a lost or dead object as a pretext for melancholy yearning.[7] In this case, the ultimate goal of the artist-aesthete, the subject lover, figured, of course, as male, is yearning for the sake of yearning, loving for the sake of love, aspiring without a determinate object in mind (see e.g. Singer 1984/1987, 292). The concept of romantic love as self-centred and individualist is developed to the extreme, since human relationships are seen as valueless in themselves: love cannot have any value as objective communication with another person, but as an awareness of the self (cf. e.g. Busst 1967, 70). These "hard boundaries" which the Decadents developed, frequently prevented them from sustaining any kind of intimacy (cf. Gagnier 1994, 271). Although it was often an image of woman that stood for the ideal as well as the muse, the symbol of artistic inspiration, woman was valuable only in this metaphorised form of abstract femininity; a real woman, viewed as a vulgar, threatening other, could only disrupt the dream, since anything real was seen as hostile to the idealised image.[8]

In *Mirdja*, the Decadent Rolf sees the heroine as a "proud dream", a "fleeting fancy" (Onerva 1908/1982, 34) and Mirdja internalises his definitions of her, admitting that her own consciousness is a mere "version of Rolf's idea" (Onerva 1908/1982, 57). The main female character in *Inari* is also supposed to act as an ideal for her lover, the artist Porkka, who convinces her that "his image [of her] corresponds to her most eternal, deepest self, which is precisely what he loves" (Onerva 1913, 48). The position of a real woman in relation to the male Pygmalion is awkward: he wants to remain in complete control of his creation, but he cannot bear any intimate relationship with her on the plane of reality: "Dreams should remain dreams. What an abysmal delusion it is to try to press them to your breast. You see now." (Onerva 1908/1982, 222.)

Nevertheless, both Mirdja and Inari attempt the impossible: to live up to the ideal, to become "symbols of their own selves" (Onerva 1913, 195) as their lovers/creators want them to be. In *Mirdja*, it is especially the heroine's narcissistic inclinations, the desire to be desired, which lead her to accept the role of the muse and the Woman-Ideal. At first, her physical, bodily existence does not seem to be an obstacle to this, since the exceptional beauty of the young heroine is repeatedly emphasised, e.g. when she is referred to as a "bayadere" (Onerva 1908/1982, 34).[9]

The bodily existence of the muse is, however, a contradiction in terms, since her real-life image associates vulgarity and disrupts the dream (cf. e.g. Buchwald 1990). Moreover, the concept of the muse-Ideal does not account for the transformations of the ageing female body. The tragedy of an ageing erotic ideal, losing her constitutive elements – eternal youth, beauty and thus, her *raison d'être*, is expressed at the end of *Mirdja*: "She used to possess brilliant youth, but nobody on earth knows where Mirdja went to grow old." (Onerva 1908/1982, 291.) An awareness of this perspective seems to be behind Mirdja's reply to the artist Bengt Iro, who styles her into the role of a "dark muse", who "does not spare souls". Mirdja reacts: "... you do not even spare bodies, but that is exactly why you are – the artist..." (Onerva 1908/1982, 99.) The transcendence of the male artist is achieved at the expense of the female body, with the relegation of the real woman to the trope of male creativity (cf. e.g. Fetterly 1986, 159). The grotesque figure of a fading beauty, often explored by the Decadents with a mixture of fascination and sadistic pleasure as a symbol of oversophistication and decay, is given voice in a number of Onerva's early texts. The narcissistic pleasure of being objectified by the creator's gaze, often experienced by Onerva's heroines, develops into shame and anxiety, as in the poem *Geisha*: "Don't look at me: I am already old, I am dancing in the glimmer of wine and the silver brooch". (Onerva 1910, 81.)

Don Juan, cerebral lecher... or virgin whore?

The status of the beloved, desired object is not only a short-lived one, but it does not leave much space to woman's agency either. Onerva's heroine Mirdja tries to acquire the status of a subject lover within the Decadent discourse by styling herself into the popular Decadent libertine figures: the Don Juan and the dandy. The "strangely complicated" Decadent version of the earlier libertine in the figure of Don Juan (e.g. Mauclair 1926) was a popular character in Finnish *fin-de-siècle* literature (see e.g. Lyytikäinen 1997 and in this volume, and Soikkeli 1998). The attempt to appropriate to a female figure the Don Juan's never-ending cycle of searching, seducing and discarding, conceived in harmony with traditional concepts of male sexuality and used as a symbol of the process of discovering one's own self, was a rather ambitous one.

Don Juan, the eternal seeker cannibalising the identities of many women, acquires from them various aspects of their selves. Mirdja tries to play the role of Don Juan during her experiments in relationships with several men, described in the section of the novel entitled "Madrigal stories". She later contemplates:

> She could not help it that she was condemned to wander the cursed paths of a seeker's connscience, as all Don Juans, those eternal wandering Jews of love who cannot be saved by any power in the world. Those to whom Rolf once referred, Mirdja now discusses better herself, even the previously unknown species: Don Juan in the figure of woman... (Onerva 1908/1982, 203.)

Mirdja soon discovers that her "quest built on variety" was in fact only a process of trying on a variety of stereotypical roles which woman can adopt in a heterosexual relationship and that it did not bring her any further in her search for subjectivity. Finally, the strategy proves to be a destructive one: contrary to Mirdja's expectations, it was *she* who was finally consumed and cannibalised by the men she "had" (cf. Lyytikäinen 1997, 158): Mirdja affirms that she does not possess a "soul of her own" (Onerva 1908/1982, 204). The older she grows, the more she becomes aware of the asymmetry of the roles available to men and women in the process of both literal and metaphorical seduction. The image of the "female Don Juan" begins to epitomise for her the image of the "loose woman", the prostitute. Though she despises and fights off these thoughts which mirror contemporary double moral standards, she cannot get rid of them and interprets her former habit of "going from man to man" as resembling the "usual development of a prostitute" (Onerva 1908/1982, 206). The second part of the novel piles up various prostitute figures, with which Mirdja identifies to the point of obsession.

Most Decadent versions of the Don Juan figure emphasise his weariness and emotional sterility. The same applies to another prototype of a Decadent lover: the dandy, the effeminate narcissistic aesthete figure who can never become emotionally involved. Moreover, he cannot become involved sexually either; any kind of emotional and physical experience leaves him cold and untouched. In this way, the dichotomy between sexual and spiritual love is erased and replaced by the dichotomy of involvement (emotional and sexual) versus cold detachment. The dandy is imprisoned by his "hard boundaries", by his fear of the other. Though sexual ecstasy fascinated Decadents since it could be seen as a rebellion against bourgeois coyness, the achievement of sexual saturation could only have a negative function as anything real and material or materialised. While in Symbolism, the discrepancy between the unreachable Ideal and the despicable reality was resolved in a complete divorce from anything material, striving towards the metaphysical altitudes of love where "the breath of no maiden can tarnish the pure mirror of the glaciers", as put by Jules Laforgue (see Balakian 1967, 118–120), the Decadent resolution of the divorce from reality meant an artistic, aestheticised though usually morbid and perverse stimulation of the senses, a kind of mental erethism, called "cerebral lechery", the Baudelairean "prostitution of the soul" (see e.g. Busst 1967, Pierrot 1981, Pynsent 1989). A strict line was drawn between "higher sensuality", depicted as metaphysical sensation though often consisting of various "perverse" desires, and "lower", literary sexual sensuality, which was associated with heterosexual intercourse, feelings of disgust, filth and debasement.

Though their bodily existence represents a burden to Onerva's Decadent heroines, they never assume the strategy of styling themselves into the figure of the effeminate man as do the female characters of some other Decadent women writers, who used such double masquerade in order to get rid of their physical femaleness and thus escape Baudelaire's famous statement about the "natural, abominable woman" who is "the opposite of the dandy" (Baudelaire 1949).[10] Onerva's Mirdja sees beauty and femininity as a constituent part of her self and is thus destined, when attempting to explore the possibilities of cerebral lechery, to choose the role of the *femme fatale*, a highly feminine figure. Though the *femme fatale* always remains object of the male gaze (cf. Belsey 1994, 177), she could be a possible candidate for the role of the male cerebral lecher's counterpart thanks to her "undefeatability", her "mercilessness" and her emotional and sexual sterility. As a *femme fatale,* Mirdja appears to prefer cool and detached observation and contemplation to the "hot orgies of life" in the manner of a Decadent analyst. However, it is repeatedly emphasised that the heroine's inability to realise her erotic dreams does not result from the sexual saturation and Decadent *ennui* but from her inability to achieve complete liberation from conventional morality, the dichotomy of love and sex, the conviction that woman is always – physically and mentally – more affected by sexual relationships than man. Even the narcissistic contemplation of her naked body at the beginning of the novel results in feelings of guilt and a horrifying nightmare (Onerva 1908/1982, 41–42), showing the woman character's difficulties with appropriating narcissism in dandy terms as a self-sufficient, self-confident aesthetic pose.

A female cerebral lecher thus ends up figuring herself as a *demi-vièrge*, a "half-virgin", a pejorative name for a woman who has avoided sexual intercourse but not all other possible ways of erotic and sexual involvement. In *Mirdja,* there is a direct allusion to Marcel Prévost's novel of the same title (Onerva 1908/1982, 201). Needless to say, the demi-vièrge's motivation for abstaining from sexual fulfilment is rather different from that of the Decadent cerebral lecher: while the Decadent dandy tries to deconstruct the model of "natural" male sexuality, the *demi-vièrge* tries to preserve her value as an object of exchange in order to escape the label of a "bad, fallen woman", again, that of a prostitute. The easiness with which these notions could collapse into each other is shown by the concept of the "virgin whore", used in certain contexts as a synonym for the *demi-vièrge*.

It is remarkable to note the extent to which the colourful variations of the figure of the prostitute pervade *fin-de-siècle* imagery. A number of critics have commented upon the significance of the prostitute figure in 19th and early 20th century social imaginary and its emblematic status in the literature and art of the period, most of them basing their approach on Walter Benjamin's ideas (e.g. Buci-Glucksmann 1986, see also Felski 1995, 19, 215). The figure yielded to a number of conflicting interpretations – the prostitute stood e.g. for the commodification of the artist in the market place, the commodification of Eros, and a threatening female sexuality as linked to ideas of contamination and disease. When projected on to the figure of the prostitute, this dangerous female sexuality was easier to control, as the figure was connected with the subordinate strata of society (see Lappalainen 1999). For many male artists and writers, the prostitute was (just as the figure of the lesbian) an emblem of "chic transgression", allowing them to explore, through metaphor or allegory, the above mentioned issues and, at the same time, to shock the bourgeoisie without necessarily challenging traditional assumptions and the privileges of masculinity (cf. Felski 1995, 21).

Due to the frequent habit of identifying the author with her heroines, the prostitute was a rather risky metaphor for a middle class New Woman writer. Women simply had more to lose in compromising their sexual reputation than men did, which Onerva herself experienced when "officially scolded" for her "immoral" novel *Mirdja* by representatives of the Finnish women's movement. Expressing any kind of sexual awareness, let alone sexual liberty by a woman (writer), was viewed as a sign of immorality and corruption by the conservative circles, to which the mainstream women's movement in Finland belonged (see e.g. Rajainen 1973, 82–83). Generally, (middle-class) women were confined to the private sphere, but by no means were they allowed to be truly active within that sphere in terms of expressing sexual desire and reflecting upon it, being bound by mythical, ideological and utilitarian discourses (cf. Karkama 1994, 153, pointing to Kaplan).

Onerva's Decadent texts open the question of how women writers could appropriate Decadent ideas on sexuality at a point in time when contemporary discourses viewed woman's sexuality as either non-existent or as "dark and mysterious", a time when female sexuality was "recognised and immediately crushed" – treated as the pathological origin of hysteria (Giddens 1992, pointing to Foucault) and demonised in various ways. This leads us to one of the fundamental questions posed within the feminist theory of sexual difference: how to problematise, deconstruct or diffuse something which has not yet been voiced, "discovered", and fully granted (cf. Braidotti 1994, 141). At the turn of the 19th and the 20th century, the various Decadent "perversions" as forms of cerebral lechery could only serve as women writers' strategy in the case of writers like the French Rachilde, who abstained from physical femininity, played sophisticated games of masquerade and were uninterested in "normal" heterosexual economy (cf. Felski 1995). There was no discursive space for the type of articulation made possible much later by feminist discourse: to use such "perverse" figurations of Eros as a positive, empowering vision of female sexuality, as not conceptualised within masculine parameters, i.e. focused around orgasm, but figured as multiple and unlocalised; based not on abrupt culmination and climax, but on "female morphology", which can offer much more versatile and sophisticated pleasures than the male model of sexuality (cf. e.g. Irigaray 1977/ 1985, 23–33).

Subterranean fire, cosmic burning and "cold intelligence, alien to erotics"

As indicated above, cerebral sensualism often offered *fin-de-siècle* men a release from the burden of physical sensuality, as well as the displacement of the dichotomy of love and sex, referred to by some Decadent writers as a "deplorable, immoral fiction of the society" (Mauclair 1926, 56), without, however, questioning this fiction from a gender viewpoint. Being at the beginning of the process of discovering and appropriating Eros on their own terms, many early 20th century women writers concentrated on exploration of "the heart of the matter", namely woman's "instincts" and bodily desires. This proved to be an exacting task, considering the nature of contemporary discourses on the subject within which women were viewed either as "pure", asexual beings or as intrinsically erotic and sexual. It is also important to note that, as already suggested, this view was class-specific: asexuality was associated with upper- and middle-class women, while sexuality was associated with lower-class prostitutes. While for men, sexuality was simply one of specialised domains, for woman it either did not exist, or it constituted her entire being.

This interest in women's "instincts" is present in Onerva's early poem *Te naiset* (You women) (Onerva 1904), where the authorial voice exposes the alleged hypocrisy of women who conform to moral double standards and conservative ideals of womanhood, who are "walking in the image of nuns". Women are required to abandon their pretence, and to admit that what they "really want" is to please men – this is their instinctual longing (Onerva 1904, 11–12). This straightforward answer to the famous question "what does a woman want?" could sound bold and provocative when read as a reaction to the conservative image of the middle-class woman as the asexual "angel in the house" or the "household nun" (cf. e.g. Dijkstra 1986), and in Onerva's case, it could be also read as a pun against the conservative Finnish women's movement. However, understood in the context of Onerva's other early texts, the closing line of the poem quoted above can be more adequately seen as an ironic comment on such a simple conclusion. Is a woman's instinctual longing really limited to the urge to please the man? And if it is, what implications would this have?

In her short stories, Onerva takes greater pain to explore the issue of female sexuality as more rooted in a contemporary context than she does in her other early texts. Onerva's middle-class female characters generally perceive their instincts as a dormant force which has to be awakened, a force of which they seem to be afraid (just as the men are), but which they believe to form an essential part of their selves, and which they wish to discover on their own terms. This is the case of the character Sinikka in the short story *Hävittävää voimaa* (Destroying Power) (Onerva 1912). While in Onerva's more Decadent works, such as *Mirdja* and *Inari*, the key male characters are artist-aesthetes who impose on the heroines Decadent ideas of love, many male counterparts of the heroines in her short stories seem, at first sight, to represent the masculine rationality of the Enlightenment, the "voice of reason", which tries to master the dangerous "nature".

One example of this is Sinikka's colleague and suitor Orismala in *Destroying Power,* who expresses his longing for a "calm partnership", while Sinikka feels attracted to what she calls "the dark side of her personality". When she speaks of a "subterranean, eternal fire, which destroys everything, which roars inside, secretly, for a long time, but then, all of a sudden, bursts into lava and a sea of fire that will swallow the world" (Onerva 1912, 60), she uses metaphors of the apocalypse and of "natural disturbance and disaster", explored within the obsessive discourse on female sexuality at the *fin-de-siècle*, but, ironically, also present as a cliché in popular romance (cf. Belsey 1994, 27–28). Sinikka, like most of Onerva's other heroines, internalises the view that the essence of woman is "dark and chaotic", but at the same time tries to break down the oppositions of mind and body by insisting that trying to combine both characteristics should not be regarded as an "unnatural principle"; that they should not be levelled and smoothed out, or the discrepancy between them overcome, because "it cannot be overcome anyway" (Onerva 1912, 61). Orismala's "reasonable" arguments about the dangers involved in the abandonment of self-control eventually prove to be the concerns of a sexually satiated man who has satisfied his erotic needs elsewhere and now longs for a comfortable relationship without much involvement and upheaval. This is what seems to be hiding behind his condemnation of passion and the emphasis on the necessity of suppressing the dangerous, "destructive force" in Sinikka.

Other heroines in Onerva's early short stories struggle, for their part, with the idea that passion and sensuality are in conflict with pure love, equated with spirituality. The protagonist of the short story *Manja Pavlovna* (Onerva 1909) questions the division of love into "pure" and "unpure": she wants her admirer Dmitri to love her both spiritually and sexually. Manja objects to her lover's definition of sexual instinct as the "dark, night side" of the human being, as "something ugly and criminal, which one is aware of but cannot do away with". She says:

> "You should have given me everything, (---), and most of all that animalistic and instinctual love. It belongs to woman, to the woman the man loves. (---) In me, there is also hidden a wild, instinctual life (---), the intoxicating craving for sensual pleasures. (Onerva 1909, 125)

However, Dmitri has also already satisfied his "instinctual needs" elsewhere and does not want Manja to disturb his understanding of the order of things, maintaining that "the idea must possess more weight than instinct..." (Onerva 1909, 135). The exposure of the hypocrisy behind the allegedly "reasonable" or "spiritual" and "sublime" attitude of some of Onerva's heroines' male counterparts also appears in her other early texts in conjunction with men's projecting the contradictory aspects of their selves on to women (cf. Parente-Čapková 1998a, 15), thus pertaining to the above concept of man as a complex being and woman as a symbol of one of the male self's aspects. The statement that woman's "natural force" has to be "kept in the oven" (Onerva 1912, 72), reveals, in this context, that behind the façade of male reason and spirituality there often lurks not only the fear of unbound female sexuality, but, most of all, the fear of the combination of female sexuality with self-awareness, intellect and independence, a combination perceived as particularly threatening.

The question of how to combine female intellect with Eros and, not less importantly, of how to achieve both intellectual and sexual partnership with man, preoccupied most early 20th century women writers and thinkers, as it was, for them, one way of dissolving the opposition of mind and soul versus body, reasonable and/or spiritual love versus passionate sexual involvement. Onerva's early work shows how painful a process this was: in the heroine's self-perception, woman's intellect is often directly contrasted with eroticism and sexuality, as for example in *Inari*. Inari dreams of love as "cosmic burning, which desires great exaltation, unrestrained, overwhelming ecstasy" (Onerva 1913, 12). However, these exalted cosmic visions contrast with Inari's sense of her inability to experience the real ecstasy of infatuation. Inari's female intellectualism is depicted as being incompatible with woman's "natural" sexuality: Inari is portrayed as possessing "cold, proud, idealistic intelligence, alien to erotics", corresponding to the 19th century belief about the incompatibility of female sexuality, intellect and creativity, expressed by philosophers, artists and "scientists" from Baudelaire and Schopenhauer to Nietzsche, Lombroso and Weininger (see e.g. Battersby 1989, 122).

Like Mirdja, Inari also tries to oppose the deeply rooted conviction that men are concerned with sex and women with romance. However, she repeatedly fails to free herself from these beliefs in practice, for example when she wants to punish her beloved but unfaithful partner Porkka by having a sexual relationship with another man. In the midst of being caressed by another man, she ponders her relationship with Porkka, and is overwhelmed by jealousy and anguish over his betrayal. Again, the figure of the prostitute haunts the scene: Inari interprets the attempt to take revenge on Porkka for his infidelity as an "insult against her body", a "sacrifice through prostitution", and the whole situation evolves into a grotesque, tragicomic scene, in which Inari frightens her accidental lover by not displaying any signs of life (Onerva 1913, 65–74).

Though the inability to subvert the rooted stereotypes and dichotomies appears often in Onerva's early texts as one of the major obstacles for the subjectivity formation of the New Woman, there is, nevertheless, one character in Onerva's early work who is able to enjoy her sexuality without feelings of guilt: Raina from the short story bearing her name (Onerva 1911). The intelligent and talented Raina enjoys her various sexual relationships and sees herself as a comrade and a companion to her lovers. The possibility that sexual love might constitute neither the unknown "dark side", nor the entire essence, but just one facet of a woman's being, a pleasure that may or may not be associated with emotional involvement and would not be at odds with a woman's intellect and creativity and which, indeed, the short story seems to open, is subverted by the closure of Raina's suicide.

The specific circumstances leading to her suicide remain unknown, but the narrator of Raina's story emphasises her obsessive conviction that because of her "free" approach to sex, no man can ever love her, though she herself is able to love and longs for affection. "To take one's life is to force others to read one's death", writes Margaret Higonnet in her study on women's suicides in literature (Higonnet 1986, 68). Raina's way of taking her life is a strong statement, differing considerably from the conventional representations of "feminine" suicides. First, she chooses a "masculine" method by shooting herself; in addition to this, her death has very little to do with the passive self-surrender motivated by unhappy love, i.e. being abandoned by a lover and thus losing her *raison d'être*. Though the lack of love is, obviously, one of the main reasons for Raina's suicide, the interpretation of the reasons for her death by the narrator and her interlocutor, emphasising Raina's inner contradictions, suggests a subversion of the traditional figurations of the feminine *mal d'amour*.

The ambivalent ending of *Raina* as in many of Onerva's other texts, opens the question of woman's agency (a crucial one as far as the representation of women's suicides are concerned): we can read Raina's suicide as a metaphor for woman's refusal to be conscripted, forcing, in Dale Bauer's words, the internal dialogue into the open, thus raising questions about sexual difference rather than closing them (Bauer 1988, 4).

The killing sun and the fearful faun

The complexity of the contradiction between woman's will to explore, express, consummate and displace her sexual desire and her inner and outer obstacles in doing so, the tension between female intellect, creativity and the ability to experience (sexual) passion, ecstasy and "true love" is most pregnantly expressed in the heroine's dreams in *Mirdja*. In Symbolism and Decadence, dreams, visions and hallucinations provide a popular means by which to refer to intermediate states which could serve as a key to a "real" reality or to a reflection of unconscious forces (e.g. Pynsent 1989). In *Mirdja*, the heroine's dreams convey the concept of physical, ecstatic love as a mixture of Eros and Thanatos, a concept familiar from Decadent imagery, often pointing to Baroque aesthetics.

Mirdja's above mentioned nightmare at the beginning of the novel reflects her fear of and fascination with "sinful, degenerate sexuality". In the latter part of the novel, Mirdja has two more dreams with strong sexual overtones. In the first of these, Mirdja experiences a strong desire to be made love to by the Apollonian Sun god. She hears a "mighty song of life", a "victorious fanfare of her hero", which calls her to live a "moment of life and death". She is blinded by light: "every cell in her body protruded, pressed itself with a violent compulsion against the unknown"; she feels like a "sunflower which becomes wide open, stretches out, straightens up towards the heavenly beams", towards their "inflamed and deadly kiss". As a result, however, her veins swell and her sinews break, her life blood trickles to the ground, and Mirdja becomes a crumpled skeleton: "The sun is not for Mirdja..." (Onerva 1908/1982, 257–259.)

In the second dream, Mirdja sees herself sitting on a welwitschia leaf looking at a big hairy faun who is sitting on another leaf, from which Mirdja is separated by a broad abyss. However, the faun jumps onto Mirdja's leaf and asks her to dance with him. At the same time, the plant starts to grow, rise and expand so that all of a sudden, they find themselves "flying in the universe". Mirdja experiences "terrible fear", as the faun's hairs seem to grow at an incredible speed. She is unable either to accept or to refuse the faun's invitation. The faun loses his temper, he starts to paw at the leaf which has turned into a dance floor; Mirdja is petrified, unable to move or leave, she becomes part of the welwitschia leaf and cannot escape... (Onerva 1908/1982, 268.)

These cosmic dimensions and the impulse at the intersection of the beautiful, the vital and the instinctual in both dreams point to Onerva's Nietzschean inspirations, namely to the contradictory Nietzschean concept of love as the "spiritualisation of sensuality", as affirmation and self-assurance (cf. Nietzsche 1964). This ecstatic love is desirable but, at the same time, deadly for Mirdja. The mighty Sun god, understood as male in most mythologies and pointing to the concept of the Apollonian as a constructive, creative force in Nietzsche's teaching, is described in Mirdja's dream as an irresistible power which turns into a cruel and hostile force, punishing Mirdja for trying to rise too high and absorb the abilities of the creative genius, as if to remind her that woman is meant to reflect the light of the moon, not the direct light of the sun. The way in which Mirdja's "life liquids" flow to the ground can be read as a direct allusion to Mirdja's infertility both as an artist, i.e. to her dilettantism, and as a woman, i.e. to her childlessness (see Parente-Čapková 1998b).

The image of the faun, a wild creature temporarily trapped by society, connotes the neo-pagan, Dionysian ecstasy in music and dance, and combines the attributes of god, man and animal, pointing directly to wild, ecstatic, instinctual animal sensuality. All this fascinates, enchants, but also frightens Mirdja. The ambivalent, even contradictory figure of the faun in Greek and Roman mythology (fauns could be helpful to humans but could conversely bring about death if they were to be viewed directly) could be easily paralleled with Onerva's heroines' complex feelings about their sexual and bodily existence.[11] As the very idea of ecstasy involves standing outside one's self, it implies the body as an essential part of the self (e.g. Pynsent 1994, 111), as expressed by the image of the ecstatic dance in Mirdja's dream. For Mirdja, however, dance remains the performance of the objectified muse and bayadere, it never becomes a metaphor for woman's rebellious self-expression and self-sufficiency, creative narcissism and initiation, a metaphor which appears in numerous *fin-de-siècle* women writers' works.

The Nietzschean idea of combining love, sex and art, the idea of love and sexuality as artefacts of aesthetic imagination, remains beyond Mirdja's reach even in her dreams. The dreams can be read as a comment on denying real women their share in the figurations of both the Apollonian and the Dionysian, in the creative forces, strong passions, imaginations and drives which the Romantics esteemed to be an essential component of creative genius (cf. Battersby 1989, 102), as well as of the Nietzschean "setting oneself to fire and proud burning". It can however also be seen as an acknowledgement of the extent to which women internalised these denials. In Onerva's *Mirdja*, a strategy for becoming a "dionysiac, affirmative woman" as an empowering interpretation of Nietzsche's thoughts on the feminine (cf. Derrida 1978/1979), which can be ascribed to some other *fin-de-siècle* women writers and thinkers inspired by Nietzsche (such as Lou Andréas Salomé), collapses into projecting woman's strength on to something or someone outside her, indeed, the danger Salomé warned of (cf. Martin 1991, 84). Mirdja's Nietzschean infatuation seems to end with a bitterly Decadent conclusion: "Now we have also burnt ourselves to ashes by the blue flames of our souls. But hardly anything is going to rise from these ashes any more..." (Onerva 1908/1982, 145.)

The Eros-Thanatos image of heat, fire and burning can also be set in juxtaposition to their cold, frosty, and yet strongly sensual counterparts in the closing lines of the novel, when the mad Mirdja roams around the bog, looking for the child she never had: "Cold vapours rise and kiss her. Frost creeps over her and covers her in a white shroud... The marsh herbs smell strong..." (Onerva 1908/1982, 297.)

Free love with a "punishing kiss"

Within the Nietzschean concept of love, Mirdja's dream can be also read as a collapsed hope for the ideal of love as a partnership between two strong, powerful, free and self-assertive beings, which points to one of the meanings of the notion of "free love", an idea widespread at the time. In the 19th century, the term "free love" was loosely applied to all ideas about human intimacy which questioned traditional restraints (Singer 1984/1987, 420). Thus the original title of Onerva's *Mirdja, Vapaa rakkaus* (Free Love), can be interpreted in a number of ways. First of all, it is connected with one of the most fundamental questions of Onerva's works, which, again, resonates a concern of many *fin-de-siècle* women writers and thinkers: is there, for a woman, any possibility of finding a balance between freedom and love, if the ideal of love amounts to a total surrender and "giving-up of oneself", as it is expressed by many of Onerva's heroines?

In Onerva's texts, the ideal of love as a partnership between two independent, equal beings, free of any restraints, is in constant dialogue with the idea of love as a "battle for power and supremacy", the relationship of domination and subordination, which seems to be the other side of the Nietzschean coin, the union of two strong beings. The master-slave dialectics of the heterosexual partnership, traditionally criticised by feminist thinkers (e.g. De Beauvoir 1949/1974), is often mentioned by Onerva's female characters as a necessary aspect of any amorous relationship. In *Mirdja*, the eroticisation of the master-slave relationship is in tune with Decadent sado-masochist imagery. The heroine maintains that one of the partners has to be the "slave" of the other (Onerva 1908/1982, 74), and she feels that she must either be worshipped or dominated as her Decadent educators taught her. The image of the slave and slavery in conjunction with love between woman and man also recurs in *Inari* and in some of Onerva's short stories.

The protagonists of the short stories *Meiri* (Onerva 1909) and *Viha* (Hatred) (Onerva 1909) are young women married to older men, who are "naturally wiser, stronger and more dominating" (Onerva 1909, 161), and treat their much younger wives as capricious children, something which they justify with the well-known 19th century concepts of woman as an immature child in need of control and education. First, the wives accept their role as a natural one and enjoy it, but gradually they grow frustrated and unhappy, knowing that they have no possibility to change the power relations in the marriage. "Woman is either a ruler or a slave" concludes Ertta in *Lankeemus* (Fall) (Onerva 1909, 176). The irony of this short story is that Ertta is encouraged into being "free and equal" by her rational husband, but she feels her nature, of which she is afraid but over which she thinks she has little control, forces her to do otherwise.

Some scenes in Onerva's short stories can be also read as ironic comments on the romanticisation of the master-slave relationship in the manner of popular romance. The short story *Destroying Power*, analysed above as an example of woman's concern to explore her sexuality, also points to another, perhaps the most widespread meaning of the concept of "free love", i.e. to the idea of the relationship between man and woman outside marriage, exclusively on the basis of love. This figuration was to be found e.g. within the radical wings of the women's movement (especially in the U.S.A. and Russia) and was largely concerned to solve the problem of double moral standards and prostitution by means of free, often almost sacral union between man and woman, which would achieve the desired union of the sexual and the spiritual. In the early 20th century Nordic context, these ideas were pioneered by the Swedish thinker Ellen Key.[12] In Finland, the concept of free love had been discussed among artists and intellectuals since the mid-19th century. However, many of the artists and writers (including the Decadents with their urge to *épater la bourgeoisie*) promoted the idea not out of sympathy with the cause for women's liberation, but primarily due to their adherence to the Schopenhaurian and Strindbergian concept of man's "natural promiscuity". Not surprisingly, the mainstream Finnish women's movement was critical of these ideas and regarded them as morally suspicious (Jallinoja 1983, 110–111).

The above mentioned character Orismala in *Destroying Power*, a divorced man with children, seeks in his colleague Sinikka a woman who could be his mistress without demanding too much of him. When talking to her, however, he emphasises the revolutionary aspect of their relationship:

> You could show the world the amazing thing that free love does not have to be the same as immorality and wanton changeability, that it does not have to lead to unhappiness and separation, that it could be beautiful, constructive, enduring. (—). You could realise [this ideal], carry the flag of radicality high till the end... (Onerva 1912, 62–63).

Sinikka accuses Orismala of hypocrisy:

> You speak of being radical, you, whose intelligence has been tamed by the comforts of society... (—) It amazingly resembles conservative principles! (Onerva 1912, 63).

The short story concludes with a tragicomic scene, in which the metaphor of the "subterranean fire" explored above, acquires other meanings. The discussion between Sinikka and Orismala culminates in a kind of a parody of the devices of popular romance: Orismala, whose speech is full of *bon mots* about women, decides, in the end, not to "argue with a woman" any more, and "shuts Sinikka's mouth with a violent kiss", which is, however, "more threatening than caressing". He then concludes:

> You are sweeter than ever. Wonder of wonders, bad temper does not make you ugly, in this respect you are a real woman too. It seems I have to put up with it for the sake of your beauty... (Onerva 1912, 67.)

Sinikka does not respond to this last platitudinous insult but she continues to feel the "dull, rebellious, menacing thunder, which forewarns of danger and revolution" (Onerva 1912, 68). The traditional way of smoothing over "sweet female anger", well-known from popular romance, does not seem to work here: the image of subterranean fire and thunder is now transformed into a symbol of the menace of female anger and revolt.[13] *Destroying Power* is Onerva's critique of the male understanding of the concept of free love as women's sexual availability, as a pretext for making "free" use of female sexuality, again, without thoroughly questioning the whole system of asymmetry and inequality between the sexes.

Middle-class marriage – trap and prostitution?

For many writers and thinkers of the early 20th century, the cardinal antithesis of the various meanings of "free love" (or sometimes of "love" in general) was the institution of marriage, the "principal battlefield between the sexes" and an example *par excellence* of the master-slave relationship. Though, as we shall see, Onerva's treatment of marriage is complex, in most of her texts she portrays marital relationships in a strongly negative way, as institutionalised or monogamous prostitution, which was in tune with the ideas of all radical critics of the 19th century society ranging from Max Nordau to Nietzsche, from the Realists to the Decadents, from misogynists to radical feminists. According not only to the Decadents, love is wholly corrupted in marriage and must always turn to its opposite. Such a process is shown in Onerva's short story *Viha* (Hatred) (Onerva 1909) which depicts the dull inertia of a married couple who just carry on perpetuating their painful relationship and seeing no way out of it.

In *Mirdja,* the Decadent Rolf sees marriage as being totally unacceptable for any thinking man and as a last resort for a woman (e.g. Onerva 1908/1982, 259), and during the first part of the novel, it seems that the heroine has totally absorbed this Decadent contempt for it. When Mirdja suspects that her young admirer Eino intends to marry her, she asks: "What has love to do with all of that?" (Onerva 1908/1982, 25.) She maintains that the economically motivated, i.e. the vulgar, pedestrian institutionalisation of the relationship between man and woman impedes upon the realisation of any higher union. In short, marriage is viewed unequivocally by the young Mirdja as a trap (e.g. Onerva 1908/1982, 53). The concept of marriage as a trap or a prison later appears in several of Onerva's short stories, most explicitly in the short story with a revealing title *Vangittuja sieluja* (Imprisoned Souls) (Onerva 1915), in which Onerva depicts two women imprisoned in marriage for two "classical" reasons: one through her child, the other out of economic dependence. Though they are planning to escape together, neither of them is able to implement the revolt. There are many other dimensions added to the socially critical idea of marriage as prison, mostly by means of questioning the extent to which the women are disabled either by outer circumstances or by their inner contradictions, their "inner imprisonment".

One of the main evils of marriage is its incompatibility with artistic aspirations, highlighted in *Mirdja* and also dealt with in *Inari*. Mirdja's Decadent dilettante father Ervin and Inari's artist lover Porkka recount stories of their nightmarish experiences with marriage, describing their former wives as petite bourgeois, unbearably jealous and possessive. We do not know the wives' rendering of the stories, a point of view which would be particularly interesting in the case of Porkka's wife, who is said to have also been an artist before she married Porkka, and consequently turned into a "motherly bore" (Onerva 1913).

The view of marriage as an obstacle to art is also internalised by Mirdja when she styles herself into the role of the Decadent artist. However, tired of her unsuccessful "Don Juan quest", she finally marries Runar, a middle-class teacher with artistic aspirations, and tortures him with constant reproaches and accusations that he is impeding her from fulfilling her artistic dreams. While constantly living at the expense of Runar, who gave up his artistic ambitions in order to make a living for the family, Mirjda openly shows her typically Decadent contempt for her husband's way of "prostituting himself" by working. This time, Mirdja's position as an economically dependent wife is, ironically enough, compatible with her gender role and can be interpreted in various ways: on the one hand, as a critique of women who take their social handicaps as an excuse for not making any effort to change the status quo, on the other hand, as an ironic comment on this critique, highlighting the obstacles and prejudice with which women artists and writers have to struggle. The second option seems justified especially when this section of *Mirdja* is juxtaposed with Onerva's short story *Jumalien hämärä* (The Twilight of Gods) (Onerva 1915), in which the male protagonist expresses the prevailing opinion on "bourgeois married women writers", saying: "Women who write and are married are writers who enjoy a pension." (Onerva 1915, 46.)

The protagonist of the short story *Marketta Salminen* (Onerva 1909) is a rather different case. *Marketta Salminen* can be read in dialogue with Rolf's, Porkka's and Edvin's opprobrium of their suffocating wives and with the "rule" that the ideal of love has to turn into its antithesis by its consummation through marriage. As a young girl, Marketta dreams of marrying an artist, just like many of Onerva's other young heroines, e.g. the main character of the short story *Elina* (Onerva 1912). In Marketta's story, the dream comes true and does quickly turn to its opposite: the reality of marriage is depicted as a catastrophe once she has to start facing the difficulties of everyday life. Marketta's marriage to a kind of a Decadent dandy, a "pale, romantically beautiful idler" who "merely claimed to be an artist" and refused to "prostitute himself" by means of working,[14] turned out to be a harsh lesson, when Marketta had to work hard in order to keep the whole family. Finally, she leaves her husband and lives alone with her daughter as a disenchanted, sour, hardworking, but independent woman.

Marketta Salminen is a bitterly sarcastic response to the Symbolist and Decadent concept of the clash of ideal and reality, of the convergence of love, art and beauty within which the artist could be a bohemian genius completely divorced from everyday life, and, unless rich enough, could live at somebody's else's expense. The image of the independent, working woman as a product of "ugly reality" is incompatible with the ideals of Love and Beauty, and she becomes, consequentially, "ugly herself" (Onerva 1909, 37). In contrast to Mirdja's husband Runar, who does not have to betray his gender role in order to support the family, Marketta loses her femininity. When trying to "save" her daughter Hellin from making the same mistakes she did, Marketta violently opposes Hellin's inclinations towards daydreaming and forbids her to read romances, while the daughter obviously enjoys them: "Love, you are reading about love all the time. I knew it! It will make you unhappy. (—) Life is no romance!" (Onerva 1909, 33.)

The short story is one of Onerva's most ironic pieces. Marketta's small business is part of the market machinery promoting and perpetuating the institutionalisation and conventionalisation of "love's life plot" for women (cf. e.g. Berlant 2002). The company produces wedding dresses and nightgowns for "true women" who, unlike Marketta, can afford to be "fine, weak and helpless". Marketta, though she tries to maintain her caustic and contemptuous stance towards all that "romantic nonsense", cannot help from feeling envious: in this light, her forced independence has little to do with woman's emancipation and liberation. Hellin's defiance against her mother appears even more ironic; rebelling against Marketta's pessimism, Hellin seems to be ready not to give up her beauty and belief in romantic love and, if necessary, to struggle for them.

Lower class marriage – prostitution or salvation?

The dangers of love and romance may be serious, but definitely less fatal for middle-class women, the typical protagonists of Onerva's texts, than for women from the lower classes. Middle-class women may feel ugly, imprisoned, or even prostituted by marriage, they may feel that "true love" is out of their reach, but the degree to which their freedom is restricted and the "ugliness" of their reality is hardly comparable with that of lower-class women. Early twentieth century lower-class women's reality of love and marriage, as well as their relationship with and response to romantic love, naturally differed from those of middle-class women, in Finland as anywhere else: the meaning that the figure of the prostitute and the image of prostitution acquired for them can serve as one indicator of this.

A very literal contrast between love and "ugliness" is present in the short story *Marja Havu* (Onerva 1911), one of the few of Onerva's texts to deal with a lower-class environment. Marja is a poor, plain girl, an "upstart" who succeeds in receiving some degree of education, but only attracts compassion mixed with disgust in the respectable middle class environment, from which she is quickly expelled once she has finished the school. As a grown-up, she keeps her alcoholic husband, the only man who was "willing to marry her" and whom she took out of pity. At the beginning of their marriage, Marja is "intoxicated by the belated sexual instinct of a virgin", which gives her the strength to carry on and work hard (Onerva 1911, 76). Gradually, she grows exhausted and desperate again. When one night she cannot sleep and goes out for a walk, contemplating her personal revolt in relation to socialist revolutionary ideas, she is labelled an "old slut" by a bypassing man. In the sadly ironic ending of the story, Marja sinks once again into her former Christian humbleness and returns home, grateful for at least having a drunk husband who will never leave her.

In the short story *Kati* (Onerva 1909), Onerva makes use of the typically Realist/Naturalist story of a seduced lower-class girl. Kati is a beautiful lower-class country girl, who has a relationship with an upper-class man, a would-be artist. She refuses to "give herself up" to her "solid" fiancé Karri, a country man himself, who wants to marry her, yet who demands pre-marital sex from her. He insists he wants "proof of Kati's love", but they both know that he wants to check if she is still a virgin, if the goods are still intact, since he will not accept anything "which has been used by the lords". (Onerva 1909, 151.) As a protest, Kati continues her relationship with the painter, which feeds her desire for romance: she is told she is "too beautiful" for the countryside, and the painter promises to take her to the city. Kati's "wild, mad laugh" at the end of the story is a dark omen of the events that might await a "fallen country girl" in the city: the most probable variant seems to be literal prostitution. Ironically, the only salvation for her would be marriage. However, a wedding with either of the two men does not seem to be a likely ending to Kati's story.

In exposing the way double morals work in the countryside, particularly in the figure of Kati's fiancé who seems honestly convinced that his demands are just and right, *Kati* disrupts the myth, popular also in *fin-de-siècle* Finland, that the countryside is "purer" and less corrupted than the city environment. The body of the lower-class woman, associating, as already indicated, available sexuality and corruption, and symbolically connected to the diseased "social body", was a token of Realist and Naturalist prose in Finland as well as elsewhere in Europe (see Lappalainen 2001, 186–192). In Decadence, it served as a symbol of the Decadents' rejoicing in the aesthetic of corruption and degeneration. In *Kati* and *Manja Havu*, the aesthetic of the lower class woman's body is discussed in two specific examples with the result that, for a real lower-class woman, beauty seems to be just as detrimental as ugliness – both can lead to bitter ends and associate her body very clearly with that of the prostitute. By foregrounding the lower class woman's point of view, *Manja Havu* twists the perspective of the above mentioned habit of projecting fantasies of woman's threatening sexuality on to lower class women, who have no defence against being labelled prostitutes. In this way, both the threat of female sexuality and that of the lower classes' rebellion are kept in check (cf. Lappalainen 1999).

In Onerva's early texts, the development of lower-class women's love stories depends on the possibility of education and on economic circumstances even more than in the case of middle-class women. However, an important aspect of both Marja's and Kati's stories is that they are not represented as mere victims of circumstance, rather as distinct individuals. They are as complex and torn by contradictions as Onerva's other female characters, yet they are also aware of their situation and of the various codes of morality and sexuality[15] in making their, albeit severely limited, choices.

Marriage as a mystical union

Though marriage in Western culture has generally been seen in contrast to romantic love (e.g. Singer 1984/1987, 237), there have been, both in philosophy and literature, continuous attempts to elevate married love, figured as romantic partnership, to the highest ideal of love (e.g. Luhmann 1982/1986). This, of course, applied to the strata of the society who could afford such luxury. The Romantics' approach to marriage as the culmination of love was also twofold: some of them (e.g. Byron) maintained the premise that no love could survive the shipwreck of an actual marriage, while others (e.g. Shelley and Schlegel) sought to unify passionate and married love in a higher kind of union, sometimes even as a "mystical marriage", i.e. a "merging" of the beloveds, a key concept of love theories since antiquity (cf. e.g. Singer 1966/1987).

However, no Romantic or other theory has provided an adequate account of how married love could be compatible with, or indeed predicated upon, the demands of sexual intimacy and passion (Singer 1987), an issue which clearly preoccupied many women writers at the beginning of the 20th century, as closely connected to questioning the dichotomy between physical and "pure" love. The rendering of the story of Tristan and Isolde by the French scholar and writer Joseph Bédier, which Onerva translated into Finnish (Bédier 1954), indicates Onerva's complex relationship with the topic: the very myth of Tristan and Isolde, resulting from the conflict between sexual love and marriage, contributes, according to some interpretations, to the idealisation of married love by manifesting a desire *not* to separate, but to harmonise passion and marriage (Singer 1987, 34).

A most interesting way of discussing the issue of marriage provides the second part of Onerva's novel *Mirdja*. As suggested above, at the beginning of the marriage, the heroine feels trapped and deceived. She bitterly regrets having a church wedding, celebrated by her husband's father, and critiques the Protestant concept of marriage when she contrasts the way in which marriage is viewed in France with its image in Northern Europe. She sees the French way, which she calls a "formality for the sake of formality" as a much better and healthier alternative to the "Nordic attitude" which "tries to realise ideal perfection in such a rude form", and "refuses to admit any form without a content, but does not dare to create new form for the content in question". (Onerva 1908/1982, 243.) What is under attack is not only double moral standards, but also the idea of marriage based on Lutheran principles which systematically advocated the mode of integrating love and marriage in a "holy form of heterosexual friendship, a source of communion or righteous intimacy between husband and wife" (Singer 1987, 5, 31–32).

In 19th century Finland this concept of marriage served as a cornerstone of the national project, developed extensively since the 1840s by the "national philosopher", the Hegelian J.V.Snellman, who elevated the family to the status of a central political idea and dedicated much attention to it in his philosophy of the state (e.g. Häggman 1994). According to Snellman, marriage was to be based on the mutual love and respect of both partners, whilst married love was to be "reasonable": it had to find the right balance between feelings and reason. Together with a sense of duty, it should contribute to the fulfilment of the crucial role of marriage: producing children and educating them as moral citizens (Snellman 1842/1993, Karkama 1985). Other dominant discourses on marriage in early 20th century Finland drew similar lines, concentrating on procreation as the main goal of marriage (e.g. Räisänen 1995).

Passionate, romantic love, "love as merging", had no place in this discourse and was seen to be largely antithetical to the sober concept of healthy society, healthy nation. This attitude was in turn adopted by the mainstream Finnish women's movement. Within Finland's women's writing, which soon entered into dialogue with the hegemonic discourse on love and marriage, the strongest current was formed by those who tried to endow the existing concept of marriage with richer meaning.[16] The most popular ideals were "love marriage" and "companionate marriage", which tried, at least to some extent, to adapt the above mentioned Snellmanian ideals to women's needs and expectations. However, even within these concepts, the tension between married love with passionate sensuality and "mystical merging" remained unresolved.

In the last part of *Mirdja*, the Decadent degradation of marriage is transformed, surprisingly, into a more Symbolist understanding of the "mystical marriage", the above mentioned merging of the beloveds, and proves to be the means by which Mirdja as an alienated, fragmented Decadent subject experiences the desired feeling of being "whole, unshattered, unfragmented". After Mirdja has struggled for years with frustration and delusion and after long episodes of torturing Runar with constant lamentations and reproaches, she begins to appreciate Runar's nurturing, "feminine" qualities. The battle for power is forgotten and the desired "fusion" is, together with intimacy found within the framework of real marriage, albeit at a price: it happens too late, on the brink of both partners' mental illness and death, which is the price Mirdja has to pay for her symbiosis with another human being, for the feeling of unity and integration that would finally help her overcome the Decadent feelings of being split, her "half-heartedness", and the split between the mind and body. Sinking into a prelinguistic, Edenic space of perfect mutual understanding, the couple seem to sink into a kind of the Kristevan Semiotic, resigning altogether to the demands of the Symbolic, including language, which used to be the major cause of misunderstanding in their relationship (cf. Parente-Čapková 2001, 230–231).

The relationship between Mirdja and Runar can be characterised as a possibility to live the relationship with the other in a different way. The hierarchy between sexes is erased. The idea of transformation through love, an important component of the myth of romantic love, happens through questioning the strictly heterosexual character of the relationship. In Runar, the feminine qualities begin to prevail and thus the "ideal fusion" of the partners resists the concept of the complementarity of the sexes, the "dream of radical heterosexuality". In this way, the story seriously subverts the plot of romantic love. It is also important to note that Runar's feminine qualities have nothing to do with abstract, aestheticised Decadent effeminacy, constructed as antithetical to real women. The late relationship between Mirdja and Runar suggests the possibility of a relationship between two subjects instead of a subject and an object, as well as a relationship in which the physical, the instinctual and the transcendental fuse. The subversion of the classical love plot can be also seen as a process leading to Mirdja's new way of contemplating her relationships with other women (cf. Rojola 1991), a way which would enable her to relate to herself and to other women not exclusively through her relationships with men. The possibility of revaluating her relationship with other women both on a concrete, physical and emotional, as well as on a transcendental level, is, however, left open.

Mature children of immature times and the possibility of new love

In Onerva's early work, fusion in love and liberation from rooted dichotomies and gender constraints is possible only outside contemporary reality, in which love and freedom are mutually exclusive. Although the Naturalist belief in woman's "hereditary", "atavistic" instincts which prevents women from being free and equal partners, something strongly present in Onerva's texts,[17] is also frequently questioned. A "longing for serfdom" is encoded in woman's blood and instincts, but, at the same time, the view of this is not totally fatalist: in the long run, it could be changed with the help of women's resolution and a determined struggle for emancipation. Since Onerva's heroines understand this resolute, rational part of their selves, i.e. their mind as masculine (cf. Lappalainen 1991), they feel that if they realise themselves through this part, they can no longer experience love as truly feminine women can. However, this view is also disturbed, at least to a certain extent, in the short stories *Itsenäinen nainen* (Independent Woman) (Onerva 1909) and *Kiusaus* (Temptation) (Onerva 1915). The characters of the protagonists, the intellectual Ilmi and the lawyer Liina Syväri, can be read as a polemic with the view that intellectual capacity (together with feminist concerns) and the ability to love passionately are mutually exclusive for woman, the view with which the protagonist of *Inari* struggles so hopelessly. Ilmi and Liina are both women in search of heterosexual union; however, they are firmly determined not to compromise their ideals and prefer to stay alone. The young protagonist of the short story *Inkeri* (Onerva 1909) also wants to preserve her personality and independence and to remain free "in all senses" because she knows her beloved would not be able to realise the relationship in the way she would like. Inkeri is said to have in her "blood and instinct" all that "half-hearted" Decadent women, whose intermediate being is "built on contradictions" and whose instinct "still longs for serfdom", have only "in their heads" (Onerva 1909).

Both Ilmi and Liina can be, in many ways, called products of male education, as was usually the case with women artists and intellectuals at the beginning of the 20th century. Ilmi seems to have remained "halfway", whilst Liina is portrayed as having slipped out of her Pygmalion's control, maintaining that he "made her unintentionally" (Onerva 1915, 136). In addition, she is remarkable for her ethical resolution: she turns down the man she loves (the Pygmalion himself) because she does not want to make his wife unhappy. Liina's ethical principles are devoid of the traditional moralist approach: as a feminist lawyer, she is severely critical of the institution of marriage, but she firmly refuses to cause a third person's, i.e. her beloved's wife's, suffering. Liina calls herself an "immature child of immature times" (Onerva 1915, 135), but she shows her maturity by being ready, both in her public and personal activities, to assume responsibility for herself and her deeds – a responsibility of which women had so far been deprived. Though female sacrifice is viewed in negative light in Onerva's early work, there is no place for the concept of freedom as total escape from constraint, responsibility or sociality.[18]

*

Numerous possibilities of figuring love differently were explored at the beginning of the 20th century through the concept of "new love". A strong current was formed by those women writers and thinkers who connected the idea of new love with motherhood as e.g. the German writer Elisabeth Dauthendey, whose book *New Love* was translated into Finnish in 1902, and Ellen Key, who introduced Dauthendey into the Nordic context. Key's concept of the new, almighty Eros drawing on Nietzsche's metaphors of maternity and birth and her Spencerean ideas, emphasising the "natural" difference between the sexes, were close to Onerva's inspirations. Onerva, however, remained sceptical about appropriating these icons of womanhood by venerating woman's reproductive capacities, while neglecting her intellectual potential, and reducing her creative forces to those of reproduction. In this context, Key's lack of trust in the creative and intellectual capacity of woman seems remote from Onerva's painful preoccupation with these issues (cf. Parente-Čapková 1998b). Although deeply concerned with the issue of motherhood, Onerva was looking for another basis for the relationship between man and woman; indeed, in the short story *Isää etsimässä* (Looking for the Father) (Onerva 1915), which advocates the idea that women should choose the fathers of their children, as also expressed by Key, the child is seen as a substitute for a happy relationship between adults, *not* as its goal.

Other trends typical of what has been called "essentialist constructivism" (Witt-Brattström 2002), i.e. various powerful *fin-de-siècle* strategies of positively constructing female subjectivity, remained alien to Onerva, as is obvious from her pessimistic Decadent treatment of the theme of narcissism, especially when compared with the erotic "narcissistic essentialism" of Lou Andréas Salomé. Salomé defined woman "exclusively through her difference from man" and tried to deconstruct the dichotomy soul/body by turning woman into the norm, the "first sex", and man into her other, basing the concept of female creativity on woman's self-sufficiency (Salomé 1899, Martin 1991).

As has been pointed out various times, namely in conjunction with *Mirdja*, the issue of female creativity was Onerva's most painful concern (Buchwald 1990, Rojola 1992). The above analyses, however, show that in Onerva's texts the identity quest through love does not bring artistic integrity to woman. The complex web of women's outer and inner restraints calls most of all for liberation in the sense of a thorough questioning of gender inequality on various levels. In Onerva's case, this project does not seem to leave much space for ecstatic venerations of femininity, though Onerva, with her interest in combining female beauty and creativity, can hardly be accused of any attempt to eradicate difference. However, given that "woman's nature" can manifest itself in Onerva's "split" woman as undesirable atavism, which can deprive her of creative freedom, it seems that freedom for Onerva, unlike for some other early 20th century women writers and thinkers, was by no means restricted to the freedom to love. Onerva's solutions thus remain remote from those of Laura Marholm, for whom woman's existence through love, the process of becoming woman through love for a man, was closely entwined with the possibility of genuine female creativity. Onerva's women prefer to live, work and create without love, and, in this way, struggle for the possibility of more democratic love relationships for future women. The idea expressed by Alexandra Kollontai, that from being the object of the love tragedy of a man the early twentieth century woman is becoming the subject of her own, independent love tragedy (cf. Porter 1980), apply very well to the complex tragedies of Onerva's New Woman heroines, who, apart from occasional nostalgia, would not exchange their unhappiness for the "Old", i.e. domesticated woman's happiness, as put in Onerva's short story *Independent Woman* (Onerva 1909, 77).

Although Onerva was much concerned with aesthetic issues and "erotic contract", it would not do justice to her work to see her as one of those New Woman writers who, at the *fin-de-siècle*, turned from the discussion of social conditions to sexual and aesthetic conditions (Witt-Brattström 2002, quoting Birgitta Holm; see also Showalter 1995). Onerva does speak mainly for educated middle-class urban women, but her short stories also show a concern for the options open to real women of the lower classes.[19] The way Onerva´s texts employ the image of the prostitute and prostitution, foregrounding its different meanings and degrees of abstraction for male aesthetes, women writers and individualised real women of the various social strata, illustrates how multifaceted an analysis Onerva's work presents of the aesthetic, gender and social issues, grounded in the early 20th-century Finnish reality.

At first sight, the dialogue between the various styles and modes in Onerva's early work suggests that the more realist style of the short stories gives more space for exploration of the possibility of new love for women, since the Decadent mode appears to offer merely an abstract, void means of transgression, based on the metaphorisation of woman, the erasure of woman's body and the reduction of woman to a male fantasy. A closer analysis, however, reveals that radically different, i.e. new figurations of love and relationships between the sexes take place namely within the Decadent mode, in the novel Mirdja. It is through Decadent poetics that both the fatal difference and the tragic misunderstanding between the sexes, which preoccupied Onerva in so many of her early texts, cease to exist. The fulfilment of love remains in an unattainable sphere, as in Symbolism and Decadence, but it is seen through women's concerns. In this sense, Decadent ambivalence works as a tool of subversion and as a *re-scripting* of traditional romance, defined as not only altering the codes and conventions of the genre, but, more importantly, as actively interrogating and destabilising the institutions in which those conventions have become embedded (cf. Pearce and Wisker 1998, 2).

Apart from Onerva's subversive re-scriptions and her efficient employment of irony and parody, which helped to reveal the hypocrisy hidden behind both the traditional double morals and some seemingly radical ideas, the ancient, "eternal" idea of heterosexual love as merging, as a total surrending of oneself to the other, remained an ideal perpetuated in her texts. The risky nature of this ideal for the early 20th century New Woman is, nevertheless, constantly emphasised. Given that the New Man, represented in Onerva's early work by the tender, nurturing, undemanding brotherly figures with "feminine" qualities (Runar in *Mirdja* and Alvia in *Inari*), seems a mere utopia, and that the question of relationship to other women remain open, the New Woman must be cautious of giving up that little bit of freedom and independence she has attained.

NOTES

1 Some 19th century feminists argued that the blind, passionate, seductive and conflictual nature of romantic love undermined women's interests (see Leach, W., True Love and Perfect Union. London: Routledge & Kegan Paul 1981, quoted in Langford 1999). Some major protagonists of "first" and "second wave" feminism also pointed out that the discourse of romantic love is a site of women's complicity in patriarchal relations (e.g. Alexandra Kollontai, Simone de Beauvoir, Germaine Greer, Kate Millet, Shulamith Firestone).

2 The most obvious example would be Luce Irigaray with her defence of the divinity in sexuality and female transcendence (e.g. Irigaray 1984, 1992). Certain currents within gender-conscious sociological research developed positive figurations of love within the concept of 'democratisation' of the love relationship (e.g. Giddens 1992), which has been recently criticised by some feminists as too optimistic and romanticising (see esp. Langford 1999).

3 Studies on the textuality of romance (starting with Tania Modleski 1982 and Janice Radway 1984) meant a radical departure with previous "anti-romance" feminist

ideology. See e.g. Pearce & Stacey 1995 and Pearce & Wisker 1998, Liljeström 1999 for negotiations of a variety of possibilities of using the discourse of romantic love in a subversive, radical and liberatory way by means of figurations of both heterosexual and queer romance.

4   I use the term "New Woman" to point to any attempt by the *fin-de-siècle* thinkers and artists/writers to create a concept of female subjectivity different from previous ones, a discursive construction based predominantly on the concerns of middle class women. However, as has been pointed out, much of it could be characterised by a Foucaldian term "reverse discourse", which uses definitions, diagnoses and categories of femininity from 19th century. The New Woman would thus be a figure negotiating between the 19th century discourses on sexuality and the contemporary feminist movement (Witt-Brattström 2002). For the Finnish context see Hapuli, Koivunen, Lappalainen, Rojola 1992, and Rojola 1999.

5   I am pointing to the discussions of the various modes of maternal love in Onerva's novel *Mirdja*, to the analysis of the character of Mirdja as a female subject, split Modernist subject and a Narcissistic figure (see e.g. Lappalainen 1991 and 1992, Rojola 1991 and 1992, Virtala 1994, Lyytikäinen 1997 and 1999, Parente-Čapková 1998a, b and 2001).

6   To my knowledge, the only texts by Onerva translated into English are an extract from the novel *Mirdja* published in Books from Finland 1/1984 (translated by Mary Lomas and introduced by Maria-Liisa Nevala), and the poem *Tropiikin alla* (In the Tropics) in the anthology *Skating on the Sea. Poetry from Finland*. Newcastle upon Tyne & Helsinki: Bloodaxe Books, 1997 (ed. and transl. by Keith Bosley). All translations in the present article are mine.

7   The points in common with the psychoanalytical concept of love and desire are more than obvious (see e.g. Pierrot 1981, Virtala 1994, Lyytikäinen 1997).

8   This idea was already articulated by some of the Romantic forerunners of Decadence, e.g. Alfred de Musset, whose work Onerva analysed and translated: "To love is the great point. What matters the mistress? What matters the flagon provided one have the intoxication?" (quoted in Singer 1984/1987, 297–299.) The hostility towards "real women" has often been explained by the homosexuality of many Decadent artists, but this was obviously only one of its components (e.g. West 1993; for the discussion on the relationship between *fin-de-siecle* feminists and gay artists see also Showalter 1995 and Ledger 1997).

9   On Mirdja as a muse figure see Buchwald 1990 and Parente-Čapková 2001.

10 The best example of such a strategy is the French writer Rachilde, who styled herself into the figure of the androgynous, effeminate (but actually male) Decadent artist, trying to escape the burden of the embodied femininity.

11 By the beginning of the 20th century, the faun as a symbol of sexuality was commonplace; let us mention Hawthorn's *Marble Faun* (1860) with its morale of losing innocence and becoming the victim of evil after giving way to demonic passions; the most Decadent image of a faun is presented by the famous poem by Mallarmé *A Faun's Afternoon* (L'Après-midi d'un faune, 1876), which is, of course, completely antithetical to Onerva's deployment of the figure.

12 In Ellen Key's case, various meanings of the notion of free love (love outside the institution of marriage and love as a union of two free beings) tend to fuse. It has also been pointed out that "love's freedom" describes better Key's concept of heterosexual love (see Key 1911 and Kinnunen 1993).

13 A similar example of the tragicomic formula "shutting woman's mouth with a kiss" is to be found in *Inari* (Onerva 1913, 77–78).

14 Another example of an artist who marries a woman in order to gain financial security is the character Eljas in the short story *Neljä ihmistä* (Four People) (Onerva 1911), which also explores the issue of the artist who is "above all morals" and "does not spare (female) bodies".

15 In this way, the stories enter into dialogue with *fin-de-siècle* Naturalist representations of lower-class women (see Lappalainen 2001, esp. 189–191).

16 A number of studies concerning women writers' response to the issue, as well as their attempts to reconcile love, duty and freedom in 19th and early 20th century Finland have appeared in the last two decades: from the most recent publications let us mention Paasonen 1999, Aalto 2000, Immonen &al. 2000 and Lappalainen, Grönstrand & Launis 2001.
17 Belief in heredity and other forms of biological determinism are present in a number of Onerva's early texts: most explicitly in *Mirdja* and in the short story *Veren ääni* (Voice of Blood) (Onerva 1911).
18 The influence of the Ibsenian ethic is, of course, more than obvious – Ibsen was a strong source of inspiration for the previous generation of Finnish women writers represented by the Realist Minna Canth. For Ibsen's reception and influence in Finland see e.g. Liukko 1980, in conjunction with the women's question e.g. Lappalainen 2001.
19 For discussion of the class aspects of New Woman writing in Finland, see e. g. Rojola 1999.

REFERENCES

AALTO, MINNA 2000: *Vapauden ja velvollisuuden ristiriita. Kehitysromaanin mahdollisuudet 1890-luvun lopun ja 1900-luvun alun naiskirjallisuudessa.* Helsinki: Suomalaisen Kirjallisuuden Seura.
BALAKIAN, ANNA 1967: *The Symbolist Movement. A Critical Appraisal.* New York: Random House.
BATTERSBY, CHRISTINE 1989: *Gender and Genius. Towards a Feminist Aesthetics.* London: The Women's Press.
BAUDELAIRE, CHARLES 1949: *Journaux intimes. Fusées. Mon Coeur mis à nu.* Carnet, ed. by J.Crepet and G. Blin, Paris.
BAUER, DALE M. 1988: *Feminist Dialogics. A Theory of Failed Community.* Albany: State University of New York Press.
BEAUVOIR, SIMONE de 1949/1974: *The Second Sex: Facts, Myths and Lived Reality* (Le deuxième sexe). London: Vintage Books.
BÉDIER, JOSEPH 1954: *Tristan ja Isolde.* Translated by L.Onerva. Helsinki: Tammi.
BELSEY, CATHERINE 1994: *Desire. Love Stories in Western Culture.* Oxford UK and Cambridge USA: Blackwell.
BERLANT, LAUREN 2002: "Remembering Love, Forgetting Everything Else: Now, Voyager". Paper presented at the conference "Naistutkimuspäivät / Kvinnoforskningsdagarna", University of Turku/Åbo akademi, 22.–23.11.2002.
BRAIDOTTI, ROSI 1991: *Patterns of Dissonance. A Study of Women in Contemporary Philosophy.* Cambridge: Polity Press.
BRAIDOTTI, ROSI 1994: *Nomadic Subjects. Embodiment and Sexual Difference in Contemporary Feminist Theory.* New York: Columbia University Press.
BUCHWALD, EVA 1990: *Ideals of Womanhood in the Literature of Finland and Russia 1894–1914.* PhD. Thesis. School of Slavonic and East European Studies, University of London.
BUCI-GLUCKSMANN, CHRISTINE 1986: "Catastrophic Utopia: The Feminine as Allegory of the Modern." Representations n. 14.
BUSST, A.J.L. 1967: The Image of the Androgyne in the Nineteenth Century. *In Romantic Mythologies.* Ed. Ian Fletcher. London: Routledge & Kegan Paul.
DAUTHENDEY, ELISABETH 1902: *Uusi rakkaus. Kirja kypsyneille hengille.* Kuopio: C. J. Bergström.
DE LAURETIS, TERESA 1986: Feminist Studies/Critical Studies. Issues, Terms and Contexts. In: De Lauretis, Teresa (ed.), *Feminist Studies Critical Studies.* Bloomington: Indiana University Press.
DE LAURETIS, TERESA 1987: *Technologies of Gender.* Bloomington: Indiana University Press.
DERRIDA, JACQUES 1978/1979: *Spurs: Nietzsche's Styles.* Transl. by Barbara Harlow. Chicago: University of Chicago Press.

DIJKSTRA, BRAM 1986: *Idols of Perversity. Fantasies of Feminine Evil in Fin-de-Siècle Culture*. Oxford: Oxford University Press.
FELSKI, RITA 1995: *The Gender of Modernity*. Cambridge (Mass.) & London: Harvard University Press.
FETTERLY, JUDITH 1986: Reading about Reading: "A Jury of Her Peers", "The Murders in the Rue Morgue", and the "Yellow Wallpaper". *In* Flynn, Elizabeth A., Schweickart, Patrocinio (eds.): *Gender and Reading. Essays on Readers, Texts, and Contexts*. Baltimore and London: The John Hopkins Univeristy Press.
GAGNIER, REGENIA 1994: A Critique of Practical Aesthetics. In Levin, G. (ed.): *Aesthetics and Ideology*. New Brunswick, New Jersey: Rutgers University Press.
GIDDENS, ANTHONY 1992: *The Transformation of Intimacy. Sexuality, Love and Eroticism in Modern Societies*. Cambridge: Polity Press.
HAPULI, RITVA, KOIVUNEN, ANU, LAPPALAINEN, PÄIVI & ROJOLA, LEA 1992: Uutta naista etsimässä. *In* Onnela T. (ed.): *Vampyyrinainen ja Kenkkuinniemen sauna. Suomalainen kaksikymmenluku ja modernin mahdollisuus*. Helsinki: Suomalaisen Kirjallisuuden Seura.
HIGONNET, MARGARET 1986: Speaking Silences: Women's Suicide. *In* Suleiman, Susan Rubin (ed.): *The Female Body in Western Culture. Contemporary Perspectives*. Cambridge, Massachusetts & London, England: Harvard University Press.
HÄGGMAN, KAI 1994: *Perheen vuosisata. Perheen ihanne ja sivistyneistön elämäntapa 1800-luvun Suomessa*. Helsinki: Suomen Historiallinen Seura, Historiallisia tutkimuksia 179.
IMMONEN, KARI, HAPULI, RITVA, LESKELÄ, MAARIT, VEHKALAHTI, KAISA 2000: *Modernin lumo ja pelko. Kymmenen kirjoitusta 1800–1900-lukujen vaihteen sukupuolisuudesta*. Helsinki: Suomalaisen Kirjallisuuden Seura.
IRIGARAY, LUCE 1977/1985: *This Sex Which Is Not One*. (Ce Sexe qui n'en pas un) Transl. by Catherine Porter with Carolyn Burke. Cornell UP, Ithaca.
IRIGARAY, LUCE 1984: *Éthique de la difference sexuelle*. Paris: Éditions de Minuit.
IRIGARAY, LUCE 1992: *J'aime à toi. Esquisse d'une félicité dans l'histoire*. Paris: Bernard Grasset.
JALLINOJA, RIITTA 1983: *Suomalaisen naisasialiikkeen taistelukaudet. Naisasialiike naisten elämäntilanteen muutoksen ja yhteiskunnallis-aatteellisen murroksen heijastajana*. Helsinki: WSOY.
KARKAMA, PERTTI 1985: *Järkevä rakkaus. J. V. Snellman kirjoittajana*. Helsinki: Suomalaisen Kirjallisuuden Seura.
KARKAMA, PERTTI 1994: *Kirjallisuus ja nykyaika. Suomalaisen sanataiteen teemoja ja tendenssejä*. Helsinki: Suomalaisen Kirjallisuuden Seura.
KEY, ELLEN 1911: *The Morality of Women*. N.B.B. Chicago: Ralph Fletcher Seymour Company.
KINNUNEN, TIINA 1993: *Ylistyslaulu naisellisuudelle. Johdatus Ellen Keyn feministiseen teoriaan*. Naistutkimus-Kvinnoforskning n. 3.
LANGFORD, WENDY 1999: *Revolutions of the Heart. Gender, Power and the Delusions of Love*. London and New York: Routledge.
LAPPALAINEN, PÄIVI 1991: Body or Mind: The Difficulty of Integration in the Representation of the Female Self. *In* Lier, A. (ed.): *Modernismen i Skandinavisk litteratur som historisk fenomen og teoretisk problem*. Trondheim: Nordisk institutt, AVH, Universitetet i Trondheim.
LAPPALAINEN, PÄIVI 1992: Jotakin vanhaa, jotakin uutta. Naisen subjektiviteetin rakentuminen L.Onervan Mirdjassa ja Aino Kallaksen Sudenmorsiamessa. *In* Onnela T. (ed.): *Vampyyrinainen ja Kenkkuinniemen sauna. Suomalainen kaksikymmenluku ja modernin mahdollisuus*. Helsinki: Suomalaisen Kirjallisuuden Seura.
LAPPALAINEN, PÄIVI 1999: "Äiti-ilon himo". Naiset ja kansakunnan rakentuminen 1800-luvulla. *In* Koistinen, Tero, Kruuspere, Piret, Sevänen, Erkki & Turunen, Risto (eds.): *Kaksi tietä nykyisyyteen*. Helsinki: Suomalaisen Kirjallisuuden Seura.
LAPPALAINEN, PÄIVI 2001: *Koti, kansa ja maailman tahraava lika. Näkökulmia 1880- ja 1890-luvun kirjallisuuteen*. Helsinki: Suomalaisen Kirjallisuuden Seura.
LAPPALAINEN, PÄIVI, GRÖNSTRAND, HEIDI, LAUNIS, KATI (eds.) 2001: *Lähikuvassa nainen. Näköaloja 1800-luvun kirjalliseen kulttuuriin*. Helsinki: Suomalaisen Kirjallisuuden Seura.

LEDGER, SALLY 1997: *The New Woman. Fiction and Feminism at the* fin-de-siècle. Manchester and New York: Manchester University Press.
LILJESTRÖM, MARIANNE 1999: Lukijalle. *In* Paasonen, Susanna (ed.): *Hääkirja. Kirjoituksia rakkaudesta, romantiikasta ja sukupuolesta.* Turku: Turun yliopisto, Taiteiden tutkimuksen laitos, Naistutkimus, Sarja A, N:o 43.
LIUKKO, PIRKKO 1980: *Ibsen ja Suomi 1880-1910. Vaikutustutkimuksen aineksia ja lähteitä.* Turku: Turun yliopisto, Kirjallisuuden ja musiikkitieteen laitos, Sarja A, N:o 3.
LUHMANN, NIKLAS 1982/1986: *Love as Passion. The Codification of Intimacy.* Transl. by Jeremy Gaines and Doris L. Jones. Cambridge: Polity Press.
LYYTIKÄINEN, PIRJO 1997: *Narkissos ja Sfinksi. Minä ja Toinen vuosisadanvaihteen kirjallisuudessa.* Helsinki: Suomalaisen Kirjallisuuden Seura.
LYYTIKÄINEN, PIRJO 1999: Mirdja – dekadentti nainen. *In* Rojola, Lea (ed.): *Suomen kirjallisuushistoria II. Järkiuskosta vaistojen kapinaan.* Helsinki: Suomalaisen Kirjallisuuden Seura.
MARHOLM, LAURA 1895/1897: *Knihažen. Podobizny časové psychologie* (Das Buch der Frauen. Zeitpsychologische Porträts). Praha.
MARTIN, BIDDY 1991: *Woman and Modernity. The (Life)Styles of Lou Andreas-Salomé.* Ithaca & London: Cornell University Press.
MAUCLAIR, CAMILLE 1926: *Kouzlo lásky.* Praha: Jan Laichter.
MODLESKI, TANIA 1982: *Loving with a Vengenace: Mass-Produced Fantasies for Women.* London: Methuen.
NIETZSCHE, FRIEDRICH 1964: *The Complete Works of Friedrich Nietzsche,* vol. 16 by Friedrich Nietzsche, ed. Oscar Levy. New York: Russell & Russell.
ONERVA, L. "Watteau, rokoko-sulotarten esiin uneksija". Käsikirjoitus. SKS:n Kirjallisuusarkisto (Literary Archive of the Finnish Literature Society).
ONERVA, L. 1904: *Sekasointuja.* Helsinki: Lilius & Hertzberg.
ONERVA, L. 1905: "Musset'n naisluonteet". Laudaturtyö. SKS:n Kirjallisuusarkisto (Literary Archive of the Finnish Literature Society).
ONERVA, L. 1908: *Runoja.* Helsinki: Vihtori Kosonen.
ONERVA, L. 1908/1982: *Mirdja.* Helsinki: Otava.
ONERVA, L. 1909: *Murtoviivoja.* Helsinki: Otava .
ONERVA, L. 1910: *Särjetyt jumalat.* Helsinki: Otava
ONERVA, L. 1911: *Nousukkaita.* Helsinki: Yrjö Weilin & kumpp.
ONERVA, L. 1912: *Mies ja nainen.* Helsinki: Kirja.
ONERVA, L. 1913: *Inari.* Helsinki: Weilin & Göös.
ONERVA, L. 1915: *Vangittuja sieluja.* Helsinki: Kirja.
PAASONEN, SUSANNA (ed.) 1999: Hääkirja. *Kirjoituksia rakkaudesta, romantiikasta ja sukupuolesta.* Turku: Turun yliopisto, Taiteiden tutkimuksen laitos, Naistutkimus, Sarja A, N:o 43.
PARENTE-ČAPKOVÁ, VIOLA 1998a: Decadent New Woman? NORA n.1, Vol.6.
PARENTE-ČAPKOVÁ, VIOLA 1998b: "Kuka, kuka sitoi?" Dekadentti äitiys L.Onervan Mirdjassa. *In* Lyytikäinen, Pirjo (ed.): *Dekadenssi vuosisadan vaihteen taiteessa ja kirjallisuudessa.* Helsinki: Suomalaisen Kirjallisuuden Seura.
PARENTE-ČAPKOVÁ, VIOLA 2001: Kuvittelija/tar. Androgyyniset mielikuvat L.Onervan varhaisproosassa. *In* Lappalainen, Päivi, Grönstrand, Heidi, Launis, Kati (eds.): *Lähikuvassa nainen. Näköaloja 1800-luvun kirjalliseen kulttuuriin.* Helsinki: Suomalaisen Kirjallisuuden Seura.
PEARCE, LYNNE & STACEY, JACKIE (eds) 1995: *Romance Revisited.* New York and London: New York University Press.
PEARCE, LYNNE & WISKER, GINA (eds) 1998: *Fatal Attractions. Rescripting Romance in Contemporary Literature and Film.* London – Sterling – Virginia: Pluto Press.
PIERROT, JEAN 1981: *The Decadent Imagination 1880–1900.* Chicago & London: The University of Chicago Press.
PORTER, CATHY 1980: *Alexandra Kollontai.* A Biography. London: Virago 1980.
PYNSENT, ROBERT 1989: Conclusory Essay: Decadence and Innovation. *In* Pynsent R. (ed.): *Decadence and Innovation: Austro-Hungarian Life and Art at the Turn of the Century.* London: Weidenfeld and Nicolson.

PYNSENT, ROBERT 1994: Decadent Self. *In Questions of Identity. Czech and Slovak Ideas of Nationality and Personality*. London: Central European University Press.
RADWAY, JANICE 1984: *Reading the Romance: Women, Patriarchy, and Popular Literature*. Chapel Hill & London: The University of North Carolina Press.
RAJAINEN, MAIJA 1973: *Naisliike ja sukupuolimoraali. Keskustelua ja toimintaa 1800-luvulla ja nykyisen vuosisadan alkupuolella noin vuoteen 1918 saakka*. Helsinki: Suomen kirkkohistoriallinen seura.
RICH, ADRIENNE 1980: Compulsory Heterosexuality and Lesbian Existence. Signs n. 5:4.
ROJOLA, LEA 1991: Plotting Her New Life: Modern Women Authors in Finland and the Conventions of the Plot. *In* Lier, A. (ed.): *Modernismen i Skandinavisk litteratur som historisk fenomen og teoretisk problem*. Trondheim: Nordisk institutt, AVH, Universitetet i Trondheim.
ROJOLA, LEA 1992: Oman sielunsa hullu morsian. Mirdjan matka taiteen maailmassa. *In* Hypén, T.-L. (ed.): *Pakeneva keskipiste. Tutkielmia suomalaisesta taiteilijaromaanista*. Turku: Turun yliopisto, Taiteiden tutkimuksen laitos, A 26 1993.
ROJOLA, LEA 1999: Modernia minuutta rakentamassa. Veren ääni. *In* Rojola, Lea (ed.): *Suomen kirjallisuushistoria II. Järkiuskosta vaistojen kapinaan*. Helsinki: Suomalaisen Kirjallisuuden Seura.
RÄISÄNEN, ARJA-LIISA 1995: *Onnellisen avioliiton ehdot. Sukupuolijärjestelmän muodostumisprosessi suomalaisissa avioliitto- ja seksuaalivalistusoppaissa 1865–1920*. Helsinki: Suomen Historiallinen Seura, Bibliotheca Historica 6.
SALOMÉ, LOU ANDREAS 1899: *Mensch als Weib*. Berlin: Neue Deutsche Rundschau 10.
SHOWALTER, ELAINE 1995: *Sexual Anarchy. Gender and Culture at the Fin-de-Siècle*. London: Virago Press.
SINGER, IRVING 1966/1987: *The Nature of Love 1. Plato to Luther*. Chicago and London: The University of Chicago Press.
SINGER, IRVING 1984/1987: *The Nature of Love 2. Courtly and Romantic*. Chicago and London: The University of Chicago Press.
SINGER, IRVING 1987: *The Nature of Love 3. The Modern World*. Chicago and London: The University of Chicago Press.
SNELLMAN, J. V. 1842/1993: *Läran om staten. Samlade arbeten III 1842–1843*. Helsingfors: Statsrådets kansli.
SOIKKELI, MARKKU 1998: *Lemmen leikkikehässä. Rakkausdiskurssin sovellukset 1900-luvun suomalaisissa rakkausromaaneissa*. Helsinki: Suomalaisen Kirjallisuuden Seura.
STACEY, JACKIE & PEARCE, LYNNE (eds.) 1995: *Romance Revisited*. New York and London: New York University Press.
VIRTALA, IRENE 1994: *Narkissos i inre exil. En studie i begärets paradoxer i L. Onerva's roman* Mirdja. Acta Universitatis Stockholmiensis, Studia Fennica Stockholmiensia 4. Stockhom: Almqvist & Wiksell.
WEST, SHEARER 1993: *Fin-de-Siècle. Art and Society in an Age of Uncertainty*. London: Bloomsbury.
WITT-BRATTSTRÖM, EBBA 2002: The "Narcissistic Turn" in the Aesthetics of the *fin-de-siècle*. Paper presented at the seminar "Changing Scenes: Naturalism, Decadence, Modernity", Helsinki, Finnish Literature Society 24th–25th May 2002.

JYRKI NUMMI

Between time and eternity
K. A. Tavaststjerna's *Barndomsvänner*

O blomsterfält! o gröna poppelunder!
Som lifvets späda *purpurknopp* förgömde!
O *silfverkällor*, vid hvars rand jag *drömde*
Elysiskt bort min barndoms snabba stunder!
–Erik Johan Stagnelius, *Minne (1819)*

A Novel of Many Failures

Karl August Tavaststjerna (1860–1898) began his literary career in 1883 by publishing a collection of lyric poetry with the fresh title *För morgonbris*. The reviews were not bad, but this was not the decade for lyrical poetry in Finland. Very soon afterwards the budding author moved on to prose. He first translated three stories by Juhani Aho, a contemporary writer and a future translator of Tavaststjerna's prose, then he experimented with short stories and sketches, as did so many of the young *débutants* of *det moderna genombrottet* in Scandinavia. Three years later Tavaststjerna published *Barndomsvänner* ("Childhood Friends"), a novel which has been considered a turning point in the Finland-Swedish literary tradition.

In a letter dated May 4th 1886 Tavaststjerna confesses to his friend Werner Söderhjelm that he did not feel confident with a manuscript he was working with: "I don't think I'm going to make it with my novel. I'm just too green in the field of prose".[1] Fifteen years later Söderhjelm recalled that he came by the manuscript in early autumn. After reading the first pages, he was taken by complete surprise:

> Redan på den allra första sidan – – fanns det icke blott en utomordentlig natursannig, utan också ett uppslag till något alldeles nytt i vår litteratur, vardagsskildringen, där alla kände igen sig.[2]

Söderhjelm regards Tavaststjerna's first full length work in prose as a "breakthrough" novel in Finland. The "novelistic subject" has been taken "from modern life in the average middle class environment – in a small town and in the capital".[3]

Söderhjelm was not the first to discover the modernity of the novel. In an extensive review, Hjalmar Neiglick, a young and talented litterateur and a friend of Tavaststjerna, wrote that *Barndomsvänner* is "the first major attempt to depict the contemporary Finland in the Swedish language, – – a modern novel on Finnish conditions".[4] The novel is "immediately written", it is not "too elaborated", "everything is experienced by the author, seen and felt by himself", and still he has "managed to hide himself behind the work". The novelist is able to create a true and lively picture of "thedeclining family" and "the philistine atmosphere" of contemporary Finland. Neiglick classifies the novel as a "story of decadence".[5]

This was the good news. Then follows a long list of critical comments and complaints. The reviewer uses no less than 14 pages and a lot of ideas from Zola's theory of *le roman naturaliste* to express his disappointment with the novel. He starts with the main character, Ben Thomén, a young man with flaws in his character but with a talent for music. Ben is "not a very good choice", not a "fitful hero in a tenor novel". He is "very near to becoming a poet, but then he is made to sing one of those old Schubert songs."[6] Ben will neither become an artist nor a tenor singer.

Ambiguity in characterisation is bad news. Schubert, the good old Romantic, is certainly bad news. Music and Ben's role as a musician is for Neiglick merely a motif in the description of the social milieu. Neiglick's rhetorics and reasoning deserve a longer quotation:

> Kvartettsången sådan den nu är, det stående programmet vid alla tillfällen af menniskolifvet der det behöfves ett program; kvartettsången, vid hvars toner vi döpas, gifta oss och begrafvas, dansa, äta bättre middagar och bekänna vår kärlek, hylla vördade personer och fira höga bemärkelsedagar; kvartettsången såsom evigt samma vehikel för alla högtidliga, glada och sorgliga känslor; kvartettsången såsom stereoupplaga af ett helt folks skönhetsbehof; kvartettsången såsom handtverk, såsom piskadt skum på tonernas vågor, såsom die Musik als Kunst des Philistethums – *denna* kvartettsång skulle förtjena sin skald; den måste vidare tänkas utöfva ett inflytande på Bens utveckling, och detta inflytande skulle det ha varit Tavststjernas skyldighet att beskrifva.[7]

Neiglick may be quite right with the idea that "quartet singing" as "the finest flower of undergraduate life" is a myth. However, I am not quite sure whether his expectations were justified when he wonders why Tavaststjerna, "in his capability as a realist", could not resist the temptation to revise this "myth". In the 1880's, not to resist the myths of contemporary society was completely out of line.

As crucial as quartet singing may be in *Barndosmvänner*, Neiglick's malicious description of it does not say much about the novel as a whole. It is, rather, a cheerful report on all the banalities of middle-class conventions, the dead rituals at dinner parties, on mediocrity in the arts and complacency in class conceptions which so irritated the generation of young and angry men during the 1880's. All this is present in the world of *Barndomsvänner*, but it is not as important as Neiglick presupposes.

When the critic concludes that "in this history song is purely accidental", that Tavaststjerna "seriously wanted to write a conventional decadence story", and that it would have been fortunate if the author had depicted Ben as a victim of quartet song convention, he comes close to admitting that he is speaking of a very different novel from the one Tavaststjerna wrote.[8]

Neiglick falls into great difficulties when he tries to examine *Barndomsvänner* using the categories that dominated the realistic novel of the 19th century. The characters should be carved from one and the same material; the story should "grow" as naturally as it might have happened in the real world; and the parts of the story should be linked to each other as in a chain, every scene and episode leading logically to another. It is *these* novelistic standards that Tavaststjerna fails to meet.

> Han har vant sig vid att skrifva små situationsbilder och rada dem efter hvarandra, att träda perlor på band och bjuda ut det som verklig kedja med länk i länk; man fick fylla i smådikternas mellanrum efter bästa förmåga, och öfver psykologiska klyftor slog Tavaststjerna en bro med två lyckliga rim.[9]

Neiglick picks up on the lyrical quality of Tavastsjterna's writing, and concludes that it is the poet who is to be blamed for the faults and weaknesses. Neiglick proceeds to a theory of the novel, but presents it in metaphors:

> Men prosan är en ärlig varelse, som icke förstår sig på det slags lättfärdigheter; prosan förhåller sig till versnovellen som hvardagskläder till en maskeraddrägt: här passera både bomullssammet och trockeltrådar, men der grina sömmarna, om det icke är ordentligt sydt.[10]

At the end of the review, Neiglick goes through some other weaknesses in the novel using this same theory.

> Ty allt som är numro ett, är på sätt och vis ett program och här väntade vi alltså att finna framför allt *hufvudsaker* ur nutidslifvet i Finland. Det tror jag derför är arbetets förnämsta konstruktionfel, att Tavaststjerna har bygt sitt hus för lågt i taket; der ryms icke det, som der framför allt borde rymmas.[11]

From the failings in composition, the faulty conception and the lack of a clear and definitive programme, it follows that *Barndomsvänner* "necessarily gives an insufficient picture of society ("en bristfällig samhällsbild")".[12] The conclusion is not only unfair but it completely misses the nature of Tavaststjerna's novel.[13]

It is a small wonder that a brilliant reader like Neiglick should pay no attention to the many failures the novel depicts. This is, indeed, a major problem in the novel, which mainly deals with failures. First of all, there is Ben's failure to become anything at all; then there is the failure of such institutions as school and family, and the failure of personal relationships, between parents and children, between and among friends and lovers. Finally, there is the failure of such educational ideas as personal development, maturing and growing up. Why does Neiglick overlook these visible problems in the novel? It seems to me that there is a simple reason for this and it is a usual one, the wrong theory. Neiglick's review is by no means meaningless or trivial. It is well written and full of brilliant formulations of contemporary literary ideas. Despite the hasty conclusions, or, perhaps, because of them, it creates a clearly outlined background of the literary expectations against which the deviations of *Barndomsvänner* can be observed.

In his critical biography of Tavaststjerna, Werner Söderhjelm points out that Neiglick's expectations steered the early reading and reception of *Barndomsvänner* in the wrong direction. First, the novel was about an individual fate, not about the society. Despite the numerous scenes of social life, gatherings, family celebration and undergraduate life, there is not a single word on the most heated contemporary political issues: the language problem (the status of Swedish and Finnish in administration and higher education); national and ethnic identity; the status of women in marriage and in society; growing social problems and the status of lower classes. All these issues were debated in public life and in university circles of the time.[14] The slice of life which *Barndomsvänner* offers is limited to the depiction of quartet singing, dinner-parties and balls, endless bar crawls and late-hour excursions to the workers' areas of Helsinki, where the young men take the opportunity to study "folk life". This undergraduate idea of "life" no doubt has a social dimension, but the presentation of such nocturnal scenes is certainly not and does not attempt to be a depiction of society.

Furthermore, the modernity in the novel cannot be found in the main character or the way his development is dealt with; it could have happened the same way in any other time. Instead, the modern elements are to be found in the compositional aspects and representative principles of the novel. Söderhjelm admits that the composition of *Barndomsvänner* could have been more solid, because the leaps from one scene to another give the impression of "a row of pictures set side by side".[15] The argument would have become interesting, had it been focussed on the context of literary changes at the *fin-de-siècle,* but it is doubtful whether Söderhjelm fully understood what he was really arguing.

From "the artistic point of view", the composition based on more or less separate, juxtaposed scenes is a genuine weakness for Söderhjelm, but the device may be motivated from the point of view of the main character: "att se livet som en räcka av tavlor och känna det endast som en följd av stämningar, utan att tränga djupare in i dess varför och huru".[16] The view of life as a series of disconnected *tableaux* or pictures dominated by the shifts of mood and atmosphere – "stämningar" – points towards the breakdown of the model of the realistic novel based on causality, temporal continuity and order.

Ruth Hedvall characterises Tavaststjerna's relationship to naturalism as being peculiarly double. The author lived intensively through the intellectual problems of his time, and was deeply affected by the feeling that a complete reorientation was taking place in the world which had recently changed so much; ideas so dear to the former generation had hardly any value for the young. Tavaststjerna pointed out that his world view was not "idealistic" but "realistic" by which he seems to have meant that he found his literary frame and ideal in naturalism. He admired Zola's *Les romanciers nauralistes*, he even preferred it to Brandes' critical writing. At the same time, he disliked the voguish ideas that had dominated the epoch and had also influenced his own thought.[17]

In *Barndomsvänner* the reader does not meet "a realist, but a lyric poet", Ellen Key wrote in an insightful essay on Tavaststjerna.[18] In order to be a realistic novel, Erik Kihlman notes nearly 30 years later in his critical study, *Barndomsvänner* is much too individual in characterisation, the relationship between the character in the foreground and the milieu in the background was not outlined in the codex of naturalism and realism; there was too much calculation and plotting; and, above all, there was too much lyrical atmosphere.[19] This double character is an important feature of *Barndomsvänner*. The repertoires of the realistic novel and lyric poetry are set, valued and balanced against each other. From a historical perspective the presence of two separate literary repertoires may be read as a sign of change; the novel articulates two artistic or literary repertoires and a break between them. From a purely synchronic perspective the double repertoire suggests the co-presence of the old and the new – an ever-lasting theme of the modern novel.

Tavaststjerna places his novel between several front lines; furthermore, he transforms the idea of being between the lines into one of the themes of his novels. The in-between space was a stock motif and a structural element in the 19th century realistic and naturalistic novel. This upstart genre and its thematic repertoire penetrated all European societies that underwent the transition from old beliefs to new concepts. This newly defined space was a sign of transition, a sign of detaching the solid, tradition-bound world and bringing it into a modern era dominated by constant movement and change.

The Novelistic Model: Bildungsroman

The Finnish Background

As a depiction of contemporary modern life, *Barndomsvänner* has been compared to Strindberg's sensational *Röda rummet* ("The Red Room", 1879). The natural connection to Swedish literature made the novel a part of a broad modern literary and artistic movement in Scandinavia which was based on naturalist agenda imported from France. What separates *Barndomsvänner* from the Scandinavian literary context is the cultural and political situation in Finland.

The Finnish literary scene in the second half of the 19th century was dominated by two influential figures, J. L. Runeberg and Zacharias Topelius. Runeberg had gained an exceptional status in Finnish literary and cultural life first with his lyric poetry, nationally oriented drama, and the epic cycle *Fänrik Ståls sägner* (*Songs of Ensign Stål*, 1846–1860). This epic was accepted as *the* expression of the spirit of the Finnish people, and Runeberg was elevated as a national cultural hero. Topelius also started as a lyric poet. He spread his literary activities over a wide range of artistic and scientific topics. In addition to his numerous plays, short stories, novels and fairy-tales for children, he also wrote books on Finnish geography and history. Topelius' famous historical novel *Fältskärns berättelser* (*Tales of a Field-Surgeon*, 1851–1867), an extensive chronicle on two families from 17th century to the end of the 18th century symbolising the unification of the Finnish people, was to overshadow Finnish fictional prose for several decades. Runeberg and Topelius do not belong exclusively to Finland's Swedish literary tradition. Although both of them wrote in Swedish, they addressed their work to the whole nation at a time when all educated people spoke and read Swedish.

Tavaststjerna's *œuvre*, novels and short stories, drama and lyric poetry, forms a turning point in the history of Swedish literature in Finland, as Thomas Warburton and Merete Mazzarella have emphasised.[20] Tavaststjerna was the last bud in the literary branch which had gradually grown apart from the stem since 1809, when Finland, the eastern part of the Swedish Great Power, was attached to Russia and achieved a new status as a Grand Duchy of the Empire. The major part of Swedish literature was to be written on the western side of the Gulf of Bothnia, and the fate of the minor part was to struggle for its existence in an environment which had fundamentally changed. The century under the new regime witnessed the gradual progress of Finnish culture and language, a process which was supported by the new rulers.

In the last decades of the 19th century, the Swedish speaking cultural elite began to feel that their leading position was seriously threatened by the growing Finnish readership; there was no market for literature in Swedish anymore. Many years earlier Topelius had already predicted that the future of the Swedish language in Finland was gloomy. In the 1880's the minority status of Swedish was a reality.[21]

In his *Finlandsvensk litteratur 1898–1948* (1951), Thomas Warburton outlined the modern development in the Finland-Swedish literary tradition, which begins with Tavaststjerna. Warburton summarises the essential characteristics of the cultural background and the peculiar status of Finland-Swedish literature between two separate literary traditions and languages.

> Finland-Swedish literature is doubly provincial. Partly it lives like a branch which has grown out from the Swedish trunk, like a Swedish literature on foreign ground. Partly it is a landscape among others in Finnish culture, closely related to them and not just geographically, but at the same separate from them and not just linguistically. The strong national consciousness which has arisen and penetrated the Swedish speaking population in Finland has coloured its modern poetry by regionalism tied to both language and locality.[22]

Warburton defines Finland-Swedish prose as socially fixed and class-bound literature of the Swedish speaking middle-class. It is written by authors from the middle-class, it deals with middle-class problems, and its perspective is middle-class whatever the time, the milieu or the characters.[23] What Warburton defines is a sub-genre in a cross-current of several literary repertoires, and it is in this unstable no-man's land that Finland-Swedish literature exists.

Merete Mazzarella has pointed out that in comparison with the preceding Finnish authors – Runeberg and Topelius – Tavaststjerna's position as a professional writer was completely different. Tavaststjerna was the first Finland-Swedish writer who really felt that he belonged to a minority, and his life may be seen as "a story with a lesson about the Finland-Swedish writer who does not know his place".[24] For Mazzarella, the Finland-Swedish novel, as a description of closed bourgeois life detached from rest of the society, exposes the Finland-Swedish bourgeois reality as "the narrow room" ("det trånga rummet") and describes the revolts the main characters of these stories attempt to make – how they try to break the tradition. *Barndomsvänner* may be read as the first modern Finland-Swedish novel and the protagonist, Ben Thomén, seems to be the first archetypal rebel against the Finland-Swedish narrow room.[25]

The idea of the rebel against established bourgeois values also dominates Tavaststjena's ideas of himself, it is not particularly original and by no means exclusive to the Finland-Swedish novel. In general and generic terms, the rebel against middle-class values is a widely used theme in 19th and early 20th century European fiction. Johan Wrede has connected the theme in *Barndomsvänner* to *fin-de-siècle* literary life and to the late 19th century *Künstlerroman*. It is a representation of a free spirit with a claim to follow his path through life without compromise and finds that he is treated badly in a world much too narrow. Behind the respectable façade of the manipulated values of religion, *patria*, language, militarism, there is a whole system of self-interested connections and loyalties, in which only those who let themselves become corrupted will succeed. According to Wrede, *Barndomsvänner* is an ordinary *Künstlerroman* ("en ordinär konstnärroman").[26] Whatever the aesthetic standards, the evaluation is historically misleading. As an example of the *Künstlerroman* the novel may well be ordinary; as a Finnish *Künstlerroman* it could not possibly be "ordinary", because it established a generic tradition in Finnish literature.[27]

The Plot for Life

As so many later Finland-Swedish novels, *Barndomsvänner* is overtly autobiographical. The main character and *alter ego*, Ben Thomén, is, like Karl August Tavaststjerna, an artist, whose free growth is hindered by ignorant adults and reluctant circumstances; on the other hand, Ben is also a Sunday child, who thinks he has the right to fulfil his natural talent rather than to make his living through hard work.

For Ben the choice between art and a bourgeois life is not an easy one but it is definite. Studies in the law school, a pre-determined career as a civil servant in state office and a profitable marriage with a girl of equal status presents an idea of life for his father, but not for Ben. He would rather sing and play piano, perform on stage or in a cheerful company of good friends and forget about studies and career. When things finally go wrong, as they usually do with an agenda like this, Ben leaves everything behind - his country, his bride, his family, his childhood friends, the University - in order to study in Milan and Paris, to become a world famous singer and make an international career in great opera houses, that's the life! The expectations at home country are high-tuned, and the Finnish public as well as Ben's numerous friends and acquaintances follow the turns of the talented singer's career in the Finnish newspapers.

An unexpected sore throat, due to the cold weather of autumnal Paris and an old "student disease" (gonorrhea), smashes his dreams. Ben loses his voice and he has to leave singing and music once and for all. He stays in Paris living with a *grisette*, the good-hearted Suzanne, who finds him when he is really down and out, and sets out to take care of him. After hearing of his father's death, Ben returns home without a penny or a future. After humiliating experiences in Mikkeli and Helsinki, disappointments with "childhood friends", who would rather not know him, and monotonous work as a petty clerk in a miserable state office, Ben is offered the position of station master in a far-away railway station in Kituri. At the end of the novel, the hero is left in the middle of a forest to lead a modest life with his old mother. The whole course of Ben's life, embodying the clash between great expectations and bitter disappointments, is not just a faithful description of many fates in Tavaststjerna's generation, but a typical outline and a well-known pattern in Finnish and Scandinavian fiction of the 1880's and early 1890's.[28]

In the first manuscript version of *Barndomsvänner,* the name of the protagonist was Emil Öhrn ("Eagle"), in the second version it was changed to Benjamin Udde. In the final version the family name was changed to Thomén, but the first name was left untouched. The new family name is a compound of two well-known Swedish speaking families (Thomé and Homén), from which many artists have come.[29] Emil, however, may be placed in a larger framework of literary traditions. The name alludes to Rousseau's *Emile*, through which the theme of education and personal growth is underlined. The first name serves as a generic signal to the *Bildungsroman*, the generic context for *Barndomsvänner.*[30]

According to an early definition by Wilhelm Dilthey a *Bildungsroman* is a story of the formative years of a young man, who enters life in a state of childlike happiness looking for kindred spirits; he finds friendship and love, then meets the harsh realities of life and finally grows into maturity through experience, finds his identity and achieves the certainty of the goals of his life. The *Bildungsroman* focusses, as François Jost has remarked, on the experience of the world that will educate the man of the world. The greatest happiness one can attain is "personality", the most solid and stabilised form of existence. The most important thing is to learn from the lessons and teachings offered by world. In an adventure novel the incidents and episodes try and age the hero; in a *Bildungsroman* they mark him, modify him in a particular way, solidify him and brighten his character. The hero's confrontation with his environment is a Goethean *Bildungsprinzip*. The world is no longer an arsenal for fate; it is an arena, an exercise field, in which the hero gains strength against his adversaries.[31] The optimism of this personal development gained its most joyful and trustful manifestation in Goethe's *Wilhelm Meisters Lehrejahre* (1795–1796).[32]

On the level of plot *Barndomsvänner* follows faithfully the outlines of the *Bildungsroman*. Ben is a sensitive child, who grows up in the countryside or in a small town where he experiences social and intellectual restrictions to the freedom of his imagination. The family, and the father in particular, turns out to be hostile to his creative instincts and imagination. He objects to his son's goals and directions and is unable to accept his ways. Conflict is inevitable. The first time Ben tries to break his chains is when after a row with his father he threatens to go to sea. His father reacts by laughing, and Ben's decision to stay firm melts into air. A few years later Ben disappears for two days after another dispute with father; a sign of the need to behave independently and to question his father's orders. The final break-up with his father takes place when Ben informs him that he will travel abroad in order to study music. In a letter of reply his father tells him that he will withdraw any responsibility for what becomes of Ben's future and finances, his son has cost him enough already.[33]

The years of real apprenticeship in the *Bildungsroman* begin in the city, but more often not just in preparation for the career the hero has chosen but for the immediate experience of urban life. The city experience includes at least two love affairs or sexual relationships; one is degrading, the other elevating. For the male protagonist the goal is a woman, whether he loves her or not. It often happens that real love is forsaken, and the hero turns to another option. The problem is hidden within the hero; sometimes the love affair which has gone wrong is just a mistake or a misjudgement, more often it is a self-deception or a moral compromise between love and passion. Usually the choice turns out to be the wrong one, and these worldly experiences require the hero to reconsider his values. When he has completed his painful quest – adjusting himself sincerely to the modern world – he has left behind his youth and achieved a mature stage of life. As his initiation is thus completed, he may visit his childhood home and indicate his success and wisdom.[34] This is precisely the opposite of what happens in *Barndomsvänner*.

The *Bildungsroman* is certainly biographical, but it is not a biography. It does not pretend to tell the whole life of the hero. In an important sense the *Bildungsroman* is rather a kind of pre-novel: in the end the hero, who seems to be fully equipped for existence, starts to live a novel of his own. The end of the novel is not more than provisional; a change of horses in a half-way inn, as François Jost remarks.[35] The life of a character is presented up to a certain point, but this is not a conclusion; his life should start at the point where the novel ends. The fact that the motif is treated ironically does not affect the argument.[36] In *Barndomsvänner* Ben's life should, thus, start in the end of the novel – after all his years of study, preparation and experience he has so dearly paid for – but this does not happen.

As Franco Moretti points out, the *Bildungsroman* was the great image for a whole social ideal. In the course of the 19th century, the *Bildungsroman* had performed a great symbolic task in containing the unpredictability of social change and representing it through the fiction of youth, in establishing this turbulent segment of life as the modality of modern experience, and in embodying in the unheroic hero a new kind of subjectivity: everyday, worldly, pliant – "normal".[37] But the problems change, Moretti notes, and old solutions stop working. At the turn of the century, there emerged short stories, novellas and novels which opened up a new phase in the history of the European *Bildungsroman*. Moretti calls these stories the Late *Bildungsroman*: they examine how the *Bildungsideal* does not work, how the model fails to provide new answers to old questions.[38] This is precisley what happens in Tavaststjerna's *Barndomsvänner*.

The Breakdown of the Bildungsmodel

Closed Space vs. Open Air

In the first sentences of *Barndomsvänner* the reader is given several generic signals of the *Bildungsroman*. At the same time, he or she may follow some counter-signals that these generic expectations will not be met. The novel begins with a description of the dining room where the women of the Thomén family are occupied with their daily jobs:

> Den gula gardinen var nedfälld för matsalsfönstret i karaktärsbyggningen, ty därinnanför slamrade syster Emmi vid symaskinen och eftermiddagssolen låg alltid och baddade in. På bordet väntade matrester, smultron och mjölk, som surnade i en porslinskanna. Inne i hällungen i köket torkade morotslådan, som skulle hållas varm. Bordduken var uppskjuten från en del av matbordet, och däröver låg syster Emmi, när hon lämnat symaskinen, och klippte till mönstret efter en modejournal. Mamma satt i soffan med en uppbyggelsebok. (*BV*, 13)[39]

The afternoon sun penetrates into the dining room, although the curtains are drawn to block the light and heat so that the two women can concentrate on their homely activities. Both mother and daughter are completely indifferent to what happens outside; sister Emmi is sewing and mending clothes, mother is sitting on a sofa reading a prayer book. There are two kinds of activity available to the Thomén women, repetitive household routines and religious meditation. Both of these activities are essentially waiting, the one waiting for life beyond every day routines; the other for life beyond this world.

The depiction of the dining room is a standard motif in the 19th century novel. The dining room was a space through which it could represent not only family life or changing familial relationships and customs but also the reactions and interpretations of an extra-familial reality – the outside world – which was mediated through the conversation around the table. In the Thomén house, however, this space is fundamentally inactive. There is no sign of the head of the family nor any trace of the son, and the women have been left to their ordinary tasks, to take care of the household - and to wait. The leftovers on the dinner table, the milk going sour in the warm summer evening, and the carrot casserole becoming dry in the oven remind the reader that the once powerful social convention of the daily family reunion has weakened.

The next paragraph is a commentary on this scene in the disguise of a narrative bridge to the next trope, which serves as a sign of a tale to come:

> Det var nu deras siesta i den fula gula dagern, där det var tryckande hett och flugorna flög upp i klungor från faten varje gång syster Emmi drog på bordduken eller sköt sin sax skramlande åt sidan.
>   Syster Emmi sydde sommarn igenom ... mest på sina toaletter, ändrade de, klippte till nya och ändrade igen. Endast någon gång, när det kom främmande, hände det att man begav sig ut i trädgården i aftonsvalkan ... eljes var trädgården blott till för att rensas och ha förargelse av, när svinen slapp dit in. (*BV*, 13)

The fact that sister Emmi is sewing all through the summer and spends her entire summer inside the house, is a sign of closing oneself away from the open air and nature. The dresses Emmi is mending are meant for balls. This reminds the reader that Emmi's thoughts centre around conventional social events, which represent the high points of small town social life. Only when occasional guests pay a visit to the house may she go to the garden in the evening twilight – otherwise the garden is simply a nuisance.

Both garden and nature refer to the erotic and sensual sphere of life which has been removed from the Thomén house. Nature is something to be looked at, tamed and controlled, something to be admired in books. Flowers deserve attention only in colour plates.

> Naturen läste man om i böcker och beundrade i stålgravyer. Blommor brydde man sig om, så vitt det gällde trädgården, – den stora, vilda växtligheten hade sitt intresse endast för att den fanns avbildad i grant färgtryck på glatt papper i den illustrerande floran för hemmet och familjen, som låg framme på salsbordet. (*BV*, 13)

The flower motif was popular in the arts of the day. As Ekelund has shown, it gives a glimpse of the whole family's attitude towards reality. Nature is appreciated through colourful pictures. It is not, of course, just family values but middle class attitudes which the Thomén family represents. Ekelund notes that Ben is an exception to this theme. The contrast is expressed through the juxtaposition of inner and outer space at the beginning of the novel.[40]

The opening scene of the dining room and the conversation between the Thomén women is followed by a change of a scene. The reader meets Ben for the first time. He is far away from home in the woods, working in beat-burning with a team of forest workers and enjoying all the heat and fatigue the effort produces. He takes a break with the others to have lunch in a barn on a lakeshore meadow. After lunch Ben and a hired hand called Adam go for a swim. When Ben dives naked into the pure waters of the forest lake, he forgets all about home, the dining room, the yellow curtains, the leftovers waiting for him, and the women sewing all day long inside the house.

Barndomsvänner is "a book of the open air", as Kihlman notes. Nearly all the happy scenes in the novel include a reference to nature and open skies; Ben's trips into nature fill the first pages of the novel. The beat-burning episode depicts nature as "the eternal fountain of youth"; later on, the duck chase is a picture of an escape to the boyhood desire for open air and adventure and the adolescent sensitivity to impressions.[41] This feverish dreaming is another version of the opposition between the open air and interior of a closed room. Later on, a youthful adventure with a group of singers also takes place outside the town in the archipelago in Lake Saimaa. Pastoral landscapes are introduced, when the young Ben meets a shepherd girl Johanna, who works as a servant at the Thomén house. Johanna later becomes Ben's first love, when he comes home for summer vacation as a first-year undergraduate student.

The depiction of Ben in the forest with the ordinary country workers is an introduction to the theme of education; without any explicit connections, it gives an idea of the natural context for a young boy to grow up. Nature, the limitless, fresh reality is out there to be reached, to be seen with open eyes, to be smelt and to be sensed on bare skin. The Rousseau-like idea of life in immediate contact with nature had a strong influence on Strindberg in the 1880's, and it was via Strindberg that many literary vogues spread throughout Scandinavia.[42] Ben's passion for the open air is strictly against his mother's ideas; she thinks that the best way to spend summer days is to sit at home and study school books; or to lead a life under the guidance of one's parents, as Ben's sister Emmi does, always at home, sewing clothes for balls and dinner parties. Ben, by way of contrast, enjoys the open air and all the pleasures nature can offer him outside his parents' jurisdiction. The nature scenes refer to the popular spatial tropes of the contemporary novel, the opposition between interior life (the workings of the psyche and the mind) and exterior life (reality, the outside world). In the two opposing scenes we find a major theme of the novel: the idea of growing up, the idea of education and growth – the haunting themes of the 19th century novelistic model, the *Bildungsroman* – which are never fulfilled in *Barndomsvänner*.

The Failure of Education

School or Life?

After the dining room exposition, a dialogue between the women is opened. The first lines give an insight into Ben and his position in the family. He seems to be a constant cause of trouble for the family:

> – Så Ben dröjer!
> Ja, det medgav syster Emmi. De talade eljes ogärna om honom, han hade blivit ett frö till stort bekymmer på senaste tiden. Kort och tvär var han sedan, så man knappt fick ett hyggligt svar ur honom på den allra vänligaste fråga.
> – Var månne han hålla hus igen?
> Det hade syster Emmi naturligtvis ingen aning om. Hon förmodade si och så.
> – Om ändå pappa vore hemma, så skulle väl Ben hållas bättre i styr.
> – Kanske.
> – Han har ju blivit nästan folkskygg ... håller uteslutande till med tjänstefolket och lär sig säkert ingenting gott bland dem.
> – Naturligtvis inte.
> – Och ingenting kan man göra åt honom, – vem förstår sig väl på en sådan vild pojkbaddare, som inte skattar hem och föräldrar det minsta – –! (*BV*, 13–14)[43]

This exchange of words reveal the tensions, personal relations and the expected behaviour in the family. Ben's undisciplined behaviour is explained as being due to the absence of his father, the authority and law in the house. As the dialogue continues, the mother and daughter move to another authority, the school. His mother complains that Ben is not interested in the same things as other boys, the good boys, such as Syberg, another childhood friend of Ben's. He is referred to as a model, because he spends all his evenings reading books on history. Emmi defends her brother and says that in the winter time Ben reads a lot. Her mother reacts severely: it is the school books she meant, not the novels Ben likes to read.

The discussion on reading conveys two major motifs common to the 19th century realistic and naturalistic novel. The first is the conception of reality as something directly observable, permanent and unambiguous. Reading history books keeps school boys on the right track, in safe past with its closed events. Reading novels, on the other hand, means stepping into a world which cannot be controlled, the world of the imagination, the world of Ben Thomén in good and bad. The other motif is the school. Every time Ben starts going to school he feels a strong change caused by moving from a free, healthy life outdoors to "the school desk and Latin", to "the whole serious, severe school order with morning prayers, discipline and punishment lessons" (*BV*, 19).

"The trouble with school", Franco Moretti notes when analysing the role of school in the late *Bildungsnovelle*, is that "it teaches this and that, stressing the objective side of socialisation – functional integration of individuals in the social system. But in so doing it neglects the subjective side of this process: the legitimation of the social system inside the mind of individuals, which had been the great achievement of the *Bildungsroman*".[44] Ben is a sensitive young man who bends easily under pressure. In the meadows among the workers his mind is open. At home and at school he becomes silent and uncertain again. "The whole school has become a masquerade", Ben thinks. "One gets the best grades by using cunning and flattery and loses one's real character behind good manners." (*BV*, 19)

The Conflicts with Father

Aside from school, there is another problem Ben has to face, namely, his father. Very early Ben had felt "almost a magic fear of parents", and "his education had mostly consisted of commands to obey his elders, to follow them and adjust his behaviour to theirs" (*BV*, 29). A small incident in Ben's school years generates a longer digression on the theme.

One day Ben asks his father's permission to join a party arranged by his class mate. His father is doubtful, yet he gives his permission on the condition that Ben later truthfully tell him, what the guests have been served in the party. Now it is Ben's turn to doubt, because he knows very well that there will be punch, perhaps even toddies. Ben decides not to drink any toddy, so that he does not have to tell his father about it. Nonethless he feels his father's penetrating stare, and at the same time he loses his courage. He decides not to go to the party, and says that he will stay at home – "if that's what Father wants" (*BV*, 47). That is, however, not what his father wants; Ben is free to go – on his father's conditions. Ben feels the spirit of opposition growing in his mind, but only for a second. He would like to tell his father, how rotten he feels about spying on his school mates, but he is afraid that his father would only laugh at him.

The party will be like young people's parties have always been. The young host has reserved ten bottles of punch, which will be consumed in merry spirits. The next day Ben's father interrogates him, and Ben admits to having two glasses of punch. This is too much for his father; he gets angry and says to his son that he "will see that this information is passed on to the teachers at the school" (*BV*, 49). However, he promises that because Ben has told him the truth (which he probably has not, at least, not the whole truth), he will take care that Ben is not be caught; only the host will be uncovered and only he will have to pay the consequences. His father's conduct could not disappoint Ben more.

Ben's trouble with his father is more personal than with school, of course, and it has very much to with a model for growth. Very soon in his early adolescence, Ben feels that he does not want to go to school anymore and asks again his father if he can leave. There follows a severe interrogation. Ben begins by stating that he is no longer very interested in school, because his studies are dragging. His father resorts to his usual strategy.

He asks questions – hands in his pockets – and if the answers do not please him, he turns to sarcasm. He never even tries to understand his sensitive son and ask himself, why, for example, Ben is so frightened and uncertain in his presence. Ben's father is a complete failure as an authority figure and as an adult person.

The conflicts with his father leads to an important change in Ben. He finds himself happy with music. After his voice breaks he resumes singing and playing the piano; music seems to offer him consolation. Gradually his voice finds the right register; Ben is a high tenor with a fine tone. His father does not like this re-orientation, because he had made his friends and acquaintances believe that his son was "a good boy with merry tricks" and that "he was glad that his son was so vigorous" (*BV*, 50). Ironically enough, Ben's father is right. Later on, music offers Ben a way out of threatening situations whenever he faces the figures of authority who try to form his behaviour, the various challenges of life, or the simple facts of the everyday world. This point is important, because there are many suggestions that the artistic career Ben finally chooses, is not merely a happy decision.

The Art of Being an Undergraduate

The Ideal Student

After Ben and his class-mates graduate from the small town high school in Mikkeli, they travel to Helsinki to take a baccalaureate exam at Helsinki University. Before the autumn leaves have fallen, most of the young men have moved to Helsinki, rented a student apartment and started their semi-independent life as undergraduate students. Ben enrolls at the Law School of the University, not because he is interested in legal studies, let alone a future career in state office, but because that is what his parents have decided for him. Ben is to follow his father's path.

From the beginning it is quite clear that law studies were never meant for Ben. His real branch is merry comradeship, *kamratlivet,* for which Helsinki is most suitable with endless parties, balls and dinners, where one could enter "looking good in a tail coat and a white scarf" (*BV*, 80). Despite the occasional *Weltschmerz* which may strike a young man, especially when there is a lack of money and he has to write home to ask for more, the first student year is a great time for Ben: "Sorrowless as a singing bird he could throw himself into life with late hours and dinners as amiably and childishly as there might be nothing after this" (*BV*, 80). The young ladies of Helsinki classify him as an interesting case, especially when he withdraws absent-mindedly just a moment before the start of a recital, seems to look at himself in the newly waxed floor and then steps into the first line of the choir, and "perform[s] his solo with such a youthful voice and sense of immediacy that all the listeners in the back row stood up" (*BV*, 80). Ben's popularity among the ladies greatly increases, when they find out that he does not socialise and may even be considered a woman hater.

As a singer and a comrade Ben is irreplaceable. He has a regular order for nocturnal serenades. His voice has such a pure and hearty sound that it is regarded as proof of the most genuine of feelings. Ben is willing, for his part, to sing wherever and whenever; he is never able – or willing – to say "no". This is the reason for his unequivocal popularity in the brotherhood of singers, which is not at all typical in such self-satisfied and pretentious company as artistic circles can be. Some people advise him not to waste his time with such "poor company", but Ben pays little attention to these warnings or to the reminders that the main reason for his being in Helsinki is the law school. Only once, due to an occasional harshness in his voice, does he open a text book and spend a little while with it, then he decides to go and see a professor and pass an exam – the first and only one. At first, Ben's father does not worry about his son's slow progress: "Let him party for his while, there will be plenty of time for studies later". Father sends him more money. Later on money will become an important problem. During the first months of the first semester Ben runs up sky high debts.

The depiction of student life in *Barndomsvänner* has usually been read as a satirical view of the social life of Swedish-speaking students. The few pages dedicated to the merry-making of undergraduates prompted Hjalmar Neiglick to state that "if the novel proves anything", it only proves that [an undergraduate student] drinks more and works less at Helsinki university than a student in any other university in the world". This may well be true, but drinking as well as other irresponsible behaviour is also a part of the literary repertoire of the time.

The undergraduate students in *Barndomsvänner* are drawn from the well-established character repertoire of the Scandinavian "University Novel" or "Student Novel" as the Finnish version of this sub-genre is called.[45] The usual tricks of adolescent undergraduate students are the stuff which August Strindberg, whose student years at Uppsala University had equipped him with lots of useful material from academic life and bred his talent for satire and irony, used in his collection of short stories *Från Fjärdingen och Svartbäcken* (1877). The collection has been regarded as the most important work in the formation of the student motif in the 1880's. The *Fjärdingen* stories are based on the classical genre of "character", such as it is known from Theophrastus to de La Bruyère, sketches on various "universal" human types. In Strindberg's version, undergraduate students discover academic life as bars and restaurants, drinking and gambling, new friends and paid love. In Tavaststjerna's novel the characters and the atmosphere of cynicism, the standards of mediocrity, malevolence, and the tradition of bullying the freshmen come directly from Strindberg's Uppsala stories.

There is, however, something more to Finnish students of the time. The role of the academic student in the Finnish cultural and political tradition was different from that of the Swedish, Norwegian or Danish model.[46] Helsinki university, founded by Queen Christina of Sweden in 1640, moved from Turku to Helsinki in 1827 where during the 19th century it became a central institution in the spreading of nationalism. The nationalist agenda was written by the patriotic intellectuals of the time, and the most influential figures in the movement – Runeberg, Lönnrot, Snellman, Topelius – held academic posts at Helsinki University.

Replacing Swedish as the language of administration, law and literature became the main goal of the Finnish-minded national movement in the 1840's. Political support was sought within the lower classes, especially within country folk, who became the object of educational and enlightenment projects initiated by the new Finnish-speaking middle classes. After the national movement progressed to a more active phase in the 1860's, the role of the academic students changed significantly. The Finnish movement took advantage of its Romantic heritage, but modified it to its own needs. It re-articulated the relationship between the student (the educator) and the people (those to be educated), so that the role of the people was to support the political goals of the rising Finnish-speaking middle classes. The student union and individual students became active political agents and opinion leaders, exercisers of power in ideological and political life of Finland.[47]

The idealism attached to students during the Romantic era was particularly generated and spread by Zacharias Topelius in his poetry and fiction. Topelius' ideal student is based on a general Scandinavian literary convention. He is a positive hero for whom Topelius gave the shape of the young Apollo or Prometheus, and thus was connected to divine spheres of the spirit. In the first case, the student embodies the Apollonian virtues, the love of knowledge and arts, balance, reason and nobility. In the second model, the student was the one who brought forth fire like Prometheus. The virtues of the latter are manifested in a popular poem by Topelius, *Studentvisa* ("Student song", 1852):

> Vi äro andens fria folk
> Som stolt att vara ljusets tolk,
> Skall evigt kämpa för dess rätt,
> Kring verlden sprida det.[48]

It is not hard to infer the neo-Platonic idea of eternal light in this stanza. The student emanates out of the light and connects the heavenly spheres to the earthly. As Päivi Molarius notes, these innocent metaphors refer to another direction as well. The references to light and freedom are conventional, veiled images of political and national resistance, a direct expression of which was impossible under the Russian regime at the time. In Topelian "student poetry" Finland is a representative of light and justice, of the fatherland which has been ordained to light. Just like the rebellious Prometheus, the student becomes a hero who struggles for the freedom of his fatherland with the light of civilisation.[49]

The idea of continuity and tradition reflected in Topelius' poem becomes problematic in the literature of the 1880's. In the third stanza of *Studentvisa,* we find the demand of absolute loyalty to the forefathers and their heritage.

Vi äro söner af vårt land,
vi älska högt dess gömda strand.
För detta land, som fostrat oss,
vi in i döden slåss.

Och ingen, ingen svika skall
vårt utaf fädren ärfda kall
att rota ljusets fana stark
i nordens ödemark.[50]

Words like this were too much for the new generation of students in the 1880's. When scepticism and doubt spread into the young minds, the high-flying ideas of the previous generation were enthusiastically turned upside down. Patriotic poetry became the target of iconoclasm in the realistic writing of the 1880's.

The Sons of Hellas

After Ben's debut in the *Akademiska Sångföreningen* the novel builds a digression into the student life of the 1880's outside the lecture halls. This aspect of academic life means merry company in cafés and restaurants, the possibility to sit through the night with a glass of punch debating, arguing and joking. Some of the notable figures of this company become particularly renown among the freshmen who eagerly gather around these heroes. There is, for example, the inveterate joker Priffe, who performs music "without cuffs and coat and his hair unkempt". His repertoire includes three songs that will be performed at a jolly drinking party or on any occasion or festivity where the main idea is to have a good time. Priffe's repertoire includes largely patriotic songs, such as Topelius' *Hellas' barn* (from the play *Prinsessan av Cypern*, 1861): "O barn av Hellas, byt ej bort, / ditt sköna fosterland! –" ("Oh, the children of Hellas, never leave / your beautiful fatherland!").[51] The point is that they are sung through the nose. Success is always guaranteed, and in the streets of Helsinki one can occasionally hear a line or two of Priffe's best numbers. In the early hours Priffe would assemble a regular clown-orchestra to accompany him with hand-clapping, chairs, glasses and the doors of tiled ovens.

There is also another idol for the freshmen, "Uncle Gullberg", an over-time student, an ex-writer, an ex-official, obviously an ex-anything. When he starts performing he stands up, blows his nose as loud as a gun shot, and presents with great pathos a paradox from the line of Runeberg's poem *Molnens broder* (from *Fänrik Ståls Stänger):* "Mera än att leva är att älska / Mera än att älska är att dö" ("More than to live is to love, / More than to love is to die..."). Uncle Gullberg's version is as follows: "Mera än leva fann jag var att älska, / mer än älska är att äta blåbär" ("More than living is loving / More than loving is eating blueberries"). The repertoire of the jokers consists of lines from two literary father figures. The lines quoted from Topelius' poem as well as the parodic modification from *Fänrik Ståls Sänger* comment on famous patriotic themes.

What has this mocking to do with the fate of Ben Thomén? The story of *Barndomsvänner* follows the author's own student years quite faithfully, his reluctant start with academic studies in Helsinki during the 1880's, conflicting aspirations towards both a professional and an artistic career, an excursion to Paris, and the final return home in "autumn rain", as Tavaststjerna expressed his mood in a later poem.[52] In addition to this resemblance in life and characterisation, the author is careful enough to point out that there is a precise link between the writer and the main character. Ben Thomén was born on May 13th 1860, which is also Karl August Tavaststjerna's birthday.

The significance of the date lies not exclusively in the relation between the real and the fictitious artist. May 13th is also Flora's Day, and it is an important historical date in Finland. In 1848, *Vårt Land* (Our Land), a song which was later to become the national anthem, was presented in public for the first time at the student festivities on Flora's Day. *Vårt land* is also the prefacing poem of the great national epic *Fänrik Ståls Sänger*, a preface to the story of a heroic Finnish army and its individual soldiers, officers and privates, fighting against the superior Russian Army, left all alone – as the legend goes – by the treacherous Swedish troops who fled away to their homeland. Loyalty is one of the central political issues in 19th century Finland. It is also a central theme in Runeberg's epic.[53] What is the connection between Flora's Day and loyalty?

Flora's Day has an important connection with the idea of rebellion and revolution. In 1848 Finland chose another way to tackle the problem of the Tzarist oppression of Russian Empire, as did, for example, Poland and other East-European countries. The festivities of Flora's Day in 1848 were a demonstration that, while Finns wanted to promote their national culture and institutions, they accepted, at the same time, the Russian rule and the Emperor as the highest authority. An attitude like this was in the long run extremely difficult to maintain, and it produced some longstanding consequences in Finnish political life. When authoritarian rule is taken for granted, the subject's behaviour will change so that it always takes account of the oppressor's views and expectations: the subject tries to create *Lebensraum* within the physical and mental confines of the status quo. Behaviour like this leads, both on a collective and an individual level, to certain character traits: an individual or a community becomes a will-less, selfless, unsure being or entity; one who wishes to please everyone and hurt no one, one who does not know why he is doing what he does, why he acts as he does, a person who is unable to resist anything, to respond to the slightest challenge, let alone any adversity; one who becomes a person like Ben Thomén.[54]

This motif is connected to a wider frame of problems between rulers and their subjects, fathers and sons, tradition and the individual. As the title of *Barndomsvänner* suggests, the question of loyalty dominates the novel: what are the ties and obligations of a person to his friends and parents and an artist to his country and cultural tradition?

The Return to Childhood

The Birds of Passage

The sixth chapter of *Barndomsvänner* begins with a curious fairy-tale exposition. A wedge of cranes is returning from the South to the North, and the birds comment on human activity on earth. The cranes first mistake the great white "handkerchief" for snow. With a closer look the piece of cloth turns out to be a big field covered with numerous white spots, white student caps in reality. The cranes are arriving to Finland on May 1st, a festival for students in Finland. What is the function of this exposition?

Erik Ekelund links the crane episode to the theme of conflict between home country and the outside world, something that is referred to for the first time in the novel.[55] The function of the crane episode may also be read as a motif of the theme of return and home-coming. There is, indeed, another home-coming episode in the twelfth chapter of *Barndomsvänner*. The scene repeats all the significant details of the crane episode: the spring time, a character returning from the South, and the grey, northern landscape.

The twelfth chapter opens with a sharp cut to an early spring landscape in the Finnish countryside. A traveller is located in the landscape, he is returning to his Nordic home from a country where "the hills [are] covered by pink apple blossoms". The recent farewell at Gare St. Lazarre are wiped away when the traveller suddenly wakes in the middle of the Finnish backwoods. Ben Thomén is back from France:

> Nu satt han här mitt i ödemarken, kärran skumpade, och skjutskarlen smackade hästen. Ben tryckte sönder någonting i ögonvrån, så livliga blev hans minnen, och han såg upp ur sina tankar först när kärran stannade inne på gästgivargården och skjutskarlen hoppade ned.
> – Vi ä' framme, sade han. (*BV*, 170)[56]

Ben takes a long, thoughtful look at the scenery. Everything seems to be in low key, something he finds distressing.

> Den första Ben såg var en stor rishög med en kubbe, där en yxa satt inhuggen, en gul grå knut av ett uthus och ett stycke svart åker bakom med en vit snöstrimma strax under en gärdesgård. – –
> Småskogen stod dåsig i bakgrunden och likasom rodnade över att icke ha blad ännu. Han steg ned på den smutsiga gårdsplanen och gick in i gästrummet för att teckna sitt namn i dagboken. Orten, varifrån han kom, skrev han icke upp ... det kunde vara hans enska. Så lutade han sig över dagboken med huvudet mellan händerna och stirrade trött ut i det dimmiga grå framför sig...
> Det här var nu hans Finland – grått och ödsligt och fattigt! (*BV*, 170–171)[57]

This attention is drawn to the interior of the inn. Ben feels that:

> Härinne var lågt till taket och kvävande luft. Och kom den över honom med ens, den där oändliga beklämningen, känslan av att vara obevekligt inklämd mellan jämngrå väggar, och det var som hade den blyfärgade himlen och det fula uthuset varit en obeveklig ridå, vilken nu för alltid föll ned bakom honom och skilde honom från allt det förflutna, – det färgrika och solljusa. Ett omätligt svårmod tog honom fången, men han var bitter och upprorisk och hade ingen resignation till hands. (*BV*, 171)[58]

It is this passage and the motif of the "narrow room", where "the ceiling is low and the air suffocating"[59], which Mazzarella takes as a starting point for modern Finland-Swedish prose. I find no reason to restrict the space or room to a small circle of Swedish speaking people of middle-class status living in Helsinki and the small towns in Southern Finland. The whole scene of return in the novel refers to a larger thematic layer, which runs through Tavaststjerna's *oeuvre*: the multi-faceted concept of *fosterland,* the key concept of 19th century Finnish culture.

Fatherland as a Childhood Friend: The Runebergian Sub-Text

Returning home is a recurrent motif in Runeberg's lyrical *oeuvre* and a major theme in his first collection of lyric poetry *Dikter* ("Poems", 1830). The chapter on Ben's return in *Barndomsvänner* is linked to some outstanding poems from this collection on two separate levels.[60] First, the connection takes place on a general thematic level. For example, in *Den hemkommande* (*The Home Returner*) or in *Flytt-fåglarna* ("Migrating Birds") the idea of return is already present in the title. In both of these poems the motif is presented as a joyful event: the one who is coming back recognizes his Nordic fatherland as his real home. The speaker gives the expression of his emotions to the dear fatherland in *Den hemkommande* as follows:

> Dagen är all,
> mörk är min bana och kall,
> dyster i skogarna här
> vintern den isiga rår;
> ljus, der du tindrar, o der
> finner jag kärlek och vår.

It is the bleak forests, the dark slopes and the icy winters which create the contrast with the spring full of love and regeneration which makes the country so unique and dear to the returner. There is, however, a more relevant connection than with mere landscape. The motif has both literary and political undertones, which have a vital connection to Tavaststjerna's novel.

During the 17th and 18th century many an outstanding literary scholar moved from Finland to mainland Sweden in order to forge a career in a state office. The path from the eastern part of the kingdom to the western administrative centre of Stockholm was natural for anyone who wanted to serve the state. Some Finns did this brilliantly. Gustav Philip Creutz (1731–1785), for example, was a poet of some real note and finally became an ambassador in Madrid and Paris. Only from a later perspective, when the status of Finland had changed, would a career move like this come to be seen anachronistically as deserting one's own country. This is true of Frans Michael Franzén (1772–1847), the first Finnish pre-romantic poet. He had visited Sweden as early as in 1793. He was elected to the Swedish Academy in 1808, and he remained in Sweden permanently from 1811 onwards.

Franzén was greatly admired by Runeberg whose *Dikter* opens with a poetic dedication addressed to the expatriated poet, *Till Franzén* ("To Franzén"). The speaker compares the poet to a lark, who has flown away when "storms and autumn" came to Finland – an allusion to the change in Finland's political status. In the second stanza the speaker expresses his fear that his home country will not see the poet's last days:

Glömmer du i Sveas blomsterdalar
Fosterlandets skog,
Och vid sångerna av näktergalar,
Huru vakan slog?[61]

In the following stanzas the speaker describes the familiar scenes of the poet's life in his home country, his home town Oulu, his *alma mater* in Turku, and the beautiful nature of Finland. The poem is, thus, a strong appeal to the dear poet to come home. The last stanza also reveals a motif which was to recur later on in Tavaststjerna's novel:

Som en saknad vårdag skola tjällen
Hälsa dig igen,
Och vart eko i de gråa fjällen
Som en barndomsvän.[62]

Runeberg's speaker reminds us that although his fatherland is poor, it should still be dear to Franzén. One's fatherland is something which cannot be replaced, because it is the environment of the genuine beginning of one's life, the *topos* of creativity and growth, something which endures through life and never loses its meaning.

The last line presents the second important connection to Tavaststjerna's novel, the landscape of poor huts and grey hills in the fatherland as a "childhood friend". Does this exact connection generate any additional meaning as regards to Tavaststjerna's novel? Let us begin by posing another question: what is the role of "childhood" in Runeberg's poetry? The question may be clarified by examining another poem in the collection, *Den gamles hemkomst* (*The Old Man's Return*). The speaker of the poem is addressing himself as a migrating bird, who is returning to the landscape of his childhood:

> Flyttfågeln lik, som efter vinterns dar besöker
> Sin insjö och sitt bo,
> Jag kommer nu till dig, min fosterdal, och söker
> Min flydda barndoms ro – –.[63]

The introduction to the second part of Tavaststjerna's novel is based on a comparison between two landscapes: the grey northern forests of Finland and the sunny valleys and hills of the South. A similar tension is the central concern of Runeberg's collection: the opposition between home and abroad. *Den gamles hemkomst* is elegiac by nature, it expresses both the weariness and the melancholic happiness of returning home.

A return to the landscape and atmosphere of one's childhood also signifies something spiritual. Another poem in Runeberg's collection, *Flytt-fåglerne,* refers to the spiritual overtones of home coming: "Du flyktande ande på främmande strand, / När söker du åter ditt fäderneland?" ("Thou, fugitive soul on a far foreign strand, / When seek'st thou again thine own dear fatherland?") The bird is the poet's soul, as Hedvall reads the lines, taking refuge on a strange beach. The trip will lead him quickly to a nest hidden in swaying branches. Only in his death will the poet find a way back home:[64]

> Då lyfter du vingen
> som foglarna små
> Väg visar dig ingen
> in villande blå,
> Du hittar ändå.[65]

The grand final accord includes in its harmony and sorrow a victory over all that life has been able to produce. Hedvall underlines this strong religious aspect in the theme of the poem: man is a visitor on earth, his real home is elsewhere. What has gone unnoticed in the motif of migration is the idea of renewal, which is contained in this restless dual existence and constant two-way movement. The bird has to leave its home country to enjoy the warmth of the sun and to feed on the fruits of the south to strengthen itself. When it finally comes back, it must be able to create something new, to build a new nest and renew life. The translation of the migrating bird trope to the language of the arts is simple: the poet or the artist must leave his home to strengthen himself in a foreign environment, but he must come back in order to renew his art.

How does this relate to Ben Thomén's artistic career? The first thing Ben does as a freshman in Helsinki is to go to a rehearsal of the *Akademiska Sångföreningen* ("Academic Society of Singing"). The rehearsal takes place in the Student House. When Ben and his friend Syberg are waiting for their turn under a starry-patterned vault ceiling, they examine a famous painting of a red-cheeked Väinämöinen by Karl Ekman. The scene functions as an ironic anticipation of Ben's fate. Will Ben become a great singer like Väinämöinen, who, in the end of *Kalevala,* leaves Finland with the promise of returning if there will be any demand for his talent in the Finland of the future?[66]

From the perspective of the allusion to *Kalevala*, Ben Thomén is a complete failure, but in a very specific sense. He has been sent abroad with the hope that one day he would return to his home country as a celebrated, internationally recognised artist; he would bring fame to his fatherland, and he would enrich the art and culture of his country, make it bloom, again. This was, however, not to be; and this is the great failure of Ben Thomén, the artist.

At Choræus Fountain

The Graveyard Episode

The title of the first manuscript version of *Barndomsvänner* was "Fantasifoster" ('a fruit of imagination'). Kihlman has taken the title as a sort of "private monologue" between the author and the first version of the would-be novel. In the second version the title was replaced by "Barndomsvänner". Kihlman remarks that the subtitle *Nutidsöde* (a modern destiny) was an admission of the spirit of the time, fate was subordinate to the influence of "le moment et le milieu" à la Taine and Naturalism. However, this "influence" does not have much impact on the novel, as Kihlman notes.[67] The subtitle, on the other hand, emphasises the individual, and the stress is on Ben's dealings. There are strong positive features in Ben, as Söderhjelm has pointed out, the strong love for Sigrid Walborg and music, for example, and these are open to lyric treatment by nature.[68] The fatal weakness in Ben is his lack of immunity to the prosaic aspects of life; his strengths are in lyric atmosphere.

The love of Ben and Sigrid is heightened in an intensive lyrical scene in a grave yard. Brilliant autumn colours surround the secret meeting of the lovers. The graveyard is a place in which they know they will be "beyond the reach of curious glances". The whole episode is written in lyrical key and full of nature descriptions, which melt into the sensual kisses and embraces of the loving couple. The lovers enter the graveyard through a great gateway with a golden cross and a torch. The gate opens a vista to a long narrowing path bordered with fir trees. Ben and Sigrid are stepping into a garden, a garden for the dead as well as for living and for their mutual love. The images of melting and blending are repeated. The episode is a great lyrical passage in the middle of the story.

One important motif is given a full realization in the episode. When the couple try to find a place as peaceful as possible, they first cross the grave-yard area for the rich people:

> Skymningen slår rot därinne i småskogens grentrassel på de rikas kyrkogård, sveper sorgflor om allvarsamma stenblock och retuscherar konturerna på järnkorsen, som sträcker ut sina magra armar efter en ny försonare för det stackars syndiga, lidande och levnadslustiga människosläktet. (*BV*, 115)[69]

After having crossed the area for the rich, they walk into the area for the poor by the seaside, where the long, similar paths are arranged so that they form regular blocks. The big elegant headstones are replaced by tin plates, where one could read names and epitaphs "like apartment numbers". This seemingly non-functional comparison between the placement of the well-to-do and not-so-well-to-do dead reminds the reader of the elegiac theme of the passage. Death levels all.

The question is, how has the narrator of the novel linked these two texts in this particular lyrical passage? The grave-yard episode has a circular plot: the couple exits through the same gate they entered and the episode ends with the same motifs which with it had started.

> Den stängda gallerporten med korsen och facklorna skulle i morgon åter öppna den eviga kärlekens säkra famn, men den timliga kärleken tog sin älskade på ett par starka armar, bar henne över stengärdsgården ned till vägen utanför och ännu ett långt stycke fram längs den, och när han slutligen återlämnade henne åt marken, viskade hon snabbt som vinden och flyktigt:
> – När träffas vi åter här? (*BV*, 119)

What we have here are the symbols of death: the gate, the cross and the torch. However, the narrator adds something which has been acquired along the story. He refers playfully to two kinds of love, the eternal and the timely, by comparing the "womb" of the grave ("den eviga kärlekens säkra famn") and the arms of the young loving man ("den timliga kärleken tog sin älskade på ett par starka armar") . The paragraph (and the chapter) ends with Sigrid's whispering words: "When shall we meet here again?" The question and the motifs of eternal and earthly love link the graveyard episode to an elegiac poem by 18th century Finnish poet Michael Choræus, *Till mina Barndoms vänner* (1801).[70]

The opposition between earthly and eternal love is a major theme in Choræus' poem too. The last section of the poem's five stanzas starts with a statement on the nature of human happiness:

> Store God! din godhet evig är,
> Och de stunder äro så korta,
> Som till glädjens njutning du beskär;
> Knappt vi se dem, och de äro borta!

The speaker says that short moments of happiness are the essence of human life, and that they are so short that we hardly see them in their evasiveness. The speaker then moves to another aspect of the problem. He ponders whether we meet our loved ones in the life beyond:

> Men än en gång, när tidens strömmar flytt
> Bort till de oändeliga hafven,
> Och ditt *varde* kallar oss på nytt
> Till ett lif, utur den mörka grafven.

The speaker evokes the idea of new life in platonic images: all streams flow back to the origins of life, to the infinite sea.

In the sea there are men who are newly born by God's command "Let there be light" (Varde, 'let it become'), and they arise from their dark grave into life. The next stanza is the most important link to which Tavaststjerna's narrator refers:

> Skola då, på evighetens strand,
> Barndoms vänner återse hvarandra,
> Och med ädla steg, och hand i hand,
> Till det aldrig nådda målet vandra?

This question in Choræus' poem is evoked in Sigrid's innocent wish to see Ben again. All the images in the stanza have been used for the depiction of the couple's wanderings in the graveyards: hand in hand they visit the beach which is situated at one end of the graveyard.

This interplay between the lyrical passages of the novel and Choræus' poem continues further on. It is completed in the final chapter of the novel, where the two last stanzas of the poem and Ben's final vision are connected in a star motif.

The Reunion in the Stars

The novel ends with a scene in Kituri railway station. Ben is spending Christmas in a small station master's apartment with his mother and sister Emmi. Christmas is over, and the New Year is coming. The scene opens with a description of a winter landscape, a snow-covered forest glimmering in a nocturnal silver-coat lit by the moon. The description starts with snow-covered spruces, then moves to pines and aspens, and ends with birches:

> [M]en björkarna slokade smäktande med sina hänggrenar och rörde dem som solfjädrar med svandunsbräm för minsta vinddrag, likasom de haft för varmt mitt i smällkalla vinternatten. (*BV*, 247)

The scene is not built only for lyrical purposes. It partly hides a motif which will fully appear in the final sentences of the episode as Ben takes a look at a shooting star in the dark winter sky.[71] After this lyrical depiction of nature there is a diagonal inversion of the dialogue of the opening scene of the novel:

> – Så Ben dröjer.
> Ja, det medgav syster Emmi. De talade gärna numera om honom, han hade blivit ett frö till stor glädje på senaste tiden. Mamma och syster Emmi, som var hemma till julen, satt i stationsinspektorns lilla sal dit det gamla bohaget flyttats in för en månad sedan. Soffan med de vita pärlemorknapparna i ryggstödet, pianot, den stoppade gungstolen och väggspegeln med sakarven i glaset och den lilla pendylen nedanför. (*BV*, 247)

The first lines are exactly the same as of the beginning of the novel with only a slight change in the judgement on Ben's behaviour. Ben's transformation from "a great cause of sorrow" to "a great cause of joy" contains an allusion to a biblical figure, Benjamin, the son of Jacob and Rachel.[72] Structurally the allusion links the beginning and the end of *Barndomsvänner*. Although Ben still arrives late for dinner, his mother and sister are now happy with him. Where does this happiness come from? After all the years of freedom – which produced nothing – Ben is now beaten, humiliated and tamed. His life in the small forest station, where he has settled after the ship-wreck, has reached an anticlimactic, colourless end. This is why Ben has turned into a great cause of joy for the family.

Things have changed in the course of events. However, there is no development in character, and there is certainly no progress; the final scene is a scene of regression. This is mirrored in the interior of Ben's new lodgings. The only heritage left from a big mansion and a city apartment is a few pieces of old furniture, which all remind the reader that something important in the story is coming to end. The sofa and the rocking chair are signs of immobile middle-class life drifting away sitting and waiting for someone to come or for something to happen; the piano is a bitter reminder of Ben's realm of freedom which has been closed to him for years; the mirror is there for him to reflect upon himself, if he dares; and there is the bell to inform us of the passing of time. Nothing has really changed, except the size of the room. It has shrunk and is now even smaller than the room in the inn, in which Ben spent the night on his return to Finland.

Ben enters the room with a letter in his hand, and he shows it to his mother, who immediately reads it. Sigrid Walborg has died in Görbesdorf. In last will, she left 2 500 marks to Ben. Immediately after reading this, his mother asks: "Will you accept it, Ben?" Ben does not answer. Instead he lifts the lid of the piano and begins to play an old melody by Rubinstein, the tune he had once upon on a time played to Sigrid. He continues to play his old repertoire for hours, the women dare not disturb him. The novel closes with the paragraph:

> När han steg upp, gick han till fönstret och såg ut i månskenet över rimfrosten. men han såg ingenting. Tonerna hade smält så mycket inom honom att det blev överfullt där. Han strök sig ett tag med näsduken över ansiktet och då kunde han se en glittrande diamant, borta på en al nära insjöisen. Bakom den långt, långt borta sköt ett stjärnskott ut i den frostklara rymden och lämnade en rök efter sig för ett ögonblick... (*BV*, 248)

This final scene is ambiguous. Even in his early teens, Ben would read a "flaming" evening prayer for Sigrid, and sometimes he would look at the starry sky, see a shooting star and make a wish that she would be his bride:

> Såg han ett stjärnfall under vinterkvällarna, glömde han aldrig att önska sig Sigrid Walborg till brud - han hade hört att en önskan, som säges högt medan en stjärna glider ned från fästet, går i fullbordan. (*BV*, 36–37)

In the end of the novel the motif pops up again. From the perspective of the naturalistic novel, Ekelund notes, the shooting star in the cold December night becomes a meaningful final vignette for the history of Ben's dream; his life's work dissolves into nothingness. Ekelund considers the star motif a recurrent one in Tavaststjerna's *œuvre*, and reads it as a symbol for the frightening feeling of the meaninglessness of an individual's life in cosmos.[73]

In the last paragraph an important motif, which recurred in the love story of Ben and Sigrid, comes forth again. The shooting star links the final episode of the novel and the last two stanzas of Michael Choræus's poem together again:

> O! skall då jag återse den dal,
> Der jag lekte bort den glada våren?
> Skall jag se den utan hjertats qval,
> Och med ögat, icke skymdt af tåren?

The speaker is referring to the youthful years in the spring of his life. This is a parallel to Ben and Sigrid's meetings.

> Enda vän på jorden, glada hopp,
> Du de sorgnas aldrig släckta stjerna!
> tindra klar mot öknen af mitt lopp,
> Tjus mitt hjerta, och bedrag det gerna!

The last stanza of Choræus' poem is tied to the theme of Tavaststjerna's novel. The speaker who has lost all his friends makes a wish that his "only friend on earth, that joyful hope" would gleam or twinkle to the speaker and to the course of his life and that she would enchant his heart and deceive him willingly. This final reunion between the lovers is only possible beyond the stars.

What is the idea of the star evading in the final episode of the novel? Ben and Sigrid's relationship represents the love of soul-mates, representing the male and female principle of the original, undivided human. The Platonic idea or myth goes through Romantic poetry and is revived again in the symbolist and Neo-Romantic literature of the last decades of the 19th century. The myth includes a dogma of the fall of the souls from the absolute, the world of ideas, to the earth where they must live apart, and to their reunion in the absolute again. In his classic study on Swedish Romanticism, Alfred Nilsson has shown that this Platonic theme was central to Swedish Romantic poetry, especially to the poetry of Erik Johan Stagnelius (1793–1823), the most original poet of the era of Swedish Romanticism.[74] Both Runeberg and Topelius were great admirers of Stagnelius, and their poetry is strongly influenced by him.[75]

A favourite theme in Stagnelius' poetry is already present in his early poetry: the pleasures of this world are empty and true joy will only meet us after death; only in the higher world is it possible to meet true love. The external symbol of this theme is his Muse and the object of his love, Amanda.[76] The conflict between "earthly and heavenly love" fighting in the poet's soul runs through his poetry but enters into a new phase, when the poet discovers the stream of Platonic mysticism and tries to quench his thirst for it. The myth of fallen and separate souls is repeated again and again in Romantic poetry. In Stagnelius' *Afsked till lifvet,* for example, the story goes as follows:

> Stolta Flickan! ej du visste,
> Att Naturen sjelf och ödet
> För hvarannan blott oss skapat;
> Att i etherns höga zoner,
> Der, af Skaparns ljus beglänste,
> Ursprungsbilderne till lifvets
> Flyktigt skimrande fantomer,
> Skönhetens idéer sväfva,
> Våra själar fordom voro
> Blott ett enda gudaväsen;
> Att när sinneverldens bojor
> Fallit af oss snart i döden,
> Våra själar åter skola
> Till en enda sammansmälta.[77]

Both Stagnelius' poem and Tavaststjerna's novel refer to the same Platonic myth: the lovers have been united in their previous existence, and they have been separated during this worldly life, as they have fallen from the absolute. The lovers will be united again after death, where they will gain their original state of mutual love: the innocence of childhood, their lost paradise.

The Sense of Ending: the Novel Turns Lyrical

Thomas Warburton and Merete Mazzarella, two commentators on the modern development of Swedish prose in Finland, have underlined the significance of Tavaststjerna as an originator in the modern tradition of Finland-Swedish prose. This view with its emphasis on times to come, tends to ignore the deep roots in the previous epoch. Tavaststjerna is certainly a founder of a modern tradition; but at the same time he is a synthesiser and a transformer of the tradition in which he grew up. He may also be read as a commentator of a tradition almost a hundred years old, and *Barndomsvänner* may be placed at the crossroads of many literary frontiers.

The presence of various literary front lines is embodied in the protagonist of the novel. Ben Thomén is an in-between character in several senses. He is a modern immigrant, a young man from the countryside who has come to the metropolis in order to be a success. On his way to power and glory, he has to make a choice between bourgeois life and the arts. This character type is familiar from the great novels of French realism and naturalism, Balzac, Flaubert, and Zola. In Tavaststjerna's novel, there are two additional metamorphoses which the young protagonist goes through. First, he becomes lyrical and moves from the position a the novelistic hero of a realistic novel to become a lyrical artist, a singer of romantic *Lied*; he becomes a character between prose and lyric poetry.

If *Barndomsvänner* is examined from the point of view of lyrical poetry, the change may be given a more literary explanation. Lyric was the dominant mode of 19th century literature. Almost every genre became at least partly lyric – in the sense that its conventions were modulated expressively, or that shape matched form with content, or that style was at least stylish. Thus, we speak of the novelistic genre which grew out of this tradition as "the lyric novel".[78] The lyric quality of *Barndomsvänner* makes it elegiac.[79]

Elegies are prolific in the times of great changes, as Alastair Fowler reminds us, and the 19th century might have been the most prolific of all literary periods in experimentation with the genre. In this sense *Barndomsvänner* touches upon the most tender and delicate point in the cultural sphere of Swedish Finland at its important turning point. The story of Ben Thomén may be read as an elegiac expression of the feeling of the end of something valuable, the loss of a culture with which to identify, or the vanishing of a tradition through which to speak and write.

Tavaststjerna was not just writing the first modern realistic novel in Finnish literature, he was participating with his work in a major change taking place in European literature, that is, transforming the mature and full-bodied novelistic model developed and refined during the century into a new kind of writing, where prose and lyric could meet each other again on a new scene in a way in which it never had done before. The generic system was undergoing a fundamental change as it evolved from the 19th century realistic paradigm to the modernism of the 20th century via the experiments of the last two decades of the *fin-de-siècle*. In prose writing this signalled a period of experimentation with various narrative, stylistic and rhetorical inventions. The most important tendency was the reorganisation of the generic borderlines of prose and lyric. The lyrical elements in Tavaststjerna's novel are a sign of a new repertoire invading the form of the novel.

NOTES

1 Quoted in Söderhjelm 1900/1924: 131.
2 Söderhjelm 1900/1924, 132. ("Even on the first pages – – one could read not only an unusually natural truth but also a turn towards something completely new in our literature, the description of everyday reality where anyone could recognise himself.")
3 Söderhjelm 1900/1924: 129.
4 Neiglick 1887: 190.
5 Neiglick 1887: 182.
6 Neiglick 1887: 183.
7 Neiglick 1887: 184. ("Quartet singing such as it is, a standard programme at all events in the course of human life whenever there is a need for entertainment; with the tones of quartet singing we are baptised, married, buried, [with the same tones] we dance, enjoy good dinners and confess our love, extol respectful per-

sons and celebrate memorable days; quartet singing as an eternally similar vehicle for all solemn, joyful and sorrowful feelings; quartet singing as a stereotype of the whole nation's need for beauty; quartet singing as an artefact, as whipped cream on tone waves, as Musik als Kunst des Philistethums – *this* quartet singing would well serve its creator; it may be thought to have influence on Ben's development, and it should have been Tavastastjerna's responsibility to describe this development.")

8   According to Söderhjelm (1900/1924: 132) there were expectations that the novel was not only going to be a biting satire but also an expression of all those wishes that lived in the minds of the young generation. Neiglick, who was strongly influenced by realistic theories of the time, was also planning to write a satirical, realistic novel, in which one simply "plodded in mud". Behind Neiglick's criticism was a belief that there was a social demand for a Great Finland-Swedish Novel à la Strindberg's *Röda rummet* (Mazzarella 1989: 47). See also Arne Toftegaard Pedersen (1995), who has recently taken up Neiglick's criticism in the context of the Scandinavian modern breakthrough.

9   Neiglick 1887: 187.
10 Neiglick 1887: 187.
11 Neiglick 1887: 194.
12 Neiglick 1887: 194.
13 In Tavaststjerna's following novel *En Inföding* ("A Native", 1887) Neiglick was portraited as a heartless man called Hård ('hard, brusque'), who betrays his friend in the same way as Neiglick "betrayed" Tavaststjerna.
14 These issues are dealt with in Arvid Järnefelt's *Isänmaa (Fatherland,* 1893, written in the mid-1880's). In an earlier version of *Barndomsvänner,* Tavaststjerna used some contemporary political motifs. Ben's school mate was first Tudde Randers (Tudde is a typical Finland-Swedish nickname), only in the final version it was changed to Syberg. In this version, Tudde becomes a Fennoman ("A Finnish-minded") (See Söderhjelm 1923: 134). Söderhjelm (1900/1924: 136–137, n. 2) has enclosed a long passage from the first version, in which the topic of student life is represented in a way quite different to that in the published one.
15 Söderhjelm 1900/1924: 147.
16 Söderhjelm 1900/1924: 148.
17 Hedvall 1919: 123.
18 Key 1898: 197.
19 Kihlman 1926b: 126.
20 This may seem a trivial problem from the perspective of Swedish literature in Sweden. In a recent history of Swedish literature, Tavaststjerna has been labelled as "a writer of local interest" (Hägg 1996: 442).
21 One of the important signs of the times to come was the fact that by the 1880's the majority of students at Helsinki University spoke Finnish. It was clear proof that there was an educated, up-and-coming Finnish speaking class in the country, and this would have great political impact in the very near future. Young Finnish writers were climbing to the literary stage: Juhani Aho, Arvid Järnefelt, Teuvo Pakkala and Minna Canth. They wrote in Finnish, but they could fluently read the Scandinavian languages and write Swedish. In addition, they also read major European languages and followed literary life outside Finland.
22 Warburton 1951: 9.
23 Warburton 1951: 11.
24 Mazzarella 1989: 5.
25 Mazzarella 1989: 9.
26 Wrede 1999: 441. See also Erdman (1887: 129) for contemporary views on educational aspects of the novel.
27 Juhani Aho's story *Muudan markkinamies* ("A Man in a Market Place", 1884) is usually mentioned as the first *Künstlerroman*. However, the story is not a novel but a novella; additionally, its theme of art and the nature of the artist does not fit

into a middle-class environment nor does it display the clash between bourgeois life and art – a prerequisite of the *Künstlerroman*.
28 See, for example, Stenström 1961.
29 The old trick of mixing real life characters with fictional ones started a peculiar convention derived from the idea of *roman de clef* and it was later used within the tradition of "det trånga rummet": real persons in the Swedish speaking cultural, political and economic elite are ridiculed in a fictional context.
30 Mazzarella (1989: 65) classifies the novel as "an autobiographically orientated *Bildungsroman*", in which the main character is presented as "a product of his heritage and milieu".
31 Jost 1968: 98.
32 On the cultural functions of *Bildungroman*, see Moretti's brilliant *The Way of the World: The* Bildungsroman *in European Culture* (1987).
33 The theme of parental opposition to a musical career is typical in German fiction of the 19th century starting with Wilhelm Hauff's *Die Sängerin* (1827). Theodor Storm's *Ein stiller Musikant* (1874–1875) introduces a theme which was to become very important for the novels and novellas of the last two decades of the century linked to the *Bildungsmodel*: the tension between a stern father and a sensitive son with artistic aspirations. The novel indicates the strongly social bias with which the mid-19th century saw the artist's problem. (Schoolfield 1956: 78.)
34 Buckley 1974: 17–18.
35 Jost 1969: 99.
36 The end of a *Bildungsroman* may be happy or unhappy, or anything in between, but there is one restriction: any character in the novel may die except the protagonist. The main character would in that case lack the goal of his education and the novel's *raison d'être*. (Jost 1969: 99–100.) The principle can be seen in the fact that such *Bildungsroman* tend to continue: *Wilhelm Meister* was followed by *Wilhelm Meisters Wanderjahre* (1821), Gottfried Keller's *Der grüne Heinrich* (1854–1855) was followed by *Martin Salander* (1886); in Finnish literature Juhani Aho's *Papin tytär* (*The Priest's Daughter*, 1885) was followed by *Papin vaimo* (*The Priest's Wife*, 1894).
37 Moretti 1992: 44.
38 Moretti 1992: 45.
39 The pagination refers to the original version of the novel, which was re-edited in 1988.
40 Ekelund 1950: 84.
41 Kihlman 1926b: 127–129.
42 See Ekelund 1950: 90. In the 1880's Strindberg wrote much of his open air stories and novels which were based on his summer experiences in the Stockholm archipelago. Such famous novels as *Hemsöborna* (1887) and *I havsband* (1890) have a close thematic connection to Tavaststjerna's critically neglected novel *Kvinnoregement* ("The Woman Regiment", 1894)
43 ("– Ben is still late.
   – Oh, yes, said sister Emmi. Otherwise they did not want talk about him, he had become a cause of trouble. Apart from that the boy was rough and moody, he would barely answer the kindest question.
   – Where on earth could he be? Sister Emmi did not have a slightest idea. She could guess, however.
   – If only father were at home, Ben would be more disciplined.
   – Perhaps.
   – He has become almost a hooligan, making friends with the servants, and will certainly not learn anything good from them
   – Certainly not.
   – And it cannot be helped – who could understand such a wild rascal who does not value his home and his parents – – !")
44 Moretti 1992: 44–45.

45 See Ahlund 1990 for a general view of academic life in the Scandinavian university novel.
46 See Klinge 1975; for the Finnish student as a national character, see Molarius 1996.
47 See Alapuro 1987 for a concise description of the Finnish-minded national movement in Finland.
48 Topelius 1877, 56. ("We are the free people of the spirit that will proudly fight, being an interpreter of light, forever for her right to spread it around the world.")
49 Molarius 1996: 11.
50 Topelius 1877, 57. ("We are the sons of our land, we deeply love her hidden coast. For this land that grew us, we will fight for until death. And no one, no one will betray our calling inherited from forefathers to root the flag of light into to desert of the North.")
51 There is a more famous version of this particular poem, which Topelius used in his *Boken om vårt land* (1875). In this version *Hellas* has been changed to *Finland* throughout the poem. Interestingly enough, Tavaststjerna does not use it here.
52 For the personal background to the novel, the dilemma between bourgeois career and artistic calling, and the doubts about his talent, see Ekelund 1950: 77–80.
53 See Klinge 1982.
54 See Siltala 1999 on the theme of psychic internalisation of the fatherland's fate in some outstanding national figures of the 19th century national movement.
55 Ekelund 1950: 84.
56 ("Now he was sitting in the middle of the wilderness, the carriage was overflowing, and the horseman was bustling the horse. Ben wiped something from the corner of his eye, so lively were his memories, and he awoke from his thoughts only when the carriage stopped in the yard of an inn. The horseman stepped down. – We've arrived, he said.")
57 ("[There was] a heap of brushwood and a log with an axe embedded deep inside, an ugly, grey corner of an outbuilding and a piece of black field behind a snowdrift. – – In the background he could see a low, leafless forest. He stepped down into the muddy yard and went into the inn – – He leaned on the desk of the reception and stared tiredly at all the dim greyness in front of him… [– –] So, this was his Finland – grey, gloomy and poor!")
58 ("Here, inside the room the ceiling was low and the air suffocating. And it was here that he felt overwhelmed by endless distress, the feeling that everything was unrelentingly compressed inside these evenly grey walls, and it was as if that leaden sky and the ugly outbuilding were an unrelenting curtain, which now fell behind him and forever parted him from his colorful, sunny past. He was taken by endless melancholy, he was bitter and rebellious and had no resignation at hand.")
59 Mazzarella 1989: 9.
60 For the literary relationship between Runeberg and Tavaststjerna, see Kihlman 1926a.
61 ("Dost forget in Sweden's flowery valleys / Native woodland's dear, / And for songs of nightingales, the sallies / Of the mavis here?" [Runeberg 1878: 1])
62 ("As a yearned-for spring-day shall each dwelling / Thee a greeting sending, / Echo hail thee, through the gray hills swelling, As thy childhood's friend." [Runeberg 1878: 3])
63 ("Like birds of passage, after winter's days returning / To lake-land home and rest, I come now unto thee, my foster-valley, yearning / For long-lost childhood's rest." [Runeberg 1878: 4])
64 Hedvall 1941:112.
65 ("On lifted wings thither, / As little birds hie, / None shows the way whither / Through wildering sky; / Yet sure dost thou fly." [Runeberg 1878: 16])
66 The possible realisation of this promise has been interpreted as the Renaissance of Finnish culture, and this indeed is what happened about ten years after the publication of *Barndomsvänner*. The decade of the 1890's – the productive years of Gallén, Sibelius, Saarinen, Enckell – is called the Golden Age of Finnish art.

67 Kihlman 1926b: 126–127.
68 Söderhjelm 1900/1924: 140.
69 ("The twilight covered the serious tombstones with its mourning veil and revealed the outlines of the iron crosses that spread out their thin and blessing arms over the sinful, suffering human race.")
70 In the first version of the novel the graveyard episode was originally subtitled "Timely love within the eternal" ("Den timliga kärleken hos den eviga"). See Söderhjelm 1900/1924: 135.
71 In the final scene the novel is not very far from a well-known fairy-tale of Topelius, A *Birch and A Star.* A brother and a sister have moved abroad after having been separated from their parents. When they grow up they wish to leave their foster parents and find their original home. Their search will be guided by a star., and the quest will be fulfilled, when they recognise a familiar birch tree in a yard which turns out to be the yard of their original home. In his *Boken om vårt land* ("The Book on Our Land", 1875) the author has explained these symbols as follows: the star represents man's divine home and the birch tree his earthly home, fatherland.
72 Benjamin was the youngest son of Jacob and the second son of Rachel, and afterwards became the name of a tribe. According to Genesis (35: 16–18) Rachel gave birth to a son while dying, naming him Ben-oni ('son of my sorrow'). Jacob, however, called him Benjamin (based on popular etymology, 'son of fortune'), because his birth compensated for the loss of his wife. Benjamin is mentioned twice in the New Testament, in Rom. 11:1 in the context of God's dealing with the New Testament Jews, in Rev. 7:8 Benjamin is one of the New Testament tribes sealed unto salvation.
73 The motif can be met in some of his sketches (*Övergivet, En isblockad på allvar* and *Marin och genre*), novellettes (*Impressionisten* and *Unga år*) and in his lyrical testament, the last collection of poems, *Laureatus* (Ekelund 1950: 85.)
74 For "earthly and heavenly love" in Stagnelius, see Nilsson 1916/1964: 243–277.
75 Topelius' *Orions bälte* (1850) has been taken as the precursor of Topelius' famous *Vintergatan* (*Milky way*) which was written six years later (1856). Both poems recount the tale of lovers' meeting "in the home of the blue heights". Vasenius (1931: 123) informs us that when Topelius and his fiancé Emilie Lundqvist were still living apart, he in Helsinki and she in Uusikaupunki, they agreed that on certain days and at certain times they would look at the same stars in the sky. In a letter from 1845 Emilie asks Zacharias that, on a certain day at eight o'clock, if it is clear weather, they once more look at Orion – – "and so our glances and thought will meet there". Olof Enckell (see Topelius 1970) suspects that the impulse for this romantic agreement, and consequently for *Orions bälte*, was taken from Runeberg's *Till Aftonstjernan* (*Dikter*, 1833).
76 According to Frederik Böök, Amanda is merely an erotic personification, a symbol. There are three phases in the evolution of this symbol in the poetry of Stagnelius. First, she is a symbol for a captivating dream of love who in herself contains all erotic temptations and pleasure; after that she symbolised the unattainable happiness in love, and finally she stood for the bride, with whom he, in his previous existence, was united and whom he would rejoin after death. (Quoted in Nilsson 1916/1964: 217.). All these "phases" may be seen in the development of Ben's feelings towards Sigrid in *Barndomsvänner*.
77 Quoted in Nilsson 1916/1964: 218–219.
78 Fowler 1982: 206.
79 See Fowler (1982: 211): "Expressive lyricism is quite foreign to the earlier novel. But it comes increasingly prominent as we move from Thackeray and Dickens, through Meredith and James to the "lyric novels" of Virginia Woolf. This whole development can be seen as a generic transformation, in which elegiac or 'lyric' modulation of the verisimilar novel is the main process."

BIBLIOGRAPHY

AHLUND CLAES 1990 *Den skandinaviska universitetsromanen 1877–1890*. Skrifter utgivna av litteraturvetenskapliga institutionen vid Uppsala universitet 26. Stockholm: Almqvist & Wiksell.

ALAPURO RISTO 1987 De intellektuella, staten och nationen. *Historisk tidskirft för Finland* 72:3/1987.

BUCKLEY JEROME HAMILTON 1974 *Season of Youth. The Bildungsroman from Dickens to Golding*. Cambridge, Massachusetts: Harvard University Press.

CHORÆUS MICHAEL 1801/1964 Till mina Barndomsvänner. *Suomen kirjallisuus* 2. Ed. Martti Rapola. Helsinki: SKS and Otava.

EKELUND ERIK 1950 *Tavastsstjerna och hans diktning*. Skrifter utgivna av Svenska Litteratursällskapet i Finland vol. 331. Helsingfors: SLS.

ERDMANN NILS 1887 En nutidsbiografi. Benjamin Thomén i Tawaststjernas "Barndomsvänner". *Framåt* 2:8/1887.

HEDVALL RUTH 1919 Tavaststjernas förhållande till naturalismen. *Festskrift tillägnad Werner Söderhjelm den 26 juli 1919*. Red. Gunnar Castrén et al. Helsingfors: Söderström.

HEDVALL RUTH 1941 *Runeberg och hans diktning*. Andra upplagan. Stockholm: Fahlcrantz & Gumaelius.

HÄGG GÖRAN 1996 *Den svenska litteraturhistorien*. Stockholm: Wahlström & Widstrand.

JOST FRANCOIS 1969 La tradition du Bildungsroman. *Comparative Literature* 21/1969.

KEY ELLEN 1898 Karl August Tavaststjerna. *Ateneum* 1/1898.

KIHLMAN ERIK 1926a Johan Ludvig, den ende, Tyrann. *Nya Argus* 19:4/1926.

KIHLMAN ERIK 1926b *Karl August Tavaststjernas diktning*. Skrifter utgivna av Svenska Litteratursällskapet i Finland vol. 188. Helsingfors: SLS.

KLINGE MATTI 1975 Suomen ja Ruotsin 1800-luvun yliopistolaitoksen ja kulttuuri-ilmapiirin vertailua. *Bernadotten ja Leninin välissä. Tutkielmia kansallisista aiheista*. Helsinki and Porvoo: WSOY.

KLINGE MATTI 1982 *Suomen sinivalkoiset värit*. Helsinki: Otava.

LEINO KASIMIR 1898 K. A. Tavaststjernan merkitys. *Nykyaika* 1898.

MAGNUSSON BO 1973 Esteticism och epikurism i Hårda tider. *Nya Argus* 4/1973.

MAZZARELLA MERETE 1988 Förord [in Tavaststjerna K. A, *Barndomsvänner*. Schildts. Sl. 1988].

MAZZARELLA MERETE 1989 *Det trånga rummet. En finlandssvensk romantradition*: Helsingfors: Söderström & C:O. Förlags AB.

MOLARIUS PÄIVI 1996 Nuoren Apollon syöksykierre. Sivistyneistö ja kansallisen ideologian murroksia. *KTSV* 49:1/1996.

MORETTI FRANCO 1987 *The Way of the World. Bildungsroman in European Culture*. London: Verso.

MORETTI FRANCO 1992 "A Useless longing for myself." The Crisis of the European Bildunsroman, 1898 - 1914. *Studies in Historical Change*. Ed. R. Cohen. Charlottsville and London: University of Virginia Press.

NEIGLICK HJALMAR 1887 Tavaststjernas "Barndomsvänner". *Finsk Tidskrift* 3/1887.

PEDERSEN ARNE TOFTGAARD 1995 Det moderne sammenbrud. Om Karl August Tavaststjernas Barndomsvänner. *Historiska och litteraturhistoriska studier* 70/1995.

RUNEBERG JOHAN LUDVIG 1878 *Lyrical songs, Idylls and Epigrams*. Transl. by Eirikr Magnusson and E. H. Palmer. London: Kegan Paul.

RUNEBERG JOHAN LUDVIG 1925 *The Songs of Ensign Stål. National Military Song-Cycle of Finland*. Clement Burbank, transl. New York: G. E. Stechert.

SCHOOLFIELD, GEORGE C. 1956/1966 *The Figure of the Musician in German Literature*. New York: AMS Press.

SILTALA JUHA 1999 *Valkoisen äidin pojat. Siveellisyys ja sen varjot kansallisessa projektissa*. Helsinki: Otava.

STRINDBERG AUGUST 1877 *Från Fjärdingen och Svartbäcken. I vårbrytningen. Samlade Verk* 2. Uppsala: Almqvist & Wiksell. 1981.

SÖDERHJELM WERNER 1900/1924 *Karl August Tavaststjerna. En levnadsteckning. Skrifter: Band I*. Helsingfors: Holger Schildts.

TAVASTSTJERNA K. A. 1924 *Barndomsvänner. Samlade skrifter*. Band I. Helsingfors: Holger Schildts.

TAVASTSTJERNA K. A. 1988 *Barndomsvänner*. Schildts. Sl.

TOPELIUS Z. 1877 *Sånger*. Stockholm: Bonniers.

TOPELIUS ZACHARIAS 1970 *120 dikter*. Med kommentar av Olof Enckell. SSLF 43i. Helsingfors: SLF.

WARBURTON THOMAS 1951 *Finlandssvensk litteratur 1898–1948*. Helsingfors: Forum.

VASENIUS VALFRID 1931 *Zacharias Topelius ihmisenä ja runoilijana*. V osa. Helsinki: Otava.

WREDE JOHAN 1999 K. A. Tavaststjerna – den hårda verkligheten. *Finlands svenska litteraturhistoria I*. Utg. av Johan Wrede. Helsingfors and Stockholm: SLS/Atlantis.

PÄIVI MOLARIUS

"Will the Human Race Degenerate?"
The individual, the family and the fearsome spectre of degeneracy in Finnish literature of the late 19th and early 20th century

The role of heredity as a factor shaping man was emphasized in the late 19th century when Charles Darwin's theory of natural selection became widely known. Following the path marked by Darwin, interest focused on the connections and differences of man and the animals. Social Darwinism transferred Darwin's concepts and trains of thought to explain the life of human communities. Progressive evolution, natural selection and the survival of the fittest steered man just like any other species. In social and political debate, Darwinism was ideologized and associated sometimes with quite original, goal-oriented cultural and racial interpretations of evolution. Alongside the faith in progress that was associated with evolution there also arose an interest in degeneracy, decay and all manner of physical, psychological and moral weakening. The scientific formulation of degeneracy was presented in the 1850s by the French psychiatrist Bénédict Augustin Morel, according to whom degeneracy was hereditary and deepened generation by generation. (Mattila 1999, 27).

Earlier research in literature has not systematically addressed the presence and significance of Darwinism and theories of degeneracy in Finnish literature.[1] The marked commitment of Finnish research in this area to the construction of national identity, the creation of a young and strong nation, and the Christian-conservative values that influence literature research for many years, eschewed these problems until recently. Development in the "wrong direction" and its various manifestations, however, were a subject of active debate in the press and in literature in late 19th-century and early 20th- century Finland. The debate analysed the weakening of Western man, the decay of civilization, the polluting effect of "the unsound human component", and the alarming spread of crime, vice and various states of nervous agitation.

In this article I analyse the depiction of these phenomena of degeneracy in literature written in Finnish, placing it in relation to models of thought concerning degeneracy. My perspective extends roughly from the 1890s to 1918. The civil war that was fought in Finland in 1918 heightened the debate on the degeneracy of the lower classes, but also introduced new features into it, which however cannot be discussed in the present article. Since degeneracy was generally associated with heredity, I specifically focus on works of literature placing the individual in his or her community of family or kin. Emphasis is given to some degree to the works of Maila Talvio, in which social inequality and the ties between the individual and his family shape people.

The context of the Finnish debate on degeneracy was not only provided by the literature of the natural sciences and the health-education magazines and guides that became widespread around the turn of the century (Lehtonen 1996, 209–213). A particularly important role was also played by active cultural contacts and a knowledge of recent European literature. In this respect Finnish literature was associated with the European literature treating the law-like properties of heredity that became widespread during the last decades of the 19th century and the early 20th century.

French literature, for example, was extensively presented to Finnish readers (among other writers, the pseudonym H. A-n. 1887, 145–154, 206–217). Contemporary debate made reference from time to time, though in an often critical and cautionary tone, to Émile Zola in particular, whose 20-volume series *Les Rougon-Macquart* follows the development and degeneration of a twin-branched family, and the underlying genetic and environmental factors. Familiarity with the works of Zola and other French naturalist literature was aided by the writings of the influential Danish cultural figure Georg Brandes, lecture tours in Finland by Brandes and the Swedish author Gustaf ad Geijerstam, among others. (Sarajas 1961, 11; 1962, 7–37)

Nordic literature, and the works of the Norwegian author Henrik Ibsen in particular, also had an important intermediary role. Ibsen's play *Gengangere* (Ghosts) from 1881 was translated into Finnish in 1886 and performed on several occasions in Helsinki around the turn of the century. The play aroused a heated debate in Finland on the moral obligations of heredity and the relationship between degeneracy and heredity (see Saarenheimo 1924, 48).

Although the Finnish debate was largely along the lines of discussions in Europe and the Nordic countries, it had particular national features in Finland, which are discussed in further detail in the present article. Special emphases were provided by the relationship with both the old and new realms and the intensifying Russification policies of the turn of the century .In 1809 Finland had been separated from the Swedish realm and annexed as an autonomous Grand Duchy to the Russian Empire. In Finland, the problematics of degeneration were closely linked to the issue of nationality, the associated debate on rave, the fragmentation of the political field and the question of being a political subject.

The accelerating vortex of degeneracy

In 1893 Vihtori Peltonen, better known to Finnish readers as the author Johannes Linnankoski who wrote of human spiritual and moral development, published an article with the heading "Why is the human race degenerating?" In this polemic article he ponders why the idea of evolution does not appear to be realized in the case of Western man. According to his observations, the course of development appears to be completely the opposite in both physical and spiritual terms: "We see again and again slack, spineless, nervous bodies lacking the bold vigour of the Lord of nature, and only having a wan life-weary tone." Like many other contemporary writers (e.g. M.o L. 1886, 178–183; Anon 1893, 99–100) he subscribes to the idea that the spread of civilization and the growth of affluence will conversely lead to growing slackness, immorality and other vices, which are alien to native peoples. The contemporary age is "an era of baldness, toothlessness, neurasthenics, weak lungs and all manner of weakness". (Peltonen 1893, 120). This is a process of ongoing degeneration that will ultimately lead to ruin. Only a vigorous intervention will change the course from degeneracy to progress and give evolution a chance to develop a healthier and stronger human race.

Peltonen /Linnankoski also dealt with these problems in his writing. One of his main works *Laulu tulipunaisesta kukasta* (The Song of the Scarlet Flower) from 1905 is an evolutionary tale in the spirit of the above article. The hero, a Finnish Don Juan character, succeeds in his own life in ending the vicious circle of sexual irresponsibility inherited from his father's family and devoting himself to a constructive role in society.[2]

Maila Talvio's (1871–1951) novel *Silmä yössä* (An Eye in the Night) also addresses the thematic of degeneration. It presents the array of vices and accelerating vortex of degeneracy introduced by affluence and civilization. The novel begins with a description of a journey by train, a symbol of the modern lifestyle in Finnish literature. A wedding party is on the train. The new marriage is a union of two influential families, the Montonens and the Rauhaniemis. But the happy mood is soon shattered. The reader gradually learns that the wedding was preceded by a crime and wrongdoings that will lead to the degeneration of the families as surely as the train rolls ahead on its tracks.

Before the end of the novel the mighty families have become corrupted and are on the brink of ruin. The head of the Montonen family, which is in the worst state, wallowing in crime, immorality and lies, is an erstwhile financial counsellor who left his sick wife to live in a free relationship with his office assistant. He drowns in a drunken state when trying to save his money from a leaking ship. His wife has died in solitude in the terrible agonies of an "inner cancer" caused by grief. The counsellor's businessman brother is financially ruined as the result of alcoholism. During an attack of delirium tremens, he cuts through his larynx with a sherd from a broken mirror. The councillor's daughter has died of an attack of illness while still in her prime, leaving ten half-orphaned children and a husband plagued by visions in his pangs of conscience. The daughter of the couple of the blissful wedding ceremony at the beginning of the novel has become an embezzler and a "kept woman". The Rauhaniemi family of respected clergymen is not doing much better: greed, disharmony, lies and resulting conflicts among and between relatives erode the family.

Morel's theory of degeneration offered a model of explanation in which problem behaviour and a variety of psychological and physical illnesses were given a basis transcending the individual and his free will. Man was subordinate to the laws of nature, and his hereditary background made it possible at least to some degree to predict his traits and tendencies. This appeared to have been convincingly proven by renowned case studies charting the history of individual families over a long period of time. These studies showed how degeneracy accumulated in certain families and recurred in them. Prediction was believed to improve considerably when knowledge of Mendel's breeding experiments spread in the early 20th century. (Mattila 1999,29–30)

Since the 1880s the theory of degeneration gained new weight, when it was linked to the idea of a special genetic substance, "protoplasm" that passed the genotype onto the following generations. The individual was only an instrument for passing on the protoplasm. Individuals, however, also had responsibilities. They were to protect their protoplasm in all ways for example against cellular toxins such as alcohol and syphilis, which would weaken it and thus undermine the health of future generations. (see Väänänen 1916, 27).

At the beginning of Maila Talvio's novel *Silmä yössä* (Eye in the Night) the fate of the families is prefigured on several occasions. In imitation of Ibsen's Ghosts , the novel speaks of children in whom the evils of their parents haunt the world. The speaker refers not only to the metaphor of the seed but also to a model of scientific explanation: the chain of cause and effect. Just as a whole ear of grain with its numerous seeds grows from a single seed, and new ears in turn from them, the forms of degeneracy are repeated time and again. A crime once committed and moral fall return repeatedly, and the evil circle spins at an ever faster rate. As interest compounds, the dimensions will swell.

The voice of truth in the novel, Jutte Cairenius, a hermit and dissenting member of the Rauhaniemi family, also predicts the events of the future with two stories, in which degeneracy accumulates in the chain of the generations: The parents tell a white lie, and a hundred years later their great-grandchildren are forcing open a safe. A young lady steals a chocolate sweet from a shop and two hundred years later her descendant, a mighty and rich man, destroys the lives of countless people with his losses in the millions. Cairenius is certain that the poison of crime will spread and degeneracy is a contagion within the family. His ominous words of warning of the "viper's foetuses", "real monsters" and "mongrels" threatening the family are realized in the aftermath of a marriage concluded in his own family (Talvio 1917/1954, 142, 134).

Morel regarded alcohol, which poisons man, but also tobacco and opium to be the main causes of degeneracy. Other factors included moral illnesses and passions of various kinds. (Väänänen 1916, 29–30; Mattila 1999, 27–28). In Talvio's novel, the ruin of the Montonen family is based not only on dishonesty motivated by hopes of riches but also in a particularly underlined fashion by drunkenness and immorality. It was typical of the moralizing tone of the discussion on degeneration that the wrong acts and vices of the individual were regarded as more dangerous than the influence of epidemics or poor and insufficient nutrition on the genotype. It was only on the foundation of mental health and virtue that physical health and a happy life could be based. The moral degeneracy of the Montonen family rotted its soul, which was at the same time the most dangerous manifestation of degeneracy and its consequence. (cf. Halmesvirta 1995, 44–45; Lehtonen 1995, 236–238).

The healthy and brutish "people"

Finland's position between its former mother country Sweden and Russia, to which it belonged since 1809, distinguished political power from cultural authority. The political power of Finland lay in St. Petersburg; its cultural and economic power was in the hands of the Swedish-speaking upper class within the country (Alapuro 1997, 18–19). The annexation of Finland as an Autonomous Grand Duchy of the Russian Empire marked a significant change in the language conditions of this new administrative area. In former Sweden-Finland speakers of Finnish had constituted a minority of only a fifth of the total population, but in autonomous Finland belonging to Russia they immediately became an absolute majority: almost 90 percent of the inhabitants of the Grand Duchy spoke Finnish as their mother tongue. But since Swedish was the language of administration and the Swedish-speaking minority held key positions in administration, the economy and cultural pursuits, this disparity had a significant impact on political and social developments. The *Fennoman* nationalist movement campaigning to improve the position of Finnish-speakers emphasized its links with the Finnish-speaking "people" and its struggles against a "foreign-language" upper class. Elements of class struggle were also involved in the language disputes.

The new educated class, Finnish-speaking or having converted to speaking Finnish, sought a strong ally, which it found in the farmers who had become affluent in the lumber trade in connection with revival of the economy in the late 19th century. This "dirt nobility" wanted to improve its social status. The alliance defined for a long time the content of Finnish-national ideology and the propaganda practised by the movement. It also entailed criticism of the Swedish-speaking upper class, as well as an idealization of the land-owning farmer class and its way of life. The nationalist admiration of the people was mixed with features of a romantic way of thinking crystallized by Rousseau, according to which the common people are noble savages and untainted children of nature. Authentic humanity at its purest could be seen in the people. The way of life of the common people, as comprehended via representations idealizing the life of farmers and peasants, was close to nature, and developed physical strength, health and endurance. This way of thinking clearly informs Vihtori Peltonen's article (1893, 121) in which one of the reasons for degeneration is the alienation of Western man from an "original", natural and hardening way of life.

Although Fennoman-oriented literature specifically understood its own ennobled image of the farmer class to be the "people, the idealization of rural life also extended to the non-land owning rural population that supported itself with its own labour. Underlying this attitude was the contemporary medical idea of the health-promoting and healing effects of fresh country air and physical labour, as opposed to a slack upper-class lifestyle and the unhealthy consequences of the foetid air of the urban environment and an unnatural lifestyle. (Halmesvirta 1995, 34–35.)

In Aino Kallas's [3] short story "Ingel" (Meren takaa I, 1904) a wet nurse hired by a manor, a strong, healthy serf woman passes on in her milk "her whole unused capital" into a frail upper-class child, whose "blood has become thin through the generations" (Kallas 1904, 78). In feeding the child, she passes on her own strength to give new vitality to a family and race that has become weakened through time. The metaphoricity of milk and blood in Ingel was common in popular discussion on heredity around the turn of the century. Mother's milk and human blood were mystically regarded as not only symbolizing but also bearing the genotype of man. Defects of the blood, its diluted state causing weakness, told of limited vitality in the genetic material. On the other hand, by nursing the strong, healthy woman of the people not only provided the child of a stranger with nutrition to fortify him but also gave of her strong, health and undegenerated genotype.

During the period of autonomy, there were, however, several competing and mixed conceptions of the common people.[4] Alongside the idealization of the people, their primitive customs, lack of education, drunkenness, sloth and lack of cleanliness were disapproved, and their obstinacy and desire for power were feared. (see Molarius 1999, 74–75).

In various parts of Europe, racial theories applied the concepts of Darwinism to hierarchies of evolution and status among the races. Indications of contacts with the lower stages of evolution were sought in the lower races. The undeveloped races, such as the black and yellow races, were brutish and their members displayed physical characteristics and behaviour that was described as ape-like (see e.g. Kilpeläinen 1985, 183). The Finns were generally classed as a primitive primal people belonging to the yellow race, as Turanians or Mongols. The Finns – and the Finnish-speaking population in Finland – were regarded to be a strange ethnic fragment in Europe. Their strange language, different physical appearance with high cheekbones and "unnoble" noses, dubious intellectual powers and even low degree of humanity were the subject of wonder (Kemiläinen 1985a, 16; Aro 1985, 195–208). In keeping with their low racial background, the Finns were regarded to be incapable of abstract thought. Racial concepts were adopted especially in Swedish-minded circles, and they associated the Finns with irrational traits threatening the established social order, such as a tendency towards nervous disorders, collectivism and mass hysteria. (Puntila 1944 ,156.) This was also combined with the threat of repressed sexuality (see Wilkuna 1915, 42; Tarvas 1916, 65). Beneath the cool exterior of the Finns were passions that could erupt with the whole strength of their brutishness.

The social significations associated with race made the latter a considerable means of constructing group identity and discrimination around the turn of the 19th and 20th centuries. The concept was used loosely in accordance with ideological objectives by grouping people according to geographic, economic, cultural and social class into different races. The workers or peasants, for example, could be distinguished as separate races distinct from the intelligentsia, while rural-dwellers and townsfolk formed their classes. It is worth noting how close the image of industrial workers, the landless rural population or even farmers was to the concepts of races regarded as lower.

The susceptibility of the lower order to degeneration was caused by their close connection with the genotypes of instinct and drives[5]; in strong blood human drives and instincts were still dangerously close. The rural populace was believed to be at the mercy of the aggressive forces, desires and unbridled "voice of the blood" of their subconscious self. The metaphor of the "voice of the blood" which was common in Finnish literature around the turn of the century has twin connotations. Not only referring to genetic heredity from one generation to another down the family line, it also points to another direction, the irrational and destructive world of human drives and instincts. The "voice of the blood" links the individual to the chain of generations and also brings to consciousness the uncontrollable world beyond it. (Molarius 1998, 109.)

Even the slightest crack in the dam could lead to a flood. The thickness of the blood could cloud the brain and lead to violent, uncontrolled reactions. The brutish lower races and orders were more susceptible than the higher races and social classes to the corrupting vices of the "protoplasm". In fact, degeneracy was recorded as spreading most active among the common people. (Mattila 1999, 32–33.)

The idea of a brutal common people steered by its drives and instincts combined Darwinist evolutionism with the theory of degeneration, but from different directions. What the supporters of evolution regarded to be a low stage of development and the close contact of man with his animal roots, was for Morel a regression from the original type of man created by God, primal man prior to his fall.

From rugged country life to the vices of the city

Although considerable power was attributed to heredity, environment and education were also believed to play a role in shaping the fate of man, as shown by the concept of the health-sustaining effects of rural life. Hippolyte Taine's theory of the environment in particular focused attention on the relationship between heredity, environment and the contemporary era. A further element in the debate was provided by urbanization and industrialization, and the changes in lifestyle caused by them. There was now talk of a "new era" and "the man of the new era", who was nervous and hurried and susceptible to physical degeneration, psychic disorders and the vices of the city.[6]

In Finnish literature of the turn of the century, the rural – urban dichotomy is largely articulated through oppositions such as healthy and sick, as well as good and evil, and pure and soiled. The polarities reiterate an old mythical image derived from Antiquity and the Old Testament. The countryside is seen as a place for harmonious, simple and natural life, while the city, despite its many opportunities and clusters of intellectual development, is a den of iniquity. It is Sodom and Gomorrah, Babel and Jericho. The rise of capitalism and industrialized society heightened many of the problems related to towns and cities. The growing scope of the problems made the old urban-rural myth topical.[7] In Finnish literature of the turn of the century, the town or city is a nest of vice producing degeneration. It threatens the firm family ties typical of the countryside, attracts healthy young people, wears them out and discards back into the countryside as physical and mental cripple.

A particularly dangerous combination with the city was that of a rural youth coming to study or a country lass entering service. Maila Talvio's novel *Tähtien alla* (Under the Stars) points to the threat posed by the city to young people from the countryside who have no resistance: "-They are often very shy, those who come straight from the plough handle. When they enter a civilized way of life it is as if one were trying to tame a wild animal of the forest. They will not succeed..." (Talvio 1910/1953, 275.)

The rugged conditions of the countryside and hard physical labour were believed to keep the instincts that were strong in man under control. For those whose self-control had not developed over the generations and whose body and its needs had not become cultivated, they served as an exterior control. On the other hand, the looser norms of the urban milieu, "freedom" with its many sensually exciting attractions set them free of their shackles in all their unbridledness. In L. Onerva's short story *Nousukkaita* (Parvenus) from 1911, the character Pentti Korjus, a young man of farmer background studying in the city is unable to still the voice of drives and instinct within himself:

He had the longing for boundlessness of the forest dweller. He was insatiable, he could never have enough... He was a child of the famine fields. The benumbed instincts of his forefather had suddenly come to violent life in this raw land with its first touch of culture. He had inherited their burning hunger. He could not pass a single set table, drinking establishment or woman with indifference in his mind. The buds of pleasure repressed for centuries brought forth demands that could not be satisfied in a single lifetime. (Onerva 1911, 15–17).

In both Eino Leino's novel *Jaana Rönty* (1907) and Arvid Järnefelt's *Veneh'ojalaiset* (1909) the transition from the countryside and rural labour to the city sets in motion the vicious circle of degeneration in families.

But similar perils did not threaten the upper class of the cities. Over the generations culture and the urban lifestyle had tamed upper-class man. Civilized life had gradually taught man to regulate and tame his atavistic instincts. Onerva's Pentti Korjus is a kind of intermediary figure between town and countryside, nature and culture. He is a poor country boy, but has set out to study at an early stage and moved to the city. Korjus represents the rural student, the first-generation intellectual figure that was popular in European literature. The popular education objectives of the nationalist movement and the late yet rapid changes of Finnish society served to underline the interesting nature of this character.

This student of the first generation combined the polarities of town and countryside, farmers and gentlefolk, upper and lower class, culture and nature. He was a character in between classes, "half gentry", onto which the progress attendant to education important to the nationalist ideology as also the degeneration arising from the unresolved conflict of heredity and environment could be projected equally well. (Molarius 1996, 17–18, 22–25.)

Parvenus wasting their vitality and old families dying out

Degeneration was not caused or manifested only by excess in the form of an uncontrolled satisfying of the needs of vitality, its "surplus", but also by vitality depleted over the generations, a shortage of vitality. Finnish health education of the late 19th century already urged people to care for their vitality or energy which was the basis of life, which appeared in two forms in man: as the more brutal (muscular) energy of labour, and the more refined intellectual (nervous) energy. Although physical strength was above all the strength of workers and intellectual energy that of the upper classes, it was still the ideal that everyone should care for both forms of energy. (Halmesvirta 1995, 34)

Especially after the 1910s these monistic trains of thought, i.e. based on a single initial premise, gained strength. Ernst Haeckel's biogenetics and Wilhelm Ostwald's energetics are particularly well known. They aroused interest and Ostwald's ideas, for example, were discussed in academic circles in Finland. His books and the journal edited by him were read and debated (Koskenniemi 1947, 74–85).

Energy, the core element of Ostwald's cosmology, conforms to two basic principles: the laws of the indestructibility and dispersion of energy. According to the first law, the amount of energy in a closed space is constant. The second law states that energy can be free or bound and it can change form. In each alteration the free component of energy diminishes, while the bound (dispersed) component increases, until all energy is bound and the available free component has disappeared. As this is a one-directional process, bound energy cannot be released any more, and the end result of all the processes is the ending of movement, rest and death. The laws are universal and thus apply to all life, including intellectual phenomena. (Ostwald 1911–1916/ 1923)

Basing on this line of thinking, Ostwald derived his energetic moral precept: Do not waste energy, for if man "disperses the free energy subordinated to his use by misuse or through carelessness instead of using it for the good of humanity and mankind, he is guilty of stealing the shared property of mankind and he can never make amends for this, because dispersed energy can never be converted into free energy." (Ostwald 1911–1916/ 1923, 77.)

In literature, monistic ideas were combined with the disappointments of the intelligentsia and focus on the individual of psychological realism in following the degeneration of families and the intellectual powers of young men waning before their time. *Nuorena nukkunut* (1931), by the Finnish Nobel-prize winning author F. E. Sillanpää, describes the gradual degeneration of a family and the quiet waning of a young life. These were themes that Finnish literature had readily addressed since the first decades of the 20th century. In them, trains of thought not far removed from energetics are entwined in a complex manner with genetic theory, Darwinism and its Spencerian cultural-evolutionist expansion, racial theory and interpretations of the philosophy of Taine. The individual begins to perceive the state of being a subject through past ancestors and their vitality and genotype inherited from them. At the same time, the development/degeneration of families could be viewed from the perspective of a closed system.

In Aino Kallas's novel *Ants Raudjalg* (1907), set in Estonia, Ants already learns in childhood from a family tree drawn by his father of his own ties with past generations. Ants's Livonian forefathers, all the way to an ancestor liberated in his old age, had been serfs. His father had taken the first steps in obtaining an education, and Ants was the first of the family to enter university. The rise had been too fast: "It was a leap that was too large, too much of an effort, for which whole generations had to suffer". (Kallas 1907, 135). Alongside the course of development of emerging education is the antithetic feature of waning vitality, from which both Ants and his father suffer. Parallel to the process of positive development, this trait also gains strength over the generations. The father, who has become an old man too soon, notices how his son has already lost his vitality in his youth: "There was no longer the old juice and sap in the boy, even though he had the shoulders and hands of a bear" (Kallas 1907, 89).

Studying his family tree, Ants finds an explanation for his fatigue:

Then it suddenly dawned on him; he shook his fist at them. They were to blame, those toilers, who had used up the energy due to him, sweating it out in the fields and meadows of the manor. The strength that was to have come to him, his property, his legal inheritance [– –] His fatigue was the fatigue of his whole nation, fatigue accumulated by past generations in their lifetime. It was from that fatigue that they withered like the grey-barked bog birches from the excess moisture of the soil. (Kallas 1907, 134, 135.)

The depletion of energy was above all the problem of families producing first-generation members of the intelligentsia. L. Onerva's Pentti Korjus, originating from a poor rural home, has also exceeded the normal pace of development and climbed the social ladder too fast, leaving neither his family nor himself time to adapt to the changes. Unaccustomed to plenty, he and those like him had become gluttons of things of the spirit, matter and experiences, trying within their personal history to catch up with "natural" evolution of several generations:

> And to find time in this one life even intellectually to pass through the stages that a civilized man must experience and which in the natural order of things would have required the work of generations, his pace had to be extremely fast. He did not have time to follow the slow laws of nature; he rushed like an arrow through the classes straight into the nobility of the intellect, but in actual fact he only became an intellectual nihilist. (Onerva 1911, 17.)

In the light of the concepts of energetics it is logical to regard depleted vitality to be the problem of not only *arriviste* families wasting their energy with no moderation but also of slowly waning old families. Moreover, a great number of degenerate features accumulated over time in the old families. In Maila Talvio's novel *Tähtien alla* a group of girls discuss the shocking fate of an old spinster. The character, Miss Silfversvärd, corresponds quite faithfully to Morel's diagnosis of degeneration, among others. This included alcoholism in the family, waning vitality in the family, insomnia, fits of hysteria, incurability and self-destructive tendencies. Miss Silfversvärd's illness begins with attacks of hysteria that recur later. Her doctor diagnoses neurasthenia, and the patient finally has to be taken by force to hospital. Miss Silfversvärd comes from an old noble family, which is said to have become impoverished and degenerated almost to the point of extinction. The gradual decline of the family was already evident in Miss Silfversvärd's father, who was known to have drunk and lived immorally.

Although degeneracy was presented in all levels of society, it found different manifestations and explanations in them. There were claims in literature that Finnish peasants could not suffer from neurotic or hysterical symptoms, because their nervous system was not sufficiently sensitive or nuanced. The country youth, Matti Mataristo, in *Tähtien alla*, is described as a "bear cub". The girls talking about him reject any possibility that he could be mentally ill in any way. Everyone who sees his clumsy and reticent country-boy bearing, knows that "he has no nerves at all" (Talvio 1910/1953, 275).

On the other hand, the upper class was "weak-nerved" because of its overly refined and excited nervous system. The degeneracy of the upper class was associated with excess cultivation, and often also the extinction of families, "anaemia" or "weak-bloodedness". This state was characterized by nervousness, neuroses, an over-nuanced relationship with life and its phenomena. Miss Silfersvärd is characterized by extreme refinement and aestheticism. Her fragile and ethereal nature is particularly underlined. She is "thin" and "delicate" with "fine features". The old lady has "sensitive antennae", and even the slightest emotion makes her shake and shiver. (Talvio 1910/1952, 272, 274.)

The thematic of fatigue was also extended to communities, races and the state of culture. In the same manner as families, communities, races and cultures were believed to be born, to flourish, and to live out their time and grow old like biological organisms, and to die once they have depleted their energy. In Toivo Tarvas's novel *Eri tasoilta* (From Different Levels) from 1916, the city is regarded as following the life cycle of a biological organism: "The city was born, and it grew up and died like a living being." The sinking of cultural standards was attributed to "its own inherited and exhausted essence." (Tarvas 1916, 29, 79.)

In debate and discussion around the turn of the century, the Finland-Swedish culture, which was generally regarded as older than Finnish-speaking culture, was assumed to be in decline and even to die out. These claims were associated with the moods of fatigue, decay and passiveness of the *fin de siècle*, which now found a response in the self-definition of the Finland-Swedish intelligentsia at the beginning of the new century. The old Finland-Swedish culture was felt to have come to the end of its course, a keeper of the illustrious graves of an overly cultivated and over-aged past. The young generation was not believed to exhibit vitality, only pessimism and mockery. On the other hand, everything was young, vigorous and just beginning on the growing and expanding Finnish-speaking side of the divide. (H. S. 1910, 154). The latter had before it the whole life cycle of culture with its expected rise. It was believed to struggle for progress, while the energies of Swedish-speaking culture were consumed by the defence of its own existence. (See e.g. Grotenfelt 1916, 178–179.)

Will the iron bands of degeneracy be broken?

Where degeneracy was seen in Morel's terms as a hereditary and cumulative phenomenon, the opportunities of the individual – bound to his genetic heritage – to break the vicious circle of degeneration were limited or even non-existent. At the same time it was pointed out that the degenerate element, which was often regarded as having an exceptionally strong sexual drive, grew in relation to the rest of the population and caused society undue costs through its crimes, alcoholism and possible need for support. Supporters of the most radical position proposed the incarceration of the degenerate element into institutions, marriage restrictions and even castration. Health-education instructions to the public called for sickly people to think of the dismal future of their offspring and to refrain from reproduction. It was regarded as irresponsible that parents, who themselves "are full of illness from tip to toe" (Anon. 1900a, 115) produce offspring. It could also be felt that social support measures also lent support to the decline of mankind and civilization in preventing the sick from giving way to the vital and healthy element as required by Darwinist natural selection. (See e.g. Väänänen 1916; Mattila 1999.)

In Ibsen's *Ghosts* (1881/1886, 89–92), a young man ruined by the degeneration of his family hears a doctor's dire prediction of his future. He does not believe that he can change the course of his life. Therefore he asks his mother to end his anguished life with morphine capsules during his next attack of illness. In Talvio's novel *Tähtien alla* young, healthy girls discuss whether death could be a suitable solution for Miss Silfversvärd. Perhaps the self-destructive old lady should have let someone kill her, or couldn't a doctor make this service to the patient and to society with a small dose of morphine?

In the novel *Silmä yössä*, no strength is found within the family to rise from the vicious circle of degeneracy. Pity and helping the degenerate are "improvements to God's work" (Talvio 1918/1954, 293) and could only lead to even worse results. With this argument, Jutte Cairenius, who is trained as a physician, refuses to help the sick and those who need help. There is a light in the darkness, however, but its rays come from outside the sphere of degeneracy: Cairenius adopts a daughter, thus bringing pure, outside blood into a polluted family. The child, the daughter of a poor clergyman's widow, comes from a family that seeks the truth. For Jutte Cairenius the biological family of the girl represents a high ethical level. For him the girl is "a child of the best people", and "the child of people who have never lied" (Talvio 1917/1954, 180). Through the child, and her children in turn, the circle of degeneracy will be broken and the opportunity for a new beginning will open up.

In the novel, Jutte Cairenius presents himself as Judas, and reminds the reader of his Biblical namesake. In relation to his own family, he takes the role of a traitor. From the point of view of the family, Jutte Cairenius "betrays" his own blood by donating his considerable wealth outside the family and by grafting a completely new branch onto the degenerate family tree. In the novel it is only through separation from one's own family background that an opportunity for a new era and a new beginning will open up.

In 1918 a civil war broke out in Finland in connection with the country's separation from Russia. In the background were serious socio-economic problems, and the conflict had strong features of a class war. It divided the population in two. One side consisted mainly of the markedly grown landless rural population and the industrial proletariat, the "Reds", who were inspired by the Bolshevik Revolution in Russia. The other side, the victorious "Whites" was composed of owners of land or other economic capital and members of the educated classes, who campaigned for national independence and the expulsion of Russian soldiers from the country (see e.g. Alapuro 1988).

Views on degeneration and disbelief in the "curing" of the degenerate element of the population increased and grew in connection with the civil war along with growing support for forced measures. The debate was marked by a metaphoricity of blood that was expanded to society as a whole. Finland was a "body" that had been polluted by "sick blood". Especially in the extreme white propaganda of the winning side it was demanded that the blood tainted by Russian bolshevism be removed. Even the author Joel Lehtonen, who was anything but a war enthusiast and whose views were liberal and problematicized the starting points of both sides reflected on how "bad blood is to be let from the body of Finland" (letter from Joel Lehtonen to Sylvia Avellan 30.4.1918; Lehtonen 1981, 381; see also Kunnas 1976, 60).

The determinism that was associated with heredity ran counter to teachings of individualism that were common around the turn of the century and underlined the power and liberty of the individual. Despite its anti-individualism, determinism was also entwined with these views with different variants. It was asked, for example, whether a criminal rising above the mass was a person realizing his own self free of general moral precepts, or a helpless victim of heredity ruined by the immoral life of earlier generations?

In Talvio's short story "Näkymätön kirjanpitäjä" (The unseen bookkeeper) from the collection of the same name from 1918 biology is made to serve the ethic world order, against which the individual cannot rebel with his arbitrary choices. Largely following the lines of Dostoyevski's *Crime and Punishment*, the principal character of the story kills an old woman who sells sly grog. Like Raskolnikov and in a state of hubris he feels that his act was justified, and like Raskolnikov the character is also plagued by guilt. But unlike in *Crime and Punishment*, guilt does not humble the principal character or make him confess. It is not until the birth of his own child that an awareness of Biblical justice arises, the avenging of the sins of the fathers on their descendants. The man begins to be obsessed by the idea of a connection between his own crime and its forces binding his son. The father's fear is justified; his son, once a good lad, also becomes a murderer.

In Talvio's short story the crime is associated with the question of the responsibility and freedom of the individual. Crime reoccurs in three generations of the family. The protagonist's own father already had a register entry noting theft. In the next generation degeneration deepens in the form of homicide. As strongly as the principal character feels he is guilty of the murder of the grog-seller, he also regards his own descendant to be innocent and himself to be guilty of the deed committed by his son. The subject of the son and the family as well is the father, the previous generation which introduced the homicide as a strain on the blood of the family. In the eyes of the father, the boy is exonerated from guilt by the legacy of his father. The father's unexpiated crime made the son an instrument, and the latter's crime something preordained and inevitable:

His beloved one was punished for his sins. The curse extended to the third and fourth generation. Unborn generations will suffer because of his evil acts. [– –] But it was in fact impossible to have the son punished for a crime that he committed as result of his heritage. He, the father, must naturally suffer the punishment. [– –]

> My child, he began, – you have not murdered: it is your father who is the murderer... your father has committed two... two murders... the first one by his own hand, and then with your hand... The unseen bookkeeper demands what is due to him: if the father will not pay, it must come from the son... He will have his own, with interest.
> (Talvio 1918/1954, 455–456)

The bearing theme of the work is the requirement of moral balance. Just as a merchant demands strict records of all things bought and sold, and for the accounts to tally, God, the heavenly bookkeeper, demands that man must settle his accounts. It is only when a crime is confessed and expiated that it is possible to be free of degeneration. Until then the crime will be repeated and it will have its destructive effect again and again. The short story ends with the joint confession of both father and son and an allusion to expiation by suffering the necessary punishment.

In "The unseen bookkeeper" the idea of biologically based hereditary degeneration is mixed with religious elements and clearly becomes a moral-ethical issue. In moral terms, the individual is not only responsible for himself. His or her wrong way of life and choices will link unborn descendants to the vicious circle of degeneration. In Talvio's works God uses the laws of heredity as a tool to maintain a moral order. The Biblical avenging of sins unto the third and fourth generation is realized as a cumulative repetition in accordance with the theories of degeneration.

In the novel *Tähtien alla*, the neurasthenic Matti Mataristo, the son of a mother who strangled her child and was committed to a mental asylum, pursues a tiring internal struggle against the necessity of repeated crime. Mataristo's struggle to conquer his homicidal passions finds a parallel in Zola's *La Bête humaine* (1890) where Jacques struggles with his animal nature, the beast within. Mataristo has attacks during which his hands begin to follow the paths of his mother's crime. The fingers of the boy, who suffered a strangling attempt by his mother in childhood, reach for the throat of his brother, and then a schoolmate and later a girl nursing him.

During these attacks Mataristo acts involuntarily. The compulsion to strangle takes control of him. His reason functions, but his will cannot take control of it. Reason coldly estimates the relationship of the fingers and the throat of the victim:

> When the youngest brother, Santeri, was playing on the floor, his hands could not help measuring if they could reach around the boy's throat, and he pulled them together only to see if he had the strength to stop the boy's breathing and whether Santeri would turn black in the face, as he had turned when his mother had strangled him, and to see how much is needed to kill someone. [– –]
> In school he caught himself eyeing and measuring the necks of his classmates. Once in religion class he had no idea of what was being asked of him, for in his mind he was removing the teacher's collar and measuring his neck with his hands. The teacher reprimanded him for not paying attention, but after class came to ask if he were ill. The boy answered "No". But his brow was clammy and when the teacher turned to leave, he thought: "My hands could reach even around the collar!" (Talvio 1910/1953, 335, 336.)

A considerable number of depictions of degeneration in Finnish literature of the turn of the century entail a crime or criminal activities. One of the most important social applications of the theory of degeneracy is associated with criminal psychology, viz. the theory proposed by the Italian Cesare Lombroso of Italy in the 1870s regarding the born criminal. According to Lombroso, the criminal is a variant of the normal person in the direction of the animal, with an inherent and inherited tendency towards crime. The criminal character is a bestial person, in whom instincts and drives have gained the upper hand. (Mattila 1999, 28; on Finnish presentations of Lombroso, see Grotenfelt 1893, 397–421; Estlander 1894, 272–283, 373–393.)

An important aspect of Mataristo's illness is a struggle against the power of instincts. He is driven by an exceptional relationship with women, inhibited sexuality and a religious crisis. Sexuality appears as a destructive, disintegrating force that Mataristo is unable to accept in himself, nor ultimately able to control. Also in the general debate on degeneration the exceptionally great sexual activity of the degenerate element of the population was also felt to be a threat. In the comments of physicians it was noted that sexual desire remained the same or was even excessively emphasized in sick individuals. The overriding power of the sexual drive combined with immoral spinelessness was even cited as grounds for castration.

The most difficult stage of Mataristo's illness involves his lust for a girl who nurses him and his denial of the presence of God. Accordingly, the turning point of the illness is his victory over lust, his acknowledgement of the presence of God, and increased self-control. Mataristo's salvation and the decisive turn of the illness in a better direction involves a Tolstoyan clarification of Platonic love; erotic desire is replaced by a relationship based on friendship with the former object of his lust. The zealous God of organized religion is now paralleled by a faith in divine powers in man himself. Thus Mataristo's solution implies a separation, as far as possible, from the aspects associated with degeneracy in debate on the subject.

Degeneration and modern man

The theory of degeneracy is associated with the question of modern man. The birth of the modern individual has been seen as the result of the loosening of traditional ties defining man, such as a focus on class or family, and added social mobility. At the same time, theories of heredity, albeit now in a new form and with new emphasis, paradoxically brought man back to the family connection that was important for traditional society.

The ideal of the freedom of the individual and internal self-determination was problematized. Heredity made man part of his family, which influence his physique and psyche and the course of his life through his innate genotype. The appearance, racial background, vitality and quality of protoplasm bequeathed to him by his ancestors staked out the course of his life in advance. If the genotype was poor, the opportunities of life were also poor. The decisive event of his fate had already occurred before his birth.

The tendency to reattach man to his family and kin can be associated not only with the spread of the scientific world view but also with a search for pre-modern connections as a counterweight to the diffuse nature of life (cf. Beck 1993, 16, 140–144). Moreover, in Finland, the features typical of traditional society were still strong, because of the slow pace of modernization. Even in the early 20th century, the Finnish intelligentsia largely defined itself in terms of family ties (Sulkunen 1989, 1995).

Linking man to family as the agent that transferred the genetic material was also made problematic by the modern conception of man as an individual, making rational solutions and acting on an autonomous basis. In Finnish literature of the turn of the 19th and 20th century, the complex and entwined representations of biological laws and supra-individual forces came to parallel reason as a defining factor of the individual. The relationship of these forces with the reason, will and aims of the individual was often complex. A split or disintegrated subject presented itself as layered and divided into the continually varying combinations of the conscious and the subconscious. The subject could no longer make the solutions defined by the classic conception of the subject, because forces beyond his will challenged his rational self, often proving to be stronger than it. On the other hand, the idea of degeneration also had a completely opposite effect in underlining the responsibility of the individual and the importance of his choices. Man was responsible not only for his own fate but also for future generations. In relation to the future, the importance of the present and its moral obligations grew. Accordingly, the development of both Matti Mataristo and the principal character of "Näkymätön kirjanpitäjä" (The Unseen Bookkeeper) to be free of the compulsion of degenerating repetition runs parallel to ideas presented by Vihtori Peltonen on the above-mentioned article. Similar views were also propagated in the press around the turn of the century. This involved a project of taking possession of the self based on developing will-power. It was self-educational in nature and it signified the taking of communal responsibility for one's own acts. At the same time it also involved a control of personal desires, a discipline of instinct and drives, which gave a central role to self-observation and the control of satisfying one's own desires.

Degeneration and the emerging nation

The freely mobile citizenship of individuals that was taking shape led to great pressure for popular educational and other tendencies seeking to steer society. The purpose was to make individuals take responsibility for themselves and in broader terms for the state of their family and the nation as a whole. The objective of a moderate, hard-working citizen who controlled his urges was sought through the self-education of the individual. "Education and self-education meant [the development of]… self-control, i.e. a preventive and controlling nervous system". The nervous system had to be trained to encounter outside impulses and temptations with responses that were socially acceptable. Through a life of moderation protected by self-control the individual could maintain his nervous health and pass on his genotype sound and strong to posterity. (Oker-Blom 1903, 82–84). This mainly involved the lifestyle of the young intelligentsia and rising bourgeoisie of the middle classes, which they sought to apply to society as a whole. These groups found the hereditary power of the old nobility and educated families as well as the mass demands of the rural commoners and the urban proletariat to be alien to them.

Criticism of the slack and idle of the upper class was associated with the world view of the rising bourgeoisie and a society gradually becoming capitalistic. In its propaganda it employed concepts borrowed from the economy in the process of becoming capitalist. Health was capitalized by making it an issue of individual and national economy. Caring for the physical and mental condition of oneself and of future generations was a "capital" that could be afforded by rich and poor alike, and it was also their obligation. Investing in one's own health paid a greater "dividend" than the fiscal capital of even the richest plutocrat. The powers residing in man were to be used for the benefit of oneself and others, because in this way it would also add to the shared national wealth. (Halmesvirta 1995, 34–35; Lehtonen 1995, 217–218).

The overflowing vitality of the common people, threatening the social order and the health well-being of future generations had to be "tamed". Its anarchistic body and soul, susceptible to uncontrolled reactions had to be taken into possession and adapted to the requirements of a responsible civic role. In this manner, requirement of self-control related to theories of degeneration was also a tendency to control the socially activated "masses".

The project of constructing self was thus also one of developing civic potential. Strong and healthy individuals also meant a strong and vigorous nation. This was particularly important for a small people such as the Finns, whose civic identity was only being shaped at the time. In various industrialized countries in different parts of Europe dropping birth-rates had been noted. It was also observed that the birth-rate decreased more in the upper and middle classes of society than in the lower class which was regarded as unworthy in terms of its genotype. With regard to conditions within the country, this was feared to lead to a situation where people of normal heredity were to be swamped by the masses with their inferior genotype. At the same time, the nation weakened in terms of quality and in numbers would be downtrodden by larger peoples. (Mattila 1999, 33; Kaikkonen 1985, 29.)

Concern for the future of the nation drew attention to the general state of health of its citizens and their moral condition. Epidemics or loss of population through infant mortality were no longer to be seen as the harsh blows of fate, but as a scourge eroding the assets of the nation which had to be addressed. In the late 19th century and in the first decades of the 20th century, health-care magazines were recurrently concerned especially about the health of young people in their estimates of the spread of degeneration among schoolchildren and soldiers. (Uimonen 1999, 10.)

A special feature in Finnish literature on degeneration was introduced by Finland's relationship with Russia and Russian policies vis-à-vis Finland. The heightening of Russification measures especially in the years 1899–1905 and 1908–1917 increased the experiences of individuals of their limited influence on matters of society and politics.[8] Caring for one's own physical and mental health and bequeathing an unpolluted genotype to posterity ensured the continuity of national existence against the threats of Russification (see Relander 1983, 20). Conversely, all action that diminished the strength of the nation, either the damaging of one's own "protoplasm" through dissipation or emigration to America were morally reprehensible.

In Finland, the themes of degeneration were linked in a particularly strong way to the issue of nationality, and the related racial debate and the fragmentation of domestic politics. Who in Finland were ultimately entitled to regard themselves to be the subject of the national struggle? Was it the slack, over-refined and infertile old upper class? Or could the leadership of the young nation be taken by the middle classes, who had consolidated their position to replace the former upper class but were spoiled by a parvenu spirit, unused to the cultivated life of the upper class and still markedly steered by their "instinctual life"? Or would the unspoilt national foundation be found in the "people" serving as the focus of the projects of the intelligentsia, who were allowed to bear the halo of authentic, sound humanity while also representing animal brutishness?

All in all, degeneracy had a varied role in Finnish literature of the turn of the century. It could be a "fearsome spectre" whose necessity of repetition paralysed man to repeat the crimes of earlier generations. Man became an animal acting out its instincts and drives. But at the same time he was approaching the state of a machine in keeping with the contemporary period and its process of modernization, like a train inexorably rolling ahead on previously built tracks or under the compulsion of repetition mechanically repeating the movements inscribed in his genotype. On the other hand, degeneracy also fostered an ethic principle to which recourse was made in the construction of a strong, responsible individual in control of his animal genetic heritage. Healthy people would pass on to posterity a healthy future and a strong nation.

Translated by Jüri Kokkonen

NOTES

1   In his study of Finnish Realism of the 1880s, Mikko Saarenheimo (1924, 34) even points out that Darwinism and the concepts of heredity hardly found any foothold in 19th-century Finnish literature. The presence of Drawinism and views on degeneracy and their significance have been briefly discussed by e.g. Sarajas (1962, 103–108), Laitinen (1973), Tarkka (1977, 59–60, 80–85, 151–158) and Aalto (2000, 29–33).

2   Linnankoski's novel received a great deal of attention upon being published. It has been translation into 16 languages (including English, French, Russian and Italian) and achieved popularity in stage and screen adaptations..
3   The works of Aino Kallas (1878–1956), who was born in Finland and lived in Estonia as a result of her marriage, are often set in Estonia, where social contradictions, in the form of serfdom and other conditions, were much more severe than in Finland.
4   On the meanings attached to the concept of the "people", see Fewster (ed.) 2000. On definitions of the people, see e.g. Sarajas 1962, 93–181; Zilliacus 1985, 65–66; Liikanen 1995; Molarius 1997, 305–312.
5   Contemporary positivistic thinking was prone to compare the history of the human race to geological observations of stratigraphy. According to Hippolyte Taine, a deep "primal granite" resides in man under varying layers of thought and emotion of different length. It is the above of instincts and drives, which is not disturbed by historical periods or changes in fashion, and is passed on in the "heritage of the blood" from one generation to another (Taine 1865–1869/1915, 457–466.) The lower social orders had a close connection with this layer of drive and instincts. On the other hand, the upper classes had over thr generation learnt the command of their instinctual life through self-control.
6   The Finnish press quoted, with moral overtones, information on the Boer War of the turn of the century, in which the Boers demonstrated superiority over the English. The Boer's military skills were attributed to his rural way of life and moral rectitude: "Lonely life on an outlying farm will not give him an opportunity to contract immoral disease." (Anon. 1900b, 51) The nerve-wracking hurry, economic uncertainty and misery of the workers' slums of England in the process of urbanization and capitalist growth were all foreign to the Boers. The sound, healthy Boer was contrasted to the disfigured bodies of the crowds in the streets of Glasgow and the pale dwarf-like figures of the Lancashire mills. (Anon. 1900b, 49–53.)
7   The Finnish press quoted, with moral overtones, information on the Boer War of the turn of the century, in which the Boers demonstrated superiority over the English. The Boer's military skills were attributed to his rural way of life and moral rectitude: "Lonely life on an outlying farm will not give him an opportunity to contract immoral disease." (Anon. 1900b, 51) The nerve-wracking hurry, economic uncertainty and misery of the workers' slums of England in the process of urbanization and capitalist growth were all foreign to the Boers. The sound, healthy Boer was contrasted to the disfigured bodies of the crowds in the streets of Glasgow and the pale dwarf-like figures of the Lancashire mills. (Anon. 1900b, 49–53.)
8   In the years 1899–1905 and 1908–1917 relations between the Imperial Russian government and the authoritieso f the Grand Duchy of Finland became strained. The Russian government wanted to curtail Finnish self-government and to link Finland more closely to the Empire, which provoked concerned reactions both in Finland and elsewhere.

SOURCES

AALTO, MINNA 2000 *Vapauden ja velvollisuuden ristiriita. Kehitysromaanin mahdollisuudet 1890-luvun lopun ja 1900-luvun alun naiskirjallisuudessa.* Suomalaisen Kirjallisuuden Seura, Helsinki.

ALAPURO, RISTO 1988 *State and Revolution in Finland.* University of California Press, Berkeley – Los Angeles – London.

ALAPURO, RISTO 1997 *Suomen älymystö Venäjän varjossa.* Tammi, Helsinki.

ANON. 1893 Siveellisyys ja siveellisyystaistelut. *Terveydenhoitolehti* 7/1893, 99–103.

ANON. 1900a Miten toinen puoli ihmissukua kuolee. *Terveydenhoitolehti* 7–8/1900, 114–117.

ANON. 1900b Mistä buurien suuri ruumiillinen voima riippuu. *Terveydenhoitolehti* 4/1900, 49–53

ARO, TUIJA Suomalaisten rotu saksalaisissa ja pohjoismaisissa tietosanakirjoissa. In: Kemiläinen, Aira (ed.) 1985 *Mongoleja vai germaaneja? – rotuteorioiden suomalaiset.* Historiallisia tutkimuksia 86. Suomen Historiallinen Seura, Helsinki, 195–208.

BECK, ULRICH 1993 *Die Erfindung des Politischen. Zu einer Theorie reflexiver Modernisierung.* Suhrkamp, Frankfurt.

ESTLANDER, ERNST 1894 Lombrosos lära om brottet samt den positivistiska skolan inom straffrätten. *Finskt Tidskrift* 1894, 272–283, 373–393.

FEWSTER, DEREK (ed.) 2000 *Folket. Studier i olika vetenskapers syn på begreppet folk.* Skrifter utgivna av Svenska litteratursällskapet i Finland nr. 626. Helsingfors.

GROTENFELT, ARVI 1893 C. Lombroson rikos-sielutiede ja kysymykset vastuunalaisuudesta sekä tahdon vapaudesta. *Valvoja* 1893, 397–421.

GROTENFELT, ERIK 1916 *Bengt Walters' lycka.* Holger Schildts förlag, Borgå.

HALMESVIRTA, ANSSI 1995 Kansallisen vastustuskyvyn puolesta. Konrad ReijoWaara ja degeneraation idea 1880–1918. In: LAHTINEN, MERJA (ed.) 1995 *Historiallinen Arkisto 105.* Suomen Historiallinen Seura, Helsinki, 13–69

H. A-n. 1887 Katsahdus viime vuoden ranskalaiseen romaani-kirjallisuuteen. *Valvoja* 1887, 145–154, 206–217.

H.S. [= SÖDERHJELM, HENNING] 1910 "De Unga". *Argus* 17/1910.

IBSEN, HENRIK 1886 *Kummittelijoita. Kolminäytöksinen perhenäytelmä.* Suom. Elias Erkko. Hjalmar Hagelberg, Tampere.

KAIKKONEN, OLLI 1985 Eriarvoisuusajattelu, rotukäsitykset ja sosiaalidarwinismi. In: Kemiläinen, Aira (ed.) 1985 *Mongoleja vai germaaneja? – rotuteorioiden suomalaiset.* Historiallinen Arkisto 86. Suomen Historiallinen Seura, Helsinki, 19–35.

KALLAS, AINO 1904 *Meren takaa.* Otava, Helsinki.

KALLAS, AINO 1907 *Ants Raudjalg. Virolainen kertomus.* Otava, Helsinki.

KEMILÄINEN, AIRA 1985 Johdanto. In: Kemiläinen, Aira (ed.) 1985 *Mongoleja vai germaaneja? – rotuteorioiden suomalaiset.* Historiallinen Arkisto 86. Suomen Historiallinen Seura, Helsinki, 11–17.

KILPELÄINEN, JOUKO I. 1985 Rotuteoriat läntisistä suomalais-ugrilaisista kansoista Keski-Euroopan antropologiassa 1800-luvulla ja suomalaisten reaktiot niihin. In: Kemiläinen, Aira (ed.) 1985 *Mongoleja vai germaaneja? – rotuteorioiden suomalaiset.* Historiallinen Arkisto 86. Suomen Historiallinen Seura, Helsinki, 163–193.

KOSKENNIEMI, V.A. 1947 *Vuosisadanalun ylioppilas.* Werner Söderström Osakeyhtiö, Porvoo.

KUNNAS, MARIA-LIISA 1972 *Mielikuvien taistelu: Psykologinen aatetausta Eino Leinon tuotannossa.* Suomalaisen Kirjallisuuden Seuran toimituksia 304. Suomalaisen Kirjallisuuden Seura, Helsinki.

LAITINEN, KAI 1973 *Aino Kallas 1879–1921. Tutkimus hänen tuotantonsa päälinjoista ja taustasta.* Otava, Helsinki.

LEHTONEN, JOEL 1981 *Valitut teokset I. Putkinotkon herra. Kirjeet Sylvia Avellanille 1907–1920.* Ed. Pekka Tarkka. Otava, Helsinki.

LEHTONEN, TURO-KIMMO 1995 Bakteerit ja henkisten ruttotautien siemenet. Puhdas elämä suomalaisessa terveysvalistuksessa 1890-luvulla. In: Joutsivuo, Timo & Mikkeli, Heikki (ed.) 1995 *Terveyden lähteillä. Länsimaisten terveyskäsitysten kulttuurihistoriaa.* Historiallinen Arkisto 106. Suomen Historiallinen Seura, Helsinki, 205–252.

LIIKANEN, ILKKA 1995 *Fennomania ja kansa. Joukkojärjestäytymisen läpimurto ja Suomalaisen puolueen synty.* Historiallisia tutkimuksia 191. Suomen Historiallinen Seura, Helsinki.

MATTILA, MARKKU 1999 *Kansamme parhaaksi: Rotuhygienia Suomessa vuoden 1935 sterilointilakiin asti.* Bibliotheca Historica 44. Suomen Historiallinen Seura, Helsinki.

MOLARIUS, PÄIVI 1996 Nuoren Apollon syöksykierre. Sivistyneistö ja kansallisen ideologian murroksia. In: Lyytikäinen, Pirjo (ed.) 1996 *Mustat merkit muuttuvat merkityksiksi. Kirjallisuudentutkijain Seuran vuosikirja 49.* Osa 1. Suomalaisen Kirjallisuuden Seura, Helsinki, 9–29.

MOLARIUS, PÄIVI 1997 "Aatteen airut ja Minä I". Fennomania ja sivistyneistö vuosisadanvaihteen suomenkielisessä kirjallisuudessa. In: KARKAMA, PERTTI –

KOIVISTO, HANNE (ed.) 1997 *Älymystön jäljillä. Kirjoituksia suomalaisesta sivistyneistöstä ja älymystöstä.* Suomalaisen Kirjallisuuden Seura, Helsinki, 297–317.

MOLARIUS, PÄIVI 1998 "Veren äänen" velvoitteet – yksilö rodun, perimän ja ympäristön puristuksessa. In: Härmänmaa, Marja & Mattila, Markku (ed.) 1998 *Uusi uljas ihminen eli modernin pimeä puoli.* Atena Kustannus Oy, Jyväskylä, 94–116.

MOLARIUS, PÄIVI 1999 Fennomaanisen merkitysjärjestelmän muotoutuminen 1800-luvun Suomessa. In: Koistinen,Tero – Kruuspere, Piret – Sevänen, Erkki – Turunen, Risto (ed.) 1999 *Kaksi tietä nykyisyyteen. Tutkimuksia kirjallisuuden, kansallisuuden ja kansallisten liikkeiden suhteista Suomessa ja Virossa.* Suomalaisen Kirjallisuuden Seuran toimituksia 755, Suomalaisen Kirjallisuuden Seura, Helsinki, 67–83.

OKER-BLOM, MAX 1903 *Heikkohermoisuus ja kasvatus neljässä luennossa.* Tieteen työmailta 3. Otava, Helsinki.

O'HEAR, ANTHONY 1998 The Myth of Nature. In: BARNETT, ANTHONY – SCRUTON, ROGER (ed.) 1998 *Town and Country.* Jonathan Cape, London, 69–80

ONERVA, L. 1911 *Nousukkaita: Luonnekuvia.* Yrjö Weilin & Kumpp. Osakeyhtiö, Helsinki.

OSTWALD, WILHELM 1911–1916/1923 *Monistisia saarnoja: I & II osa.* Suom. Edvard Walpas. Työväen Sanomalehti Osakeyhtiö, Helsinki.

PELTONEN, VIHTORI 1893 Miksi kehnonee ihmissuku? *Suomen Terveydenhoito-lehti.* 6/1893, 120–125.

PUNTILA, L.A. 1944 *Ruotsalaisuus Suomessa: aatesuunnan synty.* Otava, Helsinki.

RELANDER, KONRAD 1893 "Alku työn kaunistaa, lopussa kiitos seisoo." *Suomen Terveydenhoitolehti 5/1893,* 17–21.

SAARENHEIMO, MIKKO 1924 *1880-luvun suomalainen realismi. Kirjallinen tutkimus.* Werner Söderström Osakeyhtiö, Porvoo.

SARAJAS, ANNAMARI 1962 *Viimeiset romantikot. Kirjallisuuden aatteiden vaihtelua 1880-luvun jälkeen.* Werner Söderström Osakeyhtiö, Porvoo – Helsinki.

SHORT, JOHN RENNIE 1991. *Imagined Contry. Society, Culture and Environment.* Routledge, London.

SULKUNEN, IRMA 1989 *Naisen kutsumus. Miina Sillanpää ja sukupuolten maailmojen erkaantuminen.* Hanki ja jää, Juva.

SULKUNEN, IRMA 1995 *Mandi Granfelt ja kutsumusten ristiriita.* Hanki ja jää, Juva.

TAINE, HIPPOLYTE 1865–1869/1915 *Taiteen filosofia.* Suom. L. Onerva. Otava, Helsinki.

TALVIO MAILA 1910/1953 *Tähtien alla.* In: Talvio, Maila 1953 *Kootut teokset III.* Werner Söderström Osakeyhtiö, Porvoo – Helsinki.

TALVIO, MAILA 1917/1954 *Silmä yössä.* In: Talvio, Maila 1954 *Kootut teokset VII.* Werner Söderström Osakeyhtiö, Porvoo – Helsinki, 123–315.

TALVIO, MAILA 1918/1954 Näkymätön kirjanpitäjä. In: Talvio, Maila 1954 *Kootut teokset VII.* WSOY, Porvoo – Helsinki, 317–457.

TANI, SIRPA 1995 *Kaupunki Taikapeilissä. Helsinki-elokuvien mielenmaisemat – maantieteellisiä tulkintoja.* Helsingin kaupungin tietokeskuksen tutkimuksia 14/1995, Helsinki.

TARKKA, PEKKA 1977 *Putkinotkon tausta. Joel Lehtosen henkilöt 1901–1923.* Otava, helsinki.

TARVAS, TOIVO 1916 *Eri tasoilta: Nykyaikainen romaani.* Otava, Helsinki.

TUAN, YI-FU 1979 *Landscapes of Fear.* The University of Minnesota Press, Minneapolis

UIMONEN, MINNA 1999 *Hermostumisen aikakausi. Neuroosit 1800- ja 1900-lukujen vaihteen suomalaisessa lääketieteessä.* Bibliotheca Historica 50. Suomen Historiallinen Seura, Helsinki.

WILKUNA, KYÖSTI 1915/1983 *Vaikea tie.* Arvi A. Karisto, Hämeenlinna.

WILLIAMS, RAYMOND 1973 *The Country and the City.* The Hogarth Press, London.

VÄÄNÄNEN, KALLE 1916 *Periytyminen ja ihmissuvun jalostaminen.* Otava, Helsinki.

ZILLIACUS, CLAS 1985 Anteckningar om pressens dopskick. In: ZILLIACUS, CLAS – KNIF, HENRIK 1985 *Opinionens tryck. En studie över pressens bildningsskede i Finland.* Svenska litteratursällskapet i Finland, Helsingfors, 43–68.

VESA HAAPALA

I am Fire and Water
Self and modernity in Edith Södergran's "Vierge moderne" (1916)

Introduction

"Jag gör icke dikter utan jag skapar mig själv, mina dikter äro mig väg till mig själv" ("I do not make poems but create myself; my poems are for me the way to myself"),[1] wrote Edith Södergran (1892–1923), one of the first and best-known Nordic modernists in describing the bases of her poetry. It is difficult to name a more powerful poet of the lyrical I in the Finnish literary tradition. In her debut collection *Dikter* (1916), the problems of writing and self are connected to the relations between sexuality and creativity. The poems criticise gender-based positions of power and culturally given roles. Important considerations are a search for one's own ethos and a sense of time associated with the problematics described above. *Dikter* thus raises a whole number of questions that find further emphasis in the collections *Septemberlyran* (1918), *Rosenaltaret* (1919) and *Framtidens skugga* (1920): What kind of an act is poetry? What relationship does it have with the writing and written self? How is it associated with a perception of temporality and identity? These questions are also touched upon in the aphorisms of *Brokiga iakttagelser* (1919) and in many poems in the posthumous collection *Landet som icke är* (1925), and elsewhere throughout the poet's oeuvre. The leitmotif of Södergran's poetry can largely be summarised as the idea of inscribing selfhood – thus giving shape to the I.

In this article I shall focus on the problem of self and modernity in Södergran's debut collection, taking the poem "Vierge moderne" as my starting point. This poem has been extensively quoted in histories of literature, and as such "it is the poem that has been the most influential in forming the general image of Edith Södergran".[2] In view of her oeuvre it is a threshold text assembling many of the ideas which appeared in her early *Vaxdukshäftet* poems (1907–1909) and prepared the way for the themes of her mature poems. "Vierge moderne" is one of the latest poems Södergran wrote for her debut collection. It manifests *Dikter*'s new style, a transition from the metre of her early poetic sketches to free verse and image poetry. Having previously written mostly in German, Södergran now establishes Swedish as her language of expression.

"Vierge moderne" also offers a way into Södergran's later collections. In terms of style it falls between the symbolist and the expressionist, the images and themes of the poem are varied on several occasions after the debut collection. "Vierge moderne" appears to prefigure the tone emphasised in the texts that followed it:

Vierge moderne

Jag är ingen kvinna. Jag är ett neutrum.
Jag är ett barn, en page och ett djärvt beslut,
jag är en skrattande strimma av en scharlakanssol...
Jag är ett nät för alla glupska fiskar,
jag är en skål för alla kvinnors ära,
jag är ett steg mot slumpen och fördärvet,
jag är ett språng i friheten och självet...
Jag är blodets viskning i mannens öra,
jag är en själens frossa, köttets längtan och förvägran,
jag är en ingångsskylt till nya paradis.
Jag är en flamma, sökande och käck,
jag är ett vatten, djupt men dristigt upp till knäna,
jag är eld och vatten i ärligt sammanhang på fria villkor...

I am no woman. I am a neuter.
I am a child, a page and a bold resolve,
I am a laughing stripe of a scarlet sun...
I am a net for all greedy fish,
I am a skoal to the glory of all women,
I am a step towards hazard and ruin,
I am a leap into freedom and self...
I am a whisper of blood in the ear of the man,
I am the soul's ague, the longing and refusal of the flesh,
I am an entrance sign to new paradises.
I am a flame, searching and brazen,
I am water, deep but daring up to the knee,
I am fire and water in free and loyal union...[3]

The strong figurativeness of the poem has permitted scholars to attempt various contextualisations of conceptual approaches. For my part I am interested in the encounter between two interpretative contexts and, at the same time, two problematics of research which studies on Södergran have charted: on the one hand a reading of the poem in relation to the philosophy of Friedrich Nietzsche, and on the other, writings on the New Woman of the turn of the 19th and 20th centuries. Early studies on Södergran already noted the textual play of this poem with Nietzsche; Gunnar Tideström saw the influence of *Also sprach Zarathustra* in the imagery of the poem[4], while Olof Enckell made reference to "Das Tanzlied" in *Zarathustra*.[5] According to Ebba Witt-Brattström, a later reader, the beginning of the poem and the claim "I am a child" could refer to Nietzsche's metaphor of the superman, one of the central themes in *Zarathustra*. Without going into further detail, Witt-Brattström notes that the poem also entails other typical Nietzschean words.[6] The vocabulary and ideas of Nietzsche's writings are evident in many of Södergran's early texts[7], and *Zarathustra* in particular provided an intellectually inspiring work for her.

Later feminist researches, including Witt-Brattström's reading, have considered the poem to be primarily a contribution to the debate on the New Woman. It supports the image of a bold female avant-gardist and displays a programmatic feminist position.[8] Birgitta Holm however seeks a more fundamental analysis. Adapting the speech act theory of J. L. Austin's *How to Do Things with Words*, she notes that a poem is "a performative act that challenges 'accepted conventions' and forges new ones. /– –/ *Vierge moderne* is a promise, a thrust into the future. /– –/ it is /– – / participating in a community, a 'movement' whose values it both shares and 'helps to form'."[9] By the term "movement" Holm is referring to the objectives of contemporary women writers in redefining the identity and values of women.

In my own reading, I shall continue outlining the tradition of interpretation by seeking the core means in terms of Södergran's tone by which the poem makes use of Nietzschean idioms and trains of thought. Despite good starts and observations of detail, earlier research has not carried out a more detailed charting of them. I shall focus on the manner in which the dynamics of the Nietzschean will to power and transgression provide strategies for the "modern virgin" of the poem. I shall also include references to Södergran's other works, for as noted above "Vierge moderne" prefigures in various ways the Nietzschean tones of Södergran's later collections. I intend to enter into dialogue with the feminist interpretations of Holm and Witt-Brattström throughout my reading. Above all they are of importance in establishing the basis of my analysis by discussing the manner of expression and title of the poem. Evaluating the mode of expression has a direct connection with the kinds of interpretations on to which the poem opens. It also relates to the question as to what kind of act it can be conceived. Holm's feminist view of the poem as a performative speech act helps in shaping my point of departure. I do not employ the concept of performativeness used by Holm, which leads to a problematic that is too complex to handle, but instead I shall enhance my own description with reflections from Holm's perspective. I shall then carry on the definitions of figurativeness, metaphor and paradox, which are noted by Ebba Witt-Brattström, to the speaker of the poem with the idea of metaphorical structure. Having made observations of the speaker in "Vierge moderne" and the manner in which the poem can be regarded as utilising Nietzsche's texts, I shall end my essay with a few additional notes on the role of the poem in Södergran's oeuvre.

On the expression of "Vierge moderne"

When reading "Vierge moderne" one must pay equal attention to the expression of the poem, its manner of being, as one does to certain themes that can be abstracted from verses and contextualised in contemporary cultural debate. The first point which cannot be bypassed is the figurative nature of the verses. The expressions of the poem are ambiguous, playful and full of lacunae. The speaker is not coherent. There is no an addressee – a you – only a group of its own figurative attributions, which, however, bear the marks of different discourses. The array of images with which the speaker characterises itself moves in unpredictable ways. The verses define the speaker emerging in speech while jeopardising the emergence of a coherent self. Self is a possible and open gesture.

An interpretation of "Vierge moderne" as a performative speech act, as done by Holm, is by no means self-evident if we think of performativeness in the linguistic or philosophical sense. Holm modifies Austin's conception of performativeness, to which she adapts the poem's expression, its manner of being. Holm thus combines the former with the idea of the poem as a deconstruction of the concepts of "woman" and "femininity": "The most evident description, in present-day terminology, is that it is a deconstruction. A deconstruction of the concept of 'woman', the concept of 'femininity'."[10] Holm links the success of speech acts in "Vierge moderne" to the following prerequisite: "*Vierge moderne* is a performative speech act. If we ever want to see it as felicitous, the prerequisite is that we bring it back in its proper context: the New Woman in the decades around the turn of the century."[11] In an earlier passage, Holm formulates her idea of "proper context": "The intertext of *Vierge moderne* is /– –/ the New Woman."[12]

To describe the poem as a performative speech act is problematic. The precise context of the poem, the speech situation, is not easily defined, although the title assigns the utterances to the "modern virgin" and directs thoughts to time, existence and gender. Holm's way of combining the terms of Austin's speech act theory and feminist deconstruction and to reflect them as properties of "Vierge moderne" is not completely thought through. Austin excludes from among performative speech acts speech that cannot be classified as serious, and poetry belongs to such speech.[13] Of course, nothing can prevent Holm from reading against the grain. Holm employs Austin's speech act theory in presenting the power of material classified as excluded: what Austin's theory finds to be parasitical becomes essential in Holm's terms. What Austin regards as straying from the ordinary and as apparent becomes something to be taken seriously in Holm's reading. "Vierge moderne" is a political act altering the way in which woman is socially defined: "'Vierge moderne' initiates something new. It embodies a promise, enunciates a new being."[14] It is easy to agree with this definition and many of the details in Holm's analysis. My critical remarks concern the fact that Holm does not reflect sufficiently on her theoretical model. On the other hand, her use of Austin's insights dominates the poem in a way which is not completely natural with regard to its expression.[15]

Holm notes, quite correctly, that in Austin's terms there is a group of expressions or speech acts whose function is not to be constatives, descriptive claims concerning facts. Their function is performative; they carry things out. Holm writes: "The poem is performative, but is has been read as constative. A personal, re-active, defensive utterance or speech act. Reading the poem like that is depriving it of its authority."[16] Ultimately, Austin himself does not lay down any definite difference between the constative and the performative. The distinction is a tentative working definition. A division into constatives and performatives requires that the performatives can be identified from amongst other types of utterances. It should therefore be possible to define a number of performative verbs, above all in the first person present singular and realising the action indicated by them ("I promise", "I command", "I declare" etc.), while in other persons and tenses they will operate differently or describe acts rather than implement them ("I promised to come", "You told him to leave", "He will declare war if they continue" etc.)[17] As the analysis progresses, Austin notices that performatives cannot be defined by listing verbs that function in the manner described here, because, for example, the command "Stop it right now!" can just as well constitute the act of telling someone to stop doing something as the sentence "I order you to stop". The apparently constative claim "I'll pay you tomorrow", which appears to be either true or false depending on what will happen tomorrow, can under the proper circumstances be a promise to pay rather than a description or prediction along the lines of "He will pay you tomorrow".[18]

The moment the presence of such "implicit performatives" is permitted, it has to be admitted that almost any expression can be performative. Austin concludes that claiming, describing and reporting are no less speech acts than the speech acts that are described as performative. Constatives too can bring about acts; acts which can be termed as claiming, describing and reporting. They are performatives *of a certain kind*.[19] As it is difficult to establish sufficient criteria to maintain the difference between constatives and performatives, Austin changes direction and decides to ignore "the initial distinction between performatives and constatives and the programme of finding a list of explicit performative words, notably verbs". Instead, he reflects on "the senses in which to say something is to do something."[20] He begins to speak of the locutionary, illocutionary and perlocutionary speech act.[21]

Holm's assumption of the performativity of "Vierge moderne" as opposed to the constative speech acts poem has previously been read as, is diffuse with regard to the starting points of the speech act theory. Considering the relationship between the syntactical form of "Vierge moderne" and Austin's tentative working definition, Holm's interpretation takes liberties which even at this point are difficult to defend. The sentences of the poem are not *explicitly* performative according to the criteria presented by Austin. Rather the poem is a group of assertions identifying the speaker, albeit for the most part markedly figurative assertions. Holm's idea of performativity is more suited to the *effect* of "Vierge moderne": the poem carries out the acts and states of affairs to which it refers. At the same time it must be noticed that in such a loose sense all language in literature is performative. Firstly, the utterances of literature create the characters, and persons of the text and their actions.

The literary text makes a whole world present, and the ideas and concepts with which it operates in this world of its creation, and which it develops and employs.[22] Holm's idea of doing things with words is no doubt central to "Vierge moderne". The poem can be called performative in the general sense of the term, for it truly achieves something with its words. However, in view of its starting points, the terminology of Austin's speech act theory and the tone of the poem, Holm's model is imprecise. Her evaluating division of a reading of the poem either as a constative or a performative speech act, her symmetrical reversal of Austin's working definition, is just as alien to a deconstructive reading as to the mode of expression of "Vierge moderne". Texts deconstructing a firm logic of thought not only overturn binary oppositions and bring forth the marginalised parts of pairs which they would then celebrate as a creative principle. Deconstruction rather tends to see a continuous unresolved state existing between real assertions and ostensible ones, rhetorical and grammatical or constative and performative language. Perhaps Holm's feminist perspective ultimately fails to accept such a description of a deconstructive procedure. A deconstructive situation, however, is the subject of reflection particularly in language criticising metaphysical combinations, and it is to such a position that Holm ascribes "Vierge moderne". All critique of metaphysics will necessarily remain in a relationship with a referential, constative model and assertion, even though it questions its logic. The words of Paul de Man concerning the philosophy of Nietzsche are also appropriate here: "the critique of metaphysics is structured as an aporia between performative and constative language."[23]

Witt-Brattström, who, like Holm, interprets the poem in the context of the New Woman, employs terminology less prone to risk. She speaks of the figurativeness of the poem, noting that the form of expression in Södergran's poetry is informed by Nietzsche: the use of opposites and paradoxes comes closest to the truth.[24] I will proceed from the same terms. Witt-Brattström writes of the ideological code provided by the contemporary perspective, the debate on the New Woman, as a solution to interpreting the poem. Without that code, the poem remains a riddle.[25] She says that the idea of an enigma is interesting in view of the poem's manner of expression and its interpretation. In *Poetics*, Aristotle writes that if a text is constructed completely of metaphors the result will be a riddle.[26] By this he means that a distinct literal level does not emerge from the text as a counterweight to the metaphorically used words that would help the reader replace the words used in an exceptional manner with the real words.[27] Witt-Brattström writes of the poem as a riddle and in the above sense it is just that. From the second verse onwards "Vierge moderne" becomes a series of metaphorical assertions, in which other tropes are also stratified.

It is nonetheless obvious that "Vierge moderne" contains numerous marks of contemporary discourses attendant to it and giving it resonance; the poem is not an enigma in the sense that it could be solved without any remainder or in final terms. Unlike classical metaphors or performatives, the expressions of the poem, whether interpreted as metaphors or performative speech acts, cannot be simply replaced with ordinary words or introduced without any problems into some actual context, which would completely describe the identity of the poem. The metaphors of "Vierge moderne" accumulate on each other so fragmentarily and in such an indefinite manner that they cannot simply be harmonised with an overriding code. What remains is an attempt to contextualise the statements concerning the speaker and to seek relevant perspectives. The metaphors of the poem can be interpreted differently and in connection with many contexts, for example the contemporary feminist discussions, as arguably done by Witt-Brattström and Holm, or in the Nietzschean perspective as I do, but no single contextualisation alone can describe the characteristic style of the poem as a whole.

It must be underlined that the speech act of the poem is entirely paradoxical; it defines identity while problematising it; it is at once controlled and uncontrolled, coherent and fragmentary, concrete and abstract, modern and archaic. Although "Vierge moderne" can be described as "performative" in some general sense, I would prefer to call it simply a group of expanding metaphorical assertions developing the opportunities of the speaker. As such, the poem achieves many of the effects of the performative speech act described by Holm. Like a performative speech act, the poem is an act of language, and like a performative speech act, the metaphors of the poem utilise the social codes expressed in language. In their starting points alone, the metaphors of person imply some kind of communication and a situation of speech. As metaphors, the utterances of the poem are not, however, a figurative expression of some other actual meaning which could be abstracted as separate from style. Metaphorical utterances are assertions per se. They are the style with which the "modern virgin" exists and utters herself. The reference of the metaphors must be understood as a network of relations. These metaphors connect with the (possible) discourses and styles that the assertions of the poem can be seen as shaping and re-describing. As an expanded metaphor, a hypertrope, "Vierge moderne" creates its own stylistic reality amidst the discourses which enframe it.[28] The poem and at the same time its self are constituted by a dynamic group of metaphors.

The metaphors of "Vierge moderne" reveal the overlapping nature of the performative and constative functions of language. The roles of the speaker are created as ironic variations and repetitions of constative language, i.e. religious and philosophical definitions and postulates. The poem lies between the constative and the performative; the identity it expresses would not be possible without the (cultural) connections of language, and nonetheless this identity does not derive from tradition. On the other hand, the poem is an assertion of a style absolutely its own, and crystallised in it are the main images of the self to be sought in Södergran's oeuvre. From my perspective, "Vierge moderne" is a rhetorical construction, a lyric correlate of the new kind of individual Södergran later declares herself to be: "Med stöd av Nietzsches auktoritet upprepar jag att jag är en individ av en ny art. Med det oerhörda i min konst avser jag icke innehållet, utan *arten*. Endast ur denna synpunkt kan man förstå min konst." ("Supported by Nietzsche's authority I repeat that I am an individual of a new kind. It is not the content of my art that is unprecedented, but its *character*. My art can only be understood from that viewpoint.")[29]

The Title. Reflections on Feminism and Modernism

The title of the poem is in French. Holm and Witt-Brattström have demonstrated the possible connections of Södergran's poetry with conceptions at the turn of the century regarding sexuality, mainly with reference to the texts of Ellen Key, Lou Salomé and Elisabeth Dauthendey.[30] The Swedish author Ellen Key wrote of the new types of women in the 20th century, one of which she termed, in French, *vierges fortes*. According to Witt-Brattström, "Vierge moderne" is a representative of this type of woman.[31] On the other hand, she points out that the speaker of "Vierge moderne", defining herself with the words "Jag är ett neutrum" ("I am a neuter") combines with the German term for the New Woman, *das neue Weib*, which is already neuter in grammatical terms.[32] This point, however, cannot be used in any relevant way as grounds for the New Woman. In just the same manner, any woman, *das Weib*, even an old woman, *das alte Weib*, is grammatically neuter.

Considering the models of thought at the turn of the century regarding people of the future, Södergran's main source of inspiration was Nietzsche's superman. In her writings, Södergran does not make reference to feminist typologies of women, but she does mention the Dionysian and the superman all the more often. She feels a physical yearning to give birth to the superman: "Gråter ibland av längtan efter övermänniskan, det är rent fysiskt den havandes nyck." ("Sometimes I weep with longing for the Superman, like the whim of a pregnant woman.")[33] For my own perspective it is interesting to note that Key, in particular, combines her New Woman and the man of the future with Nietzsche's superman. Key maintained that cooperation among the sexes would solve the future and the fate of mankind. Here, she largely thinks along the lines of Nietzsche. Although Key recognises the limitations of Nietzsche's conception of women and sexuality, she nonetheless underlines the opportunities accorded to women by Nietzsche's philosophy. According to Key, woman can be the first pillar of the bridge leading to the superman; the proud, strong certainty of the liberated modern woman that the riches of her human nature are the preconditions of the realisation of love and motherhood.[34] "Vierge moderne" contains constructs similar to those of the above-quoted *Lifslinjer I* essays, yet Södergran emphasises the connections with the superman in a manner different to Key, as will be argued below.[35] Lou Salomé also has obvious connections with Nietzsche. The notion of the ideal of the strong individual is mainly constructed through Salomé's complex conception of Eros. Compared to Södergran, Salomé's interpretations of Nietzsche are restricted by literal-biographic emphases, as noted by Witt-Brattström.[36]

As much as "Vierge moderne" has in common with the women types of Key and Salomé and the concept of love of the new era, in one, and perhaps the most essential, respect Södergran differs from her predecessors – viz. her mode of expression. Södergran is conscious of the significance of the manner of saying and its different implications. This is a central aspect in an understanding of Nietzsche's philosophy.[37] Like Key and Salomé, she employs the philosophical starting points of Nietzsche's philosophy in imagining strong roles for her self, but at the same time Södergran inscribes her "modern virgin" beyond all attempts at definition. Instead of emancipatory projects, she writes an open poem: figurative roles and a voice for the poetic I. In "Vierge moderne" a distance-retaining and open metaphoricity, paradoxically posed terms and a deep-running irony are the epithets of the speaker, the conditions for inscribing the self. Therefore Södergran breaks with unequivocal assent in her relation to Nietzsche. Looking at the expression of "Vierge moderne", it is natural to say that the poem is a singular attempt at the style of being of a certain virgin, and as such it cannot be derived from any feminist or philosophical ideal. Holm, who reads the poem in a close relationship with the emancipatory texts of the turn oxf the century, must also note that it only "touches upon common concepts of the time; *femme fatale*, *femme fragile* and *dandy type*."[38]

In addition to the feminist context, the French title can also be seen as an indication of the sense of time in contemporary poetry and its style of presenting the starting-points of self. "Vierge moderne" shares the attempt of Charles Baudelaire's "Le peintre de la vie moderne" to find a new beginning in the present moment and the pleasure derived from presenting the present.[39] Baudelaire seeks an immediacy of observation and writing in order to forget history which threatens the experience of the present. In Baudelaire's terms, modernity is "/– –/ le transitoire, le fugitif, le contingent, la moitié de l'art, dont l'autre moitié est l'éternel and l'immuable".[40] A similar attitude is expressed by Arthur Rimbaud. The speaker of *Une Saison en Enfer* claims that he lacks predecessors in the history of France and can only find himself in the present. Therefore, "il faut être absolument moderne".[41] Baudelaire's conception of "modernity" (*la modernité*) and the absolute nature of Rimbaud's both modern approach the idea of modernity conceded by Nietzsche, called "life" (*Leben*) in *Unzeitgemässe Betrachtungen*.[42] Like the above authors, Södergran's poems express the will to inscribe a modern self which has its own origin and cannot be solely explained from the perspective of the past. "Vierge moderne" provides one of the rhetoric roles of the *Dikter* collection, the possibility of life having an important relationship with the contemporary presentation of self and eroticism.

In their quest for an undisturbed point of origin, all the above authors notice the absolutely modern or life, that the new is possible only in the form of a denial or a transformation of tradition. In its origins, the new of the modern is dispute and the transgression of tradition. I trace its manifestations in analysing the Nietzschean features of "Vierge moderne".

I am no woman. I am a neuter

The poem begins with a denial: "Jag är ingen kvinna" ("I am no woman"). The speaker denies that definition as a woman would describe her being. Witt-Brattström explains the negation typical of Södergran's early works, by the fact that the New Woman can only be defined as the opposite of the old.[43] Although this interpretation is relevant in its own perspective, for "kvinna" ("woman") is the term denied in the first line, it is not entirely unproblematic to assume that after the denial the speaker of the poem is still a woman in terms of gender identity, now the New Woman, as interpreted by Witt-Brattström and Holm.[44] No index in the poem defines the speaker, the "modern virgin", as a woman, although the features of courage and independence of the New Woman are attendant to it. Strictly speaking, it is not unproblematic to say that the speaker is a woman in terms of gender identity, new or old, even before the denial. The denial of the "woman" in the first line applies not only to the identity of the speaker at the moment of utterance but also to the *femme nouvelle* interpretation which could be made from the title. If the speaker is to be identified as a woman, this is justified only with reference to the features acquired by the speaker in the figurative discourse constituted by "Vierge moderne". The speaker, the "modern virgin" is a sexually empty sign, a neuter, and this position is explicitly affirmed in the first line: "Jag är ett neutrum." The speaker expresses a fantasy of what it means to be a creative force, without any ontological connections with gender identity.

After declaring herself to be a neuter, the speaker becomes a transient group of metaphors. It hovers between yearning and denial, between fire, air and water; the speaker desires, seduces and takes a distance to things. It is the movement of surface and depth; surrender to self and a depth which extends only to the knees.[45] The poem's sun metaphor "jag är ett skrattande strimma av en scharlakansol..." ("I am a laughing stripe of a scarlet sun...") underlines the state of being between night and day, and the dawning of a new beginning. The initial line, in which the speaker liberates herself from being a woman into a neuter, can be read as a variation of the bluster of Nietzsche's *Ecce Homo*, speaking of a new self and destroying everything regarded as true: "Ich bin kein Mensch, ich bin Dynamit."[46] "Jag är ett neutrum" denotes the lines of the poem in which the speaker disputes and changes position. By declaring herself to be a neuter the speaker can deconstruct and re-read the dichotomies defining identity, the epithets of self and sexuality.

The Death of God

How can "Vierge moderne", this fantasy of creative power and self, be considered in terms of the cultural debate of its day? Why did Södergran write the speaker in this manner? I regard the poem as having a connection with Nietzsche's allegory of the "Death of God", which was a central theme of cultural discussion at the turn of the 19th and 20th centuries that inspired contemporary literature. För Södergran herself Nietzsche was "the king of thought".[47] The modern era is characterised above all by the need to redefine the basis of values and identity in the state in which the "Death of God" has left people. Nietzsche's allegory opens up to become a series of changes related to values, power and the unjustified conception of truth posed by metaphysics, but also the opportunities of the future. Nietzsche seeks to prove how metaphysical assumptions of an idea assuring history and identity will distort the unresolved and non-linear nature of reality, and will debase instincts and life. He feels it is his mission to combat the shadows of God, to formulate new ways of evaluation.

For Nietzsche the "Death of God" was not a single abstract event. Although a rationalist Europe had ceased to believe in God as the guarantor of history, identity or personality, the rejection of transcendent and transcendental principles known as the "Death of God" is not certain. According to Nietzsche, "wir haben alle die Schlechten Instinkte, die christlichen, irgendwie noch im Leibe".[48] Theist structures influence the manner in which language is understood. Insofar as grammar is regarded as proof of the being of absolute substances and a uniform self, it remains metaphysical: "Ich fürchte, wir werden Gott nicht los, weil wir noch an die Grammatik glauben..."[49] Nietzsche maintained that a belief in the self or consciousness as the absolute substance of thought is only a new name for that which religion and metaphysics have called the soul.[50] For Nietzsche, the "Death of God" is an endless task. Its realisation requires not only the destruction of one universal truth and the pluralisation of truth but also the reinforcement of a new nobility in that event: "Vieler Edlen nämlich bedarf es und vielerlei Edlen, *dass es Adel gebe*! Oder, wie ich einst im Gleichniss sprach:'Das eben is Göttlichkeit, dass es Götter, aber keinen Gott giebt!"[51]

With reference to Nietzsche, Södergran writes in her letters to her friend, the Finland-Swedish author Hagar Olsson, of a desire to separate herself from the transcendental, which disturbs her inspiration. In order to create, Södergran finds it necessary to capture the mood to which Eros, "die Wille zur Macht" in its continuous state of aspiration, invites.[52] Södergran was acquainted with Nietzsche's critique of metaphysics and the idea that after the "Death of God" existence *is* the will to power. First of all for Södergran, the "Death of God" represents the possibility of redefining the human self. In a Nietzschean mood she writes of her interest to "dödandet av tyngdens ande".[53]

The distance from the transcendental which Södergran sought is already present in the structure of the poem. The way in which she wrote the tropes creating identity is essentially Nietzschean. The self speaks with metaphors and combinations of concepts which have not been heard before.[54] It is an almost material array of tropes, an open and expanded series of the possibilities of the proposition. At the same time, the metaphors of the new self break down the core narrative which has shaped the Western history of concepts, branding throughout history the ways in which identity is comprehended. In Judaeo-Christian thought God is the word that endows existence, the root cause and basis for all that is. This is given in "I am", the Biblical attribute for eternal existence, which also describes the presence of God in time, creation and the human soul. "I am that I am" was the answer of the God of the Old Testament to Moses when he asked what to tell the Israelites when they wanted to know the name of God.[55]

In "Vierge moderne" God as a guarantee of identity and the world is broken down along with an integrated self. In the utterances of the "modern virgin" ("jag är" – "I am"), the attribute of God ("I am") and the identity it guarantees are dispersed. The verbs of the "Jag är" metaphors must be read as ironic copulas enforcing the declaration of the self as neuter, a radically decentralized centre. Along with the copula, the verbs are signs of difference, replacement and plurality. Being is not derived from any unchanging self or divine *causa prima*. There is no longer any single soul or self, any more than any mystical or legal equality of souls before God.[56] The self flows like fire and water. This gesture reinforces the author's own style and bears inspiration. The next line of the poem confirms the point that the "modern virgin" is a bold resolve, a child and servant of the new era: "Jag är ett barn, en page och ett djärvt beslut" ("I am a child, a page and a bold resolve"). The self moves towards the future by overturning the starting points of the metaphysical-moral heritage with objections, infidelities and gay distrust. The self is presented as a play of corporeal and discursive forces and the mutual relationship of instincts.[57]

A laughing sun

After the first two lines, the existence of the speaker is combined with the epithets of sound ("laughing"), sight ("scarlet sun") and touch ("a laughing stripe of sun"): "I am a laughing strip of a scarlet sun..." The senses are made a comprehensive part of the fantasy of self, "a laughing sun". The rays of the rising and setting sun play an important role in Södergran's works. In her letters, she dreamed of a new literature, marking the dawn of a day of creation that will break down all barriers.[58] For Södergran, the sun symbolised ethos, will and vitality. Light takes concrete form in the individuals that bear it and is on the side of the forces of life.[59] The sun is specifically associated with the veracity of literature. Södergran thanks the author Elmer Diktonius for sending his collection *Hårda sånger* (Hard songs), noting that the book was "like sunshine to me, I love the quality of truth in it."[60]

Recollections of the imagery of Plato's writings (the sun as the image of good and truth) can be seen in the epithets attached to the sun by Södergran. Now they interpret modern, essentially Nietzschean themes: the idols of the old world, the shadows of the former truths, giving way. The self-reflective solar metaphor of "Vierge moderne" is closely connected with the images of the sun constructing Nietzsche's superman[61] and also used by Nietzsche to describe his work. The *Götzen-Dämmerung* is "ein Sonnenfleck", "ein Dämon, welcher lacht", and the philosopher himself is the "Freher Botschaftler", "ein Schicksal" of civilisations pointing the way to the future.[62]

As in Nietzsche's imagery, laughter and new veracity run parallel in Södergran's sensuous sun synesthesia. This attitude persists throughout her oeuvre.[63] In "Vierge moderne" the dawn is above all associated with virginal power, a "neuter" not clearly belonging to either day or night, to man or woman. Södergran's "neuter", which is the basis of the "modern" self, could be imagined to refer beyond gendered man – man and woman – to the superman and the will to power, the possibility of combining and redefining features marked as necessities.

The honour of all women

In its figurativeness, the following line, "jag är ett nät för all glupska fiskar" ("I am a net for all greedy fish") is a manifold metaphor. It makes several readings possible. Interpreting this line, Gunnar Tideström refers to both the characters "Fischer" and "Netz-Auswerfer" of Nietzsche's *Zarathustra* and Sigmund Freud's dream symbols. The fish is a well-known element of dreams, most often a symbol of male sexuality.[64] One does not have to be a psychoanalyst to see that the poem does not mask its erotic allusions; the speaker later calls herself "a whisper of blood in the ear of the man".

I follow Tideström's first suggestion and associate the capturing eroticism of the line with its Nietzschean sense: Eros as the will to power, Eros as the creative principle. According to Nietzsche, the will to power is the instinct of freedom (*Instinkt der Freiheit*) and a will for the future.[65] These are important features for Södergran. Writing to Hagar Olsson in 1919, she uses an expression similar to the net image in "Vierge moderne". She asks Olsson about the cause of new humanity: "Do you work for the cause in general sense or are you anxious to meet particular individuals? Give me a list. There are several souls I'd like to capture: Hemmer for instance to sing for the cause and Grotenfelt to sing or rasp away."[66] Both the line in "Vierge moderne" and Södergran's reference to "capturing certain souls" echo Zarathustra's idea of poets: "Ach, ich warf wohl mein Netz in ihre Meere und wollte gute Fische fangen; aber immer zog ich eines alten Gottes Kopf herauf."[67] Södergran set out to capture certain individuals in order to "sing" of the future and a higher humanity.

Södergran wants to be like Zarathustra, to have a good catch. Perhaps the "modern virgin" is a net in this specific sense: the self catches and captures all "greedy" ("glupska") fish – that small yet good portion of humanity yearning enough for the future and not for any "head of an old god".[68] Even in the collection *Framtidens skugga* (The Shadow of the Future) in the poem "Nätet" ("The net") Södergran writes: "Jag har nätet i vilket alla fiskar gå. / Saligt häver sig fiskerskans lugna bröst." ("I have the net into which all fish go./ Blissfully the fisherwoman's quiet breast heaves /– –/.") The speaker bears her catch, "the silver load", to "a fairytale pond", where there is a fisherman straight out of Zarathustra: "Upon the shore stands a fisherman with golden fishing rod." The end of the poem speaks of a yearning for "the burning sun of the future".[69]

The two usages of the words "alla" and "för" interestingly link the above verse with "jag är en skål för alla kvinnors ära ("I am a skoal to the glory of all women"). Firstly, "alla" and "för" characterise the speaker's being as a capturing net, and then its being as a skoal or toast to the honour of all women. The ambiguous "net for all greedy fish" changes to the expression "för all kvinnors ära", which is more abstract yet thematically more characteristic of the *Dikter* collection, in which creativity is mainly emphasized as a feminine opportunity and a question related to the honour of women.

In the poem, the negation of woman is paradoxically combined with celebrating the value of all women. Some of the paradoxes which the utterances form are resolved by the fact that the word "kvinnor" now refers to the biological sex and not so much to the gender identity denied in the opening line.[70] The speaker herself is a neuter, neither man nor woman, an example of the "modern virgin". It is specifically in this position that the speaker can be a power affirmative of all women; a toast in their honour. No woman has to commit herself to any preordained gender identity and gender roles laid down in advance. The "Death of God" also provides an opportunity to redefine gender identity: there is no woman – there are women, the possibility of "all women". The paradoxical terms of the poem thus mean that there is an innumerable number of women and creative bodies. A single truth of women and woman as a single truth are rejected.

The next line "jag är att steg mot slumpen och fördärvet" ("I am a step towards hazard and ruin") continues in ambiguous fashion, expressing simultaneously transgressive play, the destruction of self and morality, and a new valuation of the marginal "glory of all women". A step towards hazard and ruin is part of the self, but at the same time the self Södergran describes entails the will to be stronger and to trample underfoot all that is regarded as chance occurrences and ruin. This idea becomes one of the main themes of Södergran's inscription of self. In the title poem of the collection *Framtidens skugga* she still notes: "då jag trampat all slump med min fot, skall jag leende/ vända mig bort ifrån livet." ("When I have crushed all chance with my foot I shall turn/ smilingly away from life.") The active simultaneity of "Vierge moderne" characterises the modern individual's radical attitude, and perhaps also the conflicting nature of the forces that structure self. In *Jenseits von Gut und Böse*, Nietzsche writes of individuals appearing at the turning points of history, strong persons liberated from the old morality. As in the case of the speaker in "Vierge moderne", good instincts and immorality are intertwined in them. In these exploding egoisms, growth and self-destruction are simultaneously present. Nothing that has gone before can provide a measure for them:

das "Individuum" steht da, genöthigt zu einer eigenen Gesetzgebung, zu eigenen Künsten und Listen der Selbst-Erhaltung, Selbst-Erhöhung, Selbst-Erlösung. /– –/ Missverständniss und Missachtung mit einander im Bunde, der Verfall, Verderb und die höchsten Begierden schauerlich verknotet, /– – / voll neuer Reize und Schleier, die der jungen, noch unausgeschöpften, noch unermüdeten Verderbniss zu eigen sind.[71]

As if underscoring the previous line, the speaker declares itself to be a leap into freedom and self: "Jag är ett språng i friheten och självet..." This line is the debut collection's most distinct formulation of Södergran's statement: "Jag gör icke dikter utan jag skapar mig själv, mina dikter äro mig väg till mig själv" ("I do not make poems but create myself; my poems are for me the way to myself"). The speaker is a leap towards a truer self. This metaphor of authentic transition carries on the dialogue with Zarathustra: "Hinter deinen Gedanken und Gefühlen, mein Bruder, steht ein mächtiger Gebieter, ein unbekannter Weiser – der heisst Selbst. In deinem Leibe wohnt er, dein Leib ist er. /– –/ Dein Selbst lacht über dein Ich und seine stolzen Sprünge."[72] The speaker is not only a step towards ruin and chance but also a leap towards the self, the corporeal wisdom of its undefined inscription. In Nietzschean terms, the conscious entity that says "I" is steered by bodily impulses, the self and rhetoric.[73]

Blood, soul and flesh

Having declared itself to be a leap, the speaker says: "Jag är blodets viskning i mannens öra,/ jag är en själens frossa, köttets längtan och förvägran /– –/." ("I am the whisper of blood in the ear of the man,/ I am the soul's ague, the longing and refusal of the flesh /– –/.") What kind of processes are brought forth when the speaker declares herself to be the whisper of blood in the ear of the man, the ague of the soul and the longing and refusal of the flesh?

In the collection *Dikter*, the word "blod" ("blood") is associated with both the problems of gender difference and the biological and artistic future. The word gains varying emphases according to the poetic roles with which it is associated. Above all, blood is associated with the forces of life and creation. The speaker of the poem "Dagen svalnar..." ("The day cools...") identifies her body with nature awakening and surrenders to the man that she is waiting for: "Drick värmen ur min hand,/ min hand har samma blod som våren." ("Drink the warmth out of my hand,/ my hand has the same blood as springtime.") In the poem "Till en ung kvinna" ("To a Young Woman"), written in 1916 but not published until the *Septemberlyran* collection, the blood of woman represents the inviolate state of the body and virginity. The blood of man can become fertile and strong only in a young woman's receptacle of motherly tenderness: "hans blod strömmar i din moderliga ömhets/ bäcken" ("his blood only streams in the basin of your motherly/ tenderness.")

What about the word "soul"? In the poems of *Dikter* this word appears more often than "flesh" ("kött"), even though that which Södergran calls flesh is one of the starting points of her poetry. In the debut collection the problem of flesh is inseparable from the soul. The operations of the soul, the spiritual principle, are often presented at the level of primitive affects. The speaker of the poem "Min själ" ("My Soul") says after an unhappy meeting with man: "Min själ kan icke berätta och veta någon sanning,/ min själ kan endast gråta och skratta och vrida sina/ händer." ("My soul cannot tell stories and know any truth,/ my soul can only weep and laugh and wring its hands."). "Min själ" gives the soul an expression; it gestures and secretes. Also in "Vierge moderne" there is a clear entwining of the spiritual and the corporeal. Self and desire are not either body or soul but both body and soul. "Soul becomes body in *the soul's shivering*, body becomes soul in *the longing and denial of the flesh*", as Holm finely interprets.[74]

In *Dikter*, the soul is a name for features assembling the roles of the self and their related desires and passions. The soul is something received by someone who surrenders to the creative process: it is given in anguish and the pain of creation. In the poem "Smärtan" ("Pain") Södergran writes: "Vad är det ännu smärtan ger åt sina älsklingar?/ Jag vet ej mer. /– –/ Hon ger oss våra sällsamma själar och besynnerliga/ tycken /– –/." ("What more does pain give her darlings?/ I know no more. /– –/ She gives us our strange souls and curious likings /– –/.") In the poem "Dagen svalnar..." ("The day cools...") the soul is central to the problematics of an erotic non-encounter between man and women. The speaker of this poem, a young woman, is fundamentally different to what the man expected from the meeting. The maturity and scope, albeit not sexual, of the maiden disappoints the man: "Du sökte en blomma/ och fann en frukt./ Du sökte en källa och fann ett hav./ Du sökte en kvinna och fann en själ –/ du är besviken." ("You looked for a flower/ and found a fruit./ You looked for a well/ and found a sea./ You looked for a woman/ and found a soul –/ you feel tricked."). The speaker or soul described in *Dikter* often finds herself within the sphere of influence of a captivating factor which threatens to limit being. It often involves a man. In "Vierge moderne" the soul is also name given to a complex tension. Crystallised in the speaker's litany "I am a whisper of blood in the ear of the man,/ I am the soul's ague, the longing and refusal of the flesh" is a large number of the themes of the *Dikter* collection discussed above. A tension is created in the speaker via "man" and the ambiguous "flesh".

In view of the context of interpretation I emphasise, the line "I am a whisper of blood in the ear of a man" resonates with "Die Frauen und ihre Wirkung in die Ferne" of *Die fröhliche Wissenschaft*. Nietzsche describes how man standing amidst the noise of his own life – his ventures and plans – has to ask "Habe ich noch Ohren? Bin ich nur noch Ohr and Nichts weiter mehr?" Amidst the bellowing of life, Nietzsche's man is enchanted by a peaceful vision representing woman which flows before his eyes. The remote feminine influence, the peace accorded by woman, appeals to the desire of man to rush over being to a better self, even though he knows the offer of woman to be for the most part only apparent.[75]

"Vierge moderne" repeats the situation described by Nietzsche. The speaker is not, however, a vision of feminine peace attracting dynamic man from a distance. The speaker herself is the din of a new identity and order of instincts in the ear of a man. The "whisper of blood" in the man's ear could be a call to create a new, super-human self ("självet") or soul ("själ") uniting will and corporeality. The invitation is appealing in Nietzschean terms, but it establishes a distance with man in a different way to that in Nietzsche's schema. In its proximity to man, the speaker, the "modern virgin", constitutes absolute distance. In "Vierge moderne", the "whisper of blood" does not complete the biologising and male-dominated heterosexual model represented, for example, by Nietzsche's ideal, the concept of superman. Although the speaker desires the carnal union ("the longing /– –/ of the flesh") which could be achieved with man, it refuses flesh and chooses a leap into herself. The speaker sacrifices the desire that yearns for sexual love, and increases the internal insight of the mind regarding its possibilities. If we emphasise the genitive structure of the line "I am /– –/ the longing and refusal of the flesh", those possibilities are rendered by the body to the self. This movement signifies the "ague" of the soul, tension and conflict within the self, but longing and its denial are fruitful, pointing the way to new paradises: "jag är en ingångsskylt till nya paradis." ("I am an entrance sign to new paradises.")

Ni Dieu, ni maître – Nietzsche and the "modern virgin"

The idea of the "Death of God", venturing beyond good and evil and the Dionysian, establishes a certain basic tone in "Vierge moderne".[76] The will to power, the factor defining being after the "Death of God", resounds in the poem. Its tension could be summarised as follows: "dass alles Geschehen in der organischen Welt ein *Überwältigen*, *Herrwerden* und dass wiederum alles Überwältigen und Herrwerden ein Neu-Interpretieren, ein Zurechtmachen ist, bei dem der bisherige "Sinn" und "Zweck" nothwendig verdunkelt oder ganz ausgelöscht werden muss."[77] The implementation of the will to power belongs to those free spirits whose time to be born will perhaps not be until the day after tomorrow, after the father has completely died, as phrased by Nietzsche.[78]

As noted above, the sun metaphor of the poem is like an echo of Nietzsche's texts. The fire image "I am a flame, searching and brazen" bears traces of Nietzsche's dithyrambs which inspired Södergran, particularly "Ecce Homo":

Ja! Ich weiss, woher ich stamme!
Ungesättigt gleich der Flamme
Glühe und verzehr' ich mich.
Licht wird Alles, was ich fasse,
Kohle Alles, was ich lasse:
Flamme bin ich sicherlich.[79]

After the "Death of God" it is necessary to look at the creative individual. It is necessary to want to go beyond the imperatives and mechanisms which control values ratified by history – by creating one's beginning again and again through active criticism. It is to this that man is guided by the will to power, the instinct of freedom, "das Gesetz der *nothwendigen* 'Selbstüberwindung' im Wesen des Lebens".[80] Zarathustra speaks: "Verbrennen musst du dich wollen in deiner eignen Flamme: wie wolltest du neu werden, wenn du nicht erst Asche geworden bist!" and continues: "Ich liebe Den, der über sich selber hinaus schaffen will und so zu Grunde geht."[81]

The speaker of "Vierge moderne" is "a flame, searching and brazen", "a step /– –/ towards ruin". Nietzsche's volleys are hurled back into the game when the speaker ambiguously presents herself as the "flame" and "beloved" (Swedish word "flamma" is polysemic) of the future sought by Nietzsche ("I am a flame"). "Vierge moderne" could certainly have been one of the flames / beloveds, one of the willing expected by Nietzsche's Zarathustra.[82] What opportunities does Nietzsche's superman offer women and what relationship, for example, does the poem's "skoal to the glory of all women" have with the affirmation seeking to transcend metaphysics as articulated by Nietzsche, or the preparation of the horizon in terms of which woman and "all women" become affirmed in the philosopher's texts?

Zarathustra humours an old wife by speaking of the womenfolk, noting: "Zweierlei will der ächte Mann: Gefahr und Spiel. Desshalb will er das Weib, als das gefährlichste Spielzeug. /– –/ Ein Spielzeug sei das Weib, rein und fein, dem Edelsteine gleich, bestrahlt von den Tugenden einer Welt, welche noch nicht da ist."[83] In "Vierge moderne" Nietzsche's words are turned against themselves. The "modern virgin" will not submit to being a plaything. The "flame" is mocking and treacherous wisdom, a journey into the self. This attitude is already evident in the previous images of the poem. The absoluteness of the verse shows the explosive power of a pure beginning: "Jag är en flamma, sökande och käck" ("I am a flame, searching and brazen") approaches the birth of a new existential situation which breaks down the old world; "flame" means a narrow, jet flame exploding from a space burnt to be void of oxygen and underpressurised. The "modern virgin" no longer looks at a man, lover or philosophical father to find a child in him and to repeat the play of his desire. The speaker steps over the shadow of her king boldly and laughs: "I am a laughing stripe of a scarlet sun"; "I am a skoal to the glory of all women"; "I am a flame, searching and brazen". The speaker denotes her absoluteness to be a strength, and it surpasses Nietzsche's flame of the superman, leaving the philosopher's attitudes of sexual policy behind.

"Vierge moderne" thus also established a distance with Nietzsche's superman, one of the ideas that inspired Södergran the most. It utilises a Nietzschean vocabulary, yet different utopias are prefigured in the speaker, plural paradises: "I am an entrance sign to new paradises." The poem points towards new kinds of fantasies of creativity.

Fire and water

In the next line, the poem, which flowed forward powerfully, appears to stop in the self-reflection of the speaker: "I am water, deep but daring up to the knee." In literature water imagery has been one of the most common means of echoing self and its secret dimensions, and this was also the case in literature at the turn of the 19th and 20th centuries.[84] The structure of the line undermines the position of the speaker. First the speaker calls herself a lake or water. "Vatten" ("water") is given the attribute "djup" ("deep"). This property is underlined when the attribute follows the main word, with a comma marking a pause. The definition of the speaker is again followed by a hiatus, the reserved "men" ("but"). Then "I am water" is given an epithet describing human activity, "dristigt" ("daring"). The conjuction "but" which interrupts the sentence is qualified. The boldness of the speaker comes as far as the knees – "daring up to the knees". At the same time, the speaker moves from the elements of nature back to the body and the mind. The interrupted and antithetic sentence makes the reader ask in what position the speaker will finally remain, and what the sentence means in general? Will the seductive power and self-confidence of the speaker give way to doubt or an ironic comment on her own incomplete state?

The line can be read as self-mockery on the part of the speaker. It is as if the speaker were looking into water sullied by its own metaphors where there is not enough truth to go deeper than the knees, and were understanding the illusoriness of everything. Witt-Brattström interprets the poem in a similar vein, although she does not present her interpretation until the final line, noting that the speaker of the poem is also in accordance with Nietzsche a paradox – being dissolved in an image of "fire and water in free and loyal union", as if the whole construction of metaphor was illusory, and the New Woman a bluff, despite the impression of fearless strength.[85] It is obvious that the poem is an explicit rhetorical construction, a metaphorical construct of the self. This, however, does not mean that the speaker is something unreal or illusory, the absolute opposite of the real. Rather, the paradoxical terms of the poem and its vocabulary of depth and texture, reflect the poem's most intrinsic power and truth. The assertions of "Vierge moderne" obviate an unequivocal dichotomy of truth and untruth. This dichotomy is replaced by the movements of depth and texture, a flowing style fleeing a structure of bimodal value. The poem seems to say that any representation of self is fiction. The truth of the poem is a moving group of metaphors, and within that truth there is room for self-mockery and an understanding of one's own artifice.

I see the status of the line "I am fire and water in free and loyal union" differently to Witt-Brattström. The line puts the assertion "I am water, deep but daring up to the knee" in a new and different position. A lake daring up to the knees turns into water. Water is now preceded by fire, perhaps the most important image of the future in Södergran's poetry. What may have remained unfinished only recently now deepens as the speaker commits herself to the illusion of the world, the metaphorical construct that is the self. The poem is conscious of its truth. Its truth is called *Schein*, a constructed idealised truth. The speaker of "Vierge moderne" is an act striving to take form aesthetically, as a will to power. The same gesture is realized in an increasingly distinct way in Södergran's later works. "För att icke dö måste jag vara viljan till makt./ För att undgå atomernas kamp under upplösning." ("In order not to die I have to be the will to power./ In order to avoid the atoms' struggle in their break-up.") are the first lines of the poem "Materialism" in Södergran's collection *Framtidens skugga* (The Shadow of the Future). The poem ends: "dock finnes ingen själ och har det aldrig funnits någon/ själ./ Det är sken, sken, sken och idel lek." ("yet there is no soul and there has never been any soul./ It is seeming, seeming, seeming, and idle play.") The last assertion of "Vierge moderne" again reveals the possibilities of strength and the unexpected; the speaker is deep but it is only at its beginning, having only presented part of her courage. The final line is an invitation to destroy the old self, to a future which will overturn all boundaries. The poem's image finds resonance in Nietzsche's fragment "Excelsior", in the tensing of today for tomorrow, in the union of water and fire:

> Es giebt einen See, der es sich eines Tages versagte, abzufliessen, und einen Damm dort aufwarf, wo er bisher abfloss: seitdem steigt dieser See immer höher. Vielleicht wird gerade jene Entsagung uns auch die Kraft verleihen, mit der die Entsagung selber ertragen werden kann; vielleicht wird der Mensch von da an immer höher steigen, wo er nicht mehr in einen Gott *ausfliesst*.[86]

Södergran ends her poem by marking it open (...). It seems as if the modern self, even when reforming cultural positions, must be presented in terms of paradox and open conditions. These modalities of self are the core of modernity – "Vierge moderne" is true to its name to the very end.

Closing remarks

The will to work for a new self and humanity is reinforced in Södergran's later works. At the same time the new self and the gender-neutral attitude anticipated in "Vierge moderne" become stronger. Although Södergran inscribes strong feminine characters, she repeatedly transcends the social conventions and norms associated with sexuality, regardless of how radical a sexuality they may apply to. Södergran's will for the superman means a desire to be her own will, her own beginning and pregnancy. The epithets with which Södergran describes her poetics are representative of this virginity. The features described as "masculine" (intellect) and "feminine" (instinct), Apollonian and Dionysian, are combined and rearticulated. The collection *Framtidens skugga* (The Shadow of the Future) no longer speaks of men or women, but of "us", those dedicated to the cause, the "playmates of Eros". Being a playmate of

Eros is not the passionate anguish caused by sexuality. It is a desire for one thing, and the sacrifice of oneself and one's own body: "Vi Eros lekkamrater, vi vilja endast ett:/ bli eld utav din eld och brinna upp " ("Eros tempel"). ("We playmates of Eros, we want only one thing:/ to be fire of your fire and to burn up", "The Temple of Eros").[88] Eros, the will to power, is the strength and the power that uses the poet as its messenger.

Translated by Jüri Kokkonen

NOTES

1. Quoted in Tideström 1949/1991: 138; Olsson 2001: 161.
2. Holm 1993: 26.
3. Södergran 1984: 59. In reference to Södergran's poems I do not use technical annotations of the source; I only mention the collection and title of the poem. All the poems to which I refer are found in *Dikter och aforismer* (1990), Volume 1 of Södergran's collected works. The translations in English are by David McDuff (1984). With regard to Södergran's correspondence, I refer to the page numbers given in *Brev* (1996), Volume 2 of the collected works. Whenever the translation is available I quote Silvester Mazzarella's translation of Södergran's letters (2001).
4. Tideström 1949: 85.
5. Enckell 1949: 101–102. Enckell leaves his interpretation only at the level of allusion. It is hard to motivate the interpretation of the speaker of the poem in relation to the depiction of life and wisdom in "Das Tanzlied" because of the difficult structure and ambiguity of the texts. The imagery of laughter, mockery and the fisherman in "Das Tanzlied" is repeated more distinctly elsewhere in *Zarathustra* and are presented in my analysis. In Södergran's works, male and female Dionysian dancers are directly present in the poems "Stormen" and "Scherzo" in the *Rosenaltaret* collection. Enckell's allusion could be interpreted further in noting that the connection tentatively demonstrated by him perhaps contains the specific observation of the tone of the poem. "Vierge moderne" has a Dionysian state of mind; the writing is a pattern similar to dance. The connections of the poem with the Nietzschean dithyramb could be addressed from this basis. Such poems of *Dikter* as "Vierge moderne", "Violetta skymningar. . ." and "Gud", almost to be defined as outcries, would thus have opened the way for the tragic verse of the *Septemberlyran* collection.
6. Witt-Brattström 1997: 210. Nietzschean vocabulary was noted at an early stage. Hagar Olsson described Södergran with vocabulary familiar from *Zarathustra*, regarding her to be "one of these 'Kinder der Zukunft'" (Olsson 1955: 20).
7. Of the debut collection, in particular the poems "Gud", "Vierge moderne", "Violetta skymningar. . .", "Färgernas längtan", "Skönhet", "Två vägar" and "Smärtan".
8. Witt-Brattström 1997: 209–210.
9. Holm 1993: 26.
10. Holm 1993: 26.
11. Holm 1993: 30.
12. Holm 1993: 27.
13. "A performative utterance will, for example, be in a peculiar way hollow or void if said by an actor on the stage, or introduced in a poem /– –/. Language in such circumstances is in special ways – intelligibly – used not seriously, but in ways parasitic upon its normal use. All this we are excluding at present from consideration." (Austin 1962: 22.)
14. Holm 1993: 30.

15 Holm takes the feminist variant of Austin's speech act theory from Tania Modelski's text "Some Functions of Feminist Criticism, or the Scandal of the Mute Body". Perhaps more solid support for investigating the performativity of the speech act and its authority could have been found in the theories of Émile Benveniste and Roman Jakobson, which deal with the structure of the linguistic act. Benveniste (1971: 195–230) writes of the two subjects of the discursive event, the subject of uttering (*le sujet d'énonciation*) and the subject of the utterance (*le sujet d'énoncé*). Roman Jakobson speaks of the "shifter", the linguistic sign in which language and discourse – code and message – merge (1971: 130–147.)
16 Holm 1993: 26.
17 Austin 1962: 4–7, 32–34. Since my intention is to present an introduction to the subject, I will only discuss Austin's speech act theory in general terms.
18 Culler 2000: 504–505.
19 Broadly speaking, Austin proceeds – Jonathan Culler's (2000: 505) interpretation from a situation in which the performative is seen as special case of the constative – as apparent propositions – and arrives at a perspective from which constatives are regarded as a special type of performatives.
20 Austin 1962: 120.
21 Austin 1962: 120.
22 Culler 2000: 506–507.
23 De Man 1979: 131.
24 Witt-Brattström 1997: 209. My idea of metaphoricity does not address the problematics of the speaking subject in as many dimensions as the speech act theory, but it does avoid a large number of problems and is sufficient for the present discussion.
25 Witt-Brattström 1997: 210.
26 Aristotle 1921: 1458a: 25–30.
27 Aristotle 1921: 1458b: 20–25.
28 Brian McHale writes of the hypertropic nature of metaphor in modern literature: "Instead of posing an expression between 'style' and 'World' one can, for example, openly display its metaphoricity but then so extend and elaborate the metaphorical frame of reference that it approaches the status of an independent fictional world of its own, an autonomous (or at any rate quasi-autonomous) imaginative reality" (1987: 137–138).
29 Guoted in Olsson 1955: 38 and Södergran 2001: 38. Södergran made this note in her "Öppet brev till recensenter och riddare" ("Open Letter to Reviewers and Knights") in the newspaper *Dagens Press* on 29 January 1919.
30 Holm 1990 ja 1993; Witt-Bratström 1997: 205–254.
31 Witt-Brattström 1997: 211.
32 Cf. Witt-Brattström 1997: 210–211.
33 Södergran 2001: 33–34; Södergran 1921/1996: 199; see also 1920/1996: 188.
34 As written by in Key *Lifslinjer I* (1903), quoted by Witt-Brattström 1997: 208.
35 In her correspondence, Södergran refers to Ellen Key, whom she otherwise respects, in an ambivalent tone with the name "la maîtresse de N." (1919/1996: 112).
36 Witt-Brattström 1997: 221–236. Salomé's concept of Eros, which interprets the Nietzschean idea of the will to power in the manner of Södergan's Eros, would be interesting, but it would entail an interpretation of unnecessarily broad scope in the present connection. At the end of my essay I shall refer in general terms to the theme of Eros in Södergran's works.
37 In a letter to Vilhelm Ekelund Södergran aptly reflects on the way in which Nietzsche's philosophy is meant to be realised and the importance of Nietzsche's style in bearing his philosophical ideas: "Undrar om tanken ensam /– –/ för över till övermänniskan, om kraften blott blir tung och ful utan den tankens mognad Nietzsche ensam ägde" (Södergran 1920/1996: 159). In her "Öppet brev till

recensenter och riddare" ("Open letter to Reviewers and Knights") Södergran claims herself to be "Den först uppträdda berättigade arvingen till Zarahustras läror" (sit. Olsson 1955:39). A self-confident position in view of the fact that Nietzsche's texts had already been interpreted three decades before Södergran.

38 Holm 1993: 27.
39 "Le plaisir que nous retirons de la représentation du présent" (Baudelaire 1924: 52). The difference of Södergan's expression and vocabularly with regard to Baudelaire are considerable. I refer here to similarities in the attitudes of both writers.
40 Baudelaire 1924: 69.
41 Rimbaud 1906: 218–219, 259.
42 See de Man 1983: 156. De Man develops further the connections between the views of Nietzsche and Baudelaire in particular.
43 Witt-Brattström 1997: 209.
44 Witt-Brattström 1997: 210; Holm 1993: 26. My interpretation of the speaker of the poem approaches Lillqvist's idea of the transendental self (2001: 72–78), although I employ a different vocabulary. The present context does not permit a further discussion of the connections between my perspective and Lillqvist's interpretation. The connection with the tradition of aesthetic idealism is nonetheless found in relation to Nietzsche.
45 Holm describes the movement of the poem with the term "desire" and goes as far as to define the speaker of the poem as "the person or desire talking, neither passive nor active" (Holm 1993: 26).
46 KSA VI_3: 363; the critical edition of Nietzsche's collected works is used here, with references to its sections and page number. The first line of "Vierge moderne" prefigures Södergran's later metapoetic proclamations, which also draw upon Nietzsche's ideas of individuals who create laws. The "Orfeus" of the *Septemberlyran* collection notes: "Jag kan sjunga hur jag vill./ Mig är allt förlåtligt." ("I can sing how I will./ All is pardoned me", "Orpheus"). and "Makt" ("Might") in the collection *Framtidens skugga* claims: "Jag följer ingen lag. Jag är lag i mig själv." ("I follow no law. I am a law unto myself.")
47 In Södergran's words, Nietzsche is "tankens konung" (Södergran 1920/1996: 159).
48 KSA VI_3: 246.
49 KSA VI_3: 72.
50 KSA VI_2: 3, 23–26.
51 KSA VI_1: 250.
52 See Södergran 1919/1996: 102–103, 140.
53 Södergran 1920/1996: 159. In an earlier connection Södergran wrote: "Jag har haft att bekämpa min stora aversion mot mystik, religion och kristendom" ("I have had to fight my strong aversion to mysticism, religion and Christianity") (1919/1996: 144; 2001: 69). As early as *Vaxdukshäftet* poem written in German and dated 4 January 1908, she notes: "Ich hab' meine Seele verloren/ Und bin ein Kind meiner Zeit,/ Und glaube nicht, an das Leben/ In ewiger Seligkeit. /– –/ aus den alten Trümmern/ Die neue Welt entsteht."
54 According to Nietzsche, man acts thus under Dionysian inspiration (KSA III_2: 382–383).
55 The expression in Ex. 3: 13–14 permits several possible interpretation, including "I am what I am", "I shall be what I shall be", or "I am because I am". On the relation of the name of God (*"ähja"*, "I am") to being and personality, see the linguistic analysis of the *Interpreter's Bible* (1952: 874–875).
56 Södergran's "jag är" ("I am") is distinct from, for example, J. L. Runeberg's romantic-mystical subject, of which one side is a uniform national-religious subject. The young Runeberg writes: "Det är förunderligt, att vi, fast vi alla säga vårt 'jag är', likväl skola så allmänt tycka oss vara så långt, så väsentligt skilda från hvarandra. Är det icke samma ande (Gud) i oss alla, som ur våra tusen munnar

säger sitt 'jag är' och besannar sig sjelf och oss" (quoted in Tideström 1941: 395). In the Runeberg's first versions the word "ande" ("spirit") is "Gud" ("God").

57 Södergran's *Vaxdukshäftet* poem "Die Zukunft" from 1907 anticipates this situation. The future is described as a young, brave and beautiful maiden greeting the land at dawn.

58 Södergran refers to these words from R. R. Eklund's *Jordaltaret* (The Earth Altar) (Södergran 1919/1996: 109, 131.)

59 Södergran writes to Hagar Olsson: "överlämna dig åt min vilja, åt solen livskraften, pranan. /– –/ jag är bliven sällheten och ljuset självt." ("surrender yourself to my will, to the sun, to the life-force, to prana. /– –/ I've become bliss and light itself")(Södergran 1919/1996: 105; 2001: 46).

60 Södergran 2001: 145. "/– –/ den har varit som ett solsken för mig – jag älskar sanningsvärdet i denna bok" (Södergran 1922/1996: 268).

61 "Dort war's auch, wo ich das Wort 'Übermensch' vom Wege auflas, und dass der Mensch Etwas sei, das überwunden werden müsse, – dass der Mensch eine Brücke sei und kein Zweck: sich selig preisend ob seines Mittags und Abends, als Weg zu *neuen Morgenröten*: – das Zarathustra-Wort vom grossen Mittage, und was sonst ich über den Menschen aufhängte, *gleich purpurnen zweiten Abendröten*" (KSA VI_1: 244, italics by V.H.).

62 KSA VI_3: 52, VI_3: 352, 353.

63 The poem "Violetta skymningar. . ." ("Violet dusks. . .") in the collection *Dikter* crushes the male, the distorting mirror: "Mannen är en falsk spegel den solens dotter vredgad/ kastar mot klippväggen /– –/." ("The man is a false mirror that the sun's daughter angrily/ throws against the rock-face /– –/.") This poems employs a variation of the sun metaphor in "Vierge moderne" in speaking of violet dusks and naked maidens that the self bears within itself as a legacy from its primal era. Where the speaker of "Vierge moderne" refuses to be a woman, "Violetta skymningar. . ." repeatedly denies the male. Also in this poem virginity is the precondition of celebration. Even in the poem "Mysteriet" ("The Mystery") of the collection *Framtidens skugga*, the speaker notes: "all litenhet vill jag hånande döda." ("jeering I want to kill all pettiness.")

64 Tideström 1949/1991: 85. Lillqvist (2001: 72) follows the idea of a working and treatment of sexuality. He writes of the self transcending sensuality: "De glupskt åtrående fiskar som simmar omkring i det södergranska, sexuellt signifikanta havet möter i diktens transcendenta jag sin överkvinna: hon är det översinnliga fångstredskap som stoppar fiskarnas framfart."

65 KSA VI_2: 342.

66 Södergran 1919/1996: 93.

67 KSA VI_2: 161.v The symbolism of hunting and fishing familiar from *Zarathustra* is also found elsewhere in Södergran's works, particularly in the poems "Vid Nietzsche's grav" and "Jägarens lycka" written around 1918.

68 Zarathustra is an Anti-Christ figure employing Biblical vocabulary. Zarathustra casts his nets and seeks the man of the future while Christ summoned fishermen from their nets and said he would make them His disciples, the fishers of men, if they would follow him (Matthew 4: 18–20). Boel Hackman interprets the metaphor of the modern virgin as a net to be connected with the apostles and reinforces the image of the self as a spiritual trailblazer (2000: 138).

69 In her "Individuell konst" ("Individual art") Södergran addresses her poetry to the few individuals who stood near the boundary of the future. See Olsson 1955: 36–37; Södergran 2001: 24–25.

70 In this respect I follow Lillqvist's (2001: 73) interpretation.

71 KSA VI_2: 226.

72 KSA VI_1: 36.

73 Corporeality is an integral feature of Södergran's representations of the act of creation. She associates corporeality with the Dionysian principle in both her po-

ems and letters. Space does not permit further analysis of corporeal features of the mode of being in the poem. Such a discussion would involve not only Zarathustra but also the idealising aspects that Södergran adopts from Nietzsche's *Die Geburt der Tragödie*.

74 Holm 1993: 56. The lines in *Dikter* on the soul describe the processes of the corporeal and the spiritual, the multiplicity of the self in them.
75 KSA V_2: 100–101.
76 These themes particularly interested Södergran in Nietzsche's works, as she writes in her letter to Vilhelm Ekelund (Södergran 1920/1996: 159–160).
77 KSA VI_2: 329–330.
78 Ks. KSA VI_3: 165.
79 KSA V_2: 39.
80 KSA VI_2: 428.
81 KSA VI_1: 78, 79.
82 See note 36.
83 KSA VI_1: 81.
84 For example, the Symbolist Maurice Maeterlinck, whom Södergran greatly valued (1920/1996: 153), writes of the inner sea of mystical morality, "la mer intérieure", to be found within man himself in *Le trésor des humbles* (Maeterlinck 1905: 67). The water imagery of the "Tief sein und tief scheinen" aphorism (KSA V_2: 178) in Nietzsche's *Die fröhliche Wissenschaft* largely corresponds to the line in "Vierge moderne".
85 Witt-Brattström 1997: 210.
86 KSA V_2: 208.
87 Södergran 1919/1996: 90.
88 "Jag känner dig, Eros –/ du är icke man och kvinnan,/ du är den kraft,/ som sitter nedhukad i templet,/ för att resande sig, vildare än ett skrän,/ häftigare än en slungad sten,/ slunga ut förkunnelsens träffande ord över världen/ ur det allsmäktiga templets dörr" ("Eros hemlighet"). "I know you, Eros –/ you are not man and woman,/ you are the power/ that sits crouched in the temple,/ before, raising itself, wilder than a scream,/ more violently than a slung stone,/ slinging out the apt words of the annuanciation over the world/ from the temple door of the almighty"("Eros' Secret").

LITERATURE

ARISTOTLE 1921: "De Poetica". Translated by Ingram Bywater. *The Works of Aristotle Translated into English. Vol XI*. Clarendon Press, Oxford.
AUSTIN, J. L. 1962: *How to Do Things with Words. The William James Lectures delivered at Harvard University in 1955*. Harvard University Press, Cambridge, Massachusetts.
BAUDELAIRE, CHARLES 1924: *L'art Romantique. Oeuvres Complètes 4*. Calmann-Lévy, Paris.
BENVENISTE, ÉMILE 1971 *Problems in General Linquistics*. University of Miami Press, Coral Gables, Florida.
CULLER, JONATHAN 2000: "Philosophy and Literature: The Fortunes of the Performative". *Poetics Today*. Volume 21, Number 3. Fall 2000.
ENCKELL, OLOF 1949: *Esteticism och nietzscheanism i Edith Södergrans lyrik. Studier i finlandssvensk modernism (I)*. Svenska litteratursällskapet i Finland, Helsingfors.
HACKMAN, BOEL 2000: *Jag kan sjunga hur jag vill. Tankevärld och konstsyn i Edith Södergrans diktning*. Söderströms & C:o, Helsingfors.
HOLM, BIRGITTA 1990: "Edith Södergran och den nya kvinnan". *Tidskrift för litteraturvetenskap* 4/1990.

HOLM, BIRGITTA 1993: "Vierge Moderne: The New Woman in Karelia". *Edith Södergran: A Changing Image. Looking for a New Perspective on the Work of a Finnish Avant-garde Poet.* Editors Petra Broomans, Adriaan van der Hoeven, Jytte Kronig. RUG, Werkgroep Vrouwenstudies Letteren, Groningen.

JAKOBSON, ROMAN 1971: "Shifters, verbal categories, and the russian verb". *Selected Writings II. Word and Language.* Mouton, The Hague.

LILLQVIST, HOLGER 2001: *Avgrund och paradis. Studier i den estetiska idealismens litterära tradition med särskild hänsyn till Edith Södergran.* Svenska litteratursällskapet i Finland, Helsingfors.

MAETERLICK, MAURICE 1905: *Le Trésor des Humbles.* Trente-et-unième édition. Société DV Mercvre de France, Paris.

DE MAN, PAUL 1979: *Allegories of reading - Figurative Language in Rousseau, Nietzsche, Rilke, and Proust.* Yale University Press, New Haven and London.

DE MAN, PAUL 1983: *Blindness & Insight. Essays in the Rhetoric of Contemporary Criticism.* University of Minnesota Press, Minneapolis.

MCHALE, BRIAN 1987: *Postmodernist Fiction.* Methuen, New York.

NIETZSCHE, FRIEDRICH: *Nietzsche Werke. Kritische Gesamtausgabe* (KSA). Volumes III_{1-2}, V_2, VI_{1-3} (1968–1973). Herausgegeben von Giorgio Colli und Mazzino Montinari. Berlin, New York: Walter de Gruyter.

OLSSON, HAGAR 1955: *Ediths brev. Brev från Edith Södergran till Hagar Olsson, med kommentar av Hagar Olsson.* Schildt, Helsingfors.

OLSSON, HAGAR 2001: "The Poet Who Created Herself". In Edith Södergran *The Poet Who Created Herself. Selected Letters of Edith Södergran.* Translated and edited by Silvester Mazzarella. Norvik Press, Norwich.

RIMBAUD, JEAN ARTHUR 1906: *Oeuvres.* Troisième Édition. Société DV Mercvre de France, Paris.

SÖDERGRAN, EDITH 1984: *Complete Poems.* Translated by David McDuff. Bloodaxe Books, Newcastle upon Tyne.

SÖDERGRAN, EDITH 1990: *Dikter och aforismer. Samlade skrifter 1.* Redigerade av Holger Lillqvist. Svenska litteratursällskapet i Finland, Helsingfors.

SÖDERGRAN, EDITH 1996: *Brev. Samlade skrifter 2.* Utgivna av Agneta Rahikainen. Svenska litteratursällskapet i Finland, Helsingfors.

SÖDERGRAN, EDITH 2001: *The Poet Who Created Herself. Selected Letters of Edith Södergran.* Translated and edited by Silvester Mazzarella. Norvik Press, Norwich.

THE INTERPRETER'S BIBLE 1952. *The Holy Scriptures in the King James and Revisited Standard Versions with General Artices and Introduction, Exegesis, Exposition for Each Book of the Bible.* Volume I. Abingdon – Cokesbury Press, Nashville, New York.

TIDESTRÖM, GUNNAR 1941: *Runeberg som estetik. Litterära och filosofiska idéer i den unge Runebergs författarskap.* Svenska litteratursällskapet, Helsingfors.

TIDESTRÖM, GUNNAR 1949/1991: *Edith Södergran.* Wahlström & Widstrand, Helsingfors.

WITT-BRATTSTRÖM, EBBA 1997: *Ediths jag. Edith Södergran och modernismens födelse.* Nordstedts, Stockholm.

LEENA KAUNONEN

The Feminine in Paavo Haavikko's *Winter Palace*

> Light boughs on the riverbank,
>   Spring, autumn and spring and autumn
> Are the four woman-seasons the hand spread on the skin,
>   Spring a reddening, autumn a moistness,
> Winter sleep and in the summer her tresses shone, and the mallards'
> Creaking trembled across her skin.... (T, 42)

One of the most impressive sequences of *Winter Palace* is the episode quoted above from the 'Seventh Poem', which charms the reader with its sensuous lyricism. It starts from a light-as-air nature image – a fleeting perception of branches on a riverbank – whereupon the angle alters. We see not trees or water but a woman-character, emerging almost imperceptibly from the background of the river landscape. The woman's being alters with the seasons: her spring has 'reddening', her autumn is characterised by 'moistness', and winter is given over to sleep. Summer's image amplifies synaesthetically into a fusion of different senses: her hair shines, and the mallard's discordance is experienced caressingly as a trembling across her skin. The changes brought about by the cycle of the seasons create movement in the scene and a feeling of animation. Most importantly, the alterations of the woman's different 'seasons' hint at the notion of change as a definable feature of womanhood.

    This delicate vignette is a rare moment of quiet water in a series of feminine metamorphoses otherwise showing capriciousness and sudden surprises. As we read the poems of *Winter Palace* we meet woman in very different forms. Woman-characters that are well-known in antique epics and nature myths appear: Helen of Troy, for instance, the Cumaean sibyl, and a caryatid supporting the world. Along with these go variously-named beings, such as 'the beautiful child' who converses about everything, 'an exalted being' and a world-creating 'rose'. Also gender concepts arise: 'universal femaleness', and a situation identified with the womb in the 'Fourth Poem'. The feminine is sometimes figured as a sibyl, sometimes a Grace or caryatid, and, at its most fearsome, as a Gorgon or ogress. Whatever face the feminine chooses, attractive or threatening, it is never enduring: the feminine soon changes its configuration.[1]

The change and modification are not confined to the feminine. They apply equally to the meta-lyrical structure, and to the story's internal world, where the personae live. The protagonist acting as the poem's central personage is, like the feminine, a many-visaged master of role-change: he is the unifier of the poem's elements or 'images', a traveller through the poems, a seeker of his own origin, and a writer writing poems. Change is also contained in the plot, which recounts the protagonist's journey, in which, along with other occurrences, the creation of poems is foregrounded.

The meta-lyrical journey through *Winter Palace* goes forward as a process of writing. The protagonist continually writes new text and moves from one already-written line to a new line. The protagonist's written lines form poems, and the poems combine into a whole, which the protagonist calls alternately 'a house' (T, 25, 43–45) and 'a Palace' (T, 52). *Winter Palace* grows into a dramatic vision of the writing of poems, the conditions for it, and the significance of poetry. The conclusion of the series switches from depicting the construction of the poems' architecture to the demolition of the whole structure.

The principle of continuous change undoubtedly puts demands on the reader. Though the plot, which recounts the protagonist's journey, forms a clear whole, the process of following the rapidly-changing speech-situations and time-relations at the level of the lines and the line-sequences is more arduous. *Winter Palace* is certainly considered a masterpiece, but a difficult one.[2]

Is it possible that the multifacedness of the feminine and its changeableness and convertibility also operate as the work's unifying theme?[3] The most important factor in the poem's unity is the relationship between the sex roles. *Winter Palace's* most exciting turns of plot are structured round the mutual encounters of the protagonist and the feminine characters, and their conversations. Within the limits of this study I cannot deal with the task and significance of the feminine in complete detail; I shall break down my many-faceted theme by concentrating on two highly important aspects: the two primary tasks the feminine characters have in the poem. First, they teach the protagonist to converse; and secondly, they help the protagonist in the creation of the meta-lyrical structures.

The Significance of Conversation

Before dealing with the tasks of the feminine in detail, I shall discuss the importance training in conversation has for the protagonist of *Winter Palace*. Speech has a greater importance than writing in the work. Though the process of writing poems is clearly foregrounded, it is still more strongly emphasised that poems speak. The poems simulate spoken language, and there are dialogues reminiscent of drama. At the commencement of the poem the protagonist forces the poem's structural elements (its 'images') into adjoinment, so that the continuum begins to 'speak'.

The strong emphasis on speech is based on the notion that the world and speech are closely intertwined. In Haavikko's volume *Leaves Leaves* this notion crystallises as follows: the world speaks '... about all things at once' (PKV, 112). Since speech acquires so fundamental a significance – that the world is organised into speech – it is no surprise that conversation, in a work like *Winter Palace*, which emphasises the function of speech, develops into a meta-concept. In the following I shall analyse the significance of conversation with the help of three examples, in order that the peculiarities of conversation may rise into clearer view. I shall select features that distinguish the protagonist's disparate speech from his speech in situations where he converses with feminine characters.

The events of the protagonist's journey towards an imaginary 'region that is not a place' create a framework and a background for all these conversations. The journey is the protagonist's attempt to define his own origin through a backwards return in time, towards a time before birth and existence. But because proceeding backwards in time, towards a beginning, is impossible, the protagonist hopes for a mythical return and creates an origin for himself: a utopia, a place created by the imagination. The thought of this utopian return receives its impetus during the conversation in the 'Second Poem'. To achieve his goal, the protagonist needs an assistant. He achieves contact with a feminine being who can help in deciding the direction. For this phase to be reached, the helper has first to be born herself. The following excerpt is taken from the phase of *Winter Palace* where things leading up to the birth of a feminine helper give rise to a functional and dramatic episode. First, a being contained within a bottle is driven out with smoke and flames, and the 'mad trip' depicted below follows (T, 14):

   ... and tinkle-tinkle, a bottle was tinkling there,

   and there was going to be some exalted being in the bottle –
      it made me almost weep,
   in the bottle – a being I wanted to meet,
      in the bottle.

   And this Fear was shouting and burning,

   and if it had a beard, it was burning, and if an archive,
      the archive too,
   and a horrifying fire was spreading from line to line,

   and the bottle was swathed in leaves,
                        it was swathed
   in newsleaves like-apple trees
      when autumn's coming,
   and it scrambled out of the bottle.

   It was a mad trip.

   It hopped from stone to stone, from line to line,
      Fifteen lines along
   everything was in flames, it hopped,

and I:

> I ask you, O exalted being, flying fox,
> Tell me, Where is the region that's not a place?

And it replied:

> It's not a place. I am a rose and I swelled,
>   out of me burst a world,
> and the shame makes me want to weep! To abort!
>   I! To miscarry!
> O to abandon my world, no one knows me here!

That was the whole conversation... (T, 14–15)

The flames and smoke generated by the protagonist force the being concealed in the bottle to come out. Wrapped round the bottle there are 'leaves', which the fire ignites. The Finnish word is ambiguous and allows two meanings of 'leaves': leaves from a tree and newspapers. The shouting and burning being is spreading destruction in its wake. Accompanying the being, the fire spreads to the lines and burns them to ashes – as the being moves along the lines, apparently. The burning of the being, as well as some possible archives, destroys old writings and the knowledge they contain. The 'archive' that is burning (T, 14) may signify memory, or part of the emerging work which remains potential and unrealised and will be irretrievably destroyed.

After the fire something quite new arises. Along with the destruction of the writings, an opposite development begins. From the ashes arises a search for something inchoate, still forming, which is linked to the being's feminine rosaceousness. 'The mad trip' (T, 14) indicates a transition of the sexual boundary: in the course of being transformed, this evidently bearded, bottle-inhabiting creature burgeons, in the final episode, into a rose – a manifestation with clearly feminine features. Although the bottle-born being's trip acquires comical and hysterical features, the being has an important role as the possessor of knowledge in this quest.

After this rapid turn of events, the protagonist and the being share a short conversation. In this phase, the poem's discourse changes to dialogue. The conversational contact between the two begins with an apostrophe, in which the protagonist 'creates' the being through the following attributes: 'O exalted being, flying fox'. (T, 15) This form of address ('O exalted being') endows the being with an important role: oracle and guide. The oracle's pronouncements are, however, notoriously obscure and mysterious.

The role given the 'exalted being' is linked to her interesting style of conversation – the way she replies obliquely to the protagonist's direct questions. When the protagonist asks for a reply to his question 'Where is the region that's not a place?' (T, 15), the 'exalted being' apparently evades the whole question initially. The being doesn't tell the protagonist straight out the location of the 'region'. Instead she directs the talk onto her own roseaceousness – blossoming into a rose and a world – and selects out of the protagonist's question the adjunct he gives the 'region' and repeats it to him with emphasis, as her own pronouncement: 'It's not a place.' (T, 15) The impression given by the exchange is that the being wishes to drop a hint concerning some knowledge about the region – knowledge the protagonist should fix in his mind.

Also, the protagonist's rejoinder is important: 'That was the whole conversation.' (T, 15) The protagonist is evidently signalling, with irony, that the conversation was extremely short. The oracle has given no clear answer, though the protagonist perhaps expected a clearer and more factual response. But just by replying obliquely – by playing back to the protagonist a part of his own question – the being gives him to understand that the knowledge he seeks is already in his possession. The seeker of knowledge has to intuit his required knowledge personally. Here, the feminine helper's role is revealed: evasive replies direct the seeker of advice to self-help.

The conversation with the oracle gives two hints about the character of the conversation. The exchange between the protagonist and the 'exalted being' seems, at first view, to nullify the usual notions of conversation between interlocutors, a situation founded on reciprocity. 'The exalted being' answers questions in sibylline fashion: the answers do not look like answers but do have the function of answers when their content is unravelled. The other feature of the conversation is reflection on the conversation itself: an ironic commentary on the interchange is given by the protagonist, who is not satisfied with the answer he gets; yet, from the angle of the poem's plot, the being's reply is revealed as advice, and extremely apposite.[4]

The protagonist does not converse with feminine beings alone. The ensuing conversation forms an interesting comparison with the previous one: this time the protagonist begins an interchange with himself. How does this discourse differ from the conversation with the feminine beings? The following excerpt is from 'Third Poem' and is also linked to the plot of the protagonist's journey. The allusion to his being on a journey to a 'region' frames the protagonist's fantasy of the place he is going towards: the protagonist pictures the situation to himself and for himself: ... I'm heading towards a region that's not a place.

> I picture a clearing there
>   In an uncleared forest,
> a hole bordered by forest, and that I'm
>   Dangling upside down in a gap
> that's the sky, I,
>   Who am not keen on talking.
> and I'm not coming back, don't want to. (T, 20)

The protagonist visualises himself in a cleared space, 'which is the sky', in the midst of an uncleared forest (T, 20). There he hangs upside down. The discourse reveals itself as a dialogue between an imagined self and a self observing itself from outside: 'I picture… that I'm / dangling upside down in a gap / that's sky, I, / who am not keen on talking, / and I'm not coming back, don't want to' (T, 20). The protagonist's first imagined role is in a gap that's the sky, but, as if from outside, a self-characterisation inserts itself: '… I, who am not keen on talking' (T, 20). The observing eye (the protagonist's other role) offers this third-person view of the imagined self.

The excerpt illustrates how the roles are split, and located, in the imagined situation. 'The region that's not a place' is, on the one hand, 'a clearing / in an uncleared forest' (T, 20), and, on the other, 'a hole bordered by forest' (T, 20). The protagonist's 'hole' indicates an upside-down angle of vision. The dangling-upside-down persona, with his upwards vista, can see an opening bordered with treetops, revealing a portion of sky. The hole and the opening cannot really be called 'a place'. This is the spot where the imagining I places himself.

The fantasy-scene stage-managed by the protagonist is also remarkable for the conception of conversation given the protagonist: it is both ambivalent and conflicting. The observing I presents the imagining I as someone who does not want to converse. The imagining I mopes on the tree and does not want to come back. But his rather ironical assertion 'and I'm not coming back' itself shows that the protagonist, is spite of his relinquishment of conversation, is conversing with himself, replying to himself. His whole imagined situation constitutes a self-contradiction.

The examples given support my view of the special position of conversation, compared with other speech. It is important to note the qualitative difference between conversation, on the one hand, and the protagonist's debate with himself on the other. Even though the protagonist is a talkative character, committed to speech, continually disputing with himself, questioning himself and replying to himself, the speech does not rise to a self-analytical meta-level defining its own specificity. In addition, the protagonist's disputes with himself do not advance the plot. Contrariwise, conversation with a feminine character does lead the protagonist forward, one way or another. Such conversation gives the protagonist an insight into important matters and helps him to help himself. To demonstrate the process whereby the protagonist's insights are initiated, it is time to move on to the third example of conversation. For the protagonist, the decisive instruction in conversing is realised in the 'Fifth Poem', where he meets a 'beautiful child'. This is the beginning of the conversation:

> A beautiful child was playing in the sand and writing with her finger:
>   Who? Where from? Where to?
> I replied:
>   O beautiful child, tell me, is
> She interrupted:
>   I'm two children and I lead myself by the hand.

I asked:

> O beautiful child who have the art of conversation,
> Tell me where the grass tree grows,
> where the grass flowers,
> the wind and the wind's breath, the strawberry,
> the hay, the rose?

She interrupted:

> I'm having a row with myself
> and full of opposites; I converse about everything,
> I'm a girl and a boy, one and two
> and are you night or day?... (T, 29–30)

The poem appears to be nullifying usual expectations of conversation as an event directed at an interlocutor and founded on reciprocity. Rather, what we have here is a competition between the participants, with the child immediately taking the lead. As the stronger participant, she dominates the conversation through a variety of tactics.

The purpose of the competition is to activate development, thus revealing before long the didactic function of the conversation. In trying the protagonist, the child is teaching him to hold his own and increase his initiative. Shortly, the participants advance from a competitive situation into a mutual understanding, useful to both. In this process of change a meta-linguistic development plays an integral role. The meta-language generated is the conception of conversation and the speakers' self-definition.[5] The conceptual and self-reflective thinking finally leads each of the participants to self-definition.

At the start of the conversation the power-relations are extremely disproportionate. The child controls the situation by interrupting the protagonist. Interruption is not, however, a phenomenon levelled at dominance in all speech situations. In principle it may signify several things. It may, for instance, be a sign of the speaker's enthusiasm, or it may reveal a familiarity between the conversers. Here, however, neither alternative is at work.

Twice the child breaks the protagonist's parley before he has had time to complete his sentence. The interruption is not merely a question of breaking off the protagonist's lines. It is also a bypassing of his initiatives. The content of the protagonist's desire to know ('tell me where the grass tree grows, where the grass flowers'... T, 30) does not interest the child. She does not seize on the topic offered but turns the speech round onto herself ('I'm having a row with myself' ... T, 30). The protagonist's initiatives bring no results. The child interrupts the queries right away and gives no reply to them.

Even though the child dominates the situation by interrupting the protagonist, bypassing the starting points he offers and controlling the conversation, this is not the complete truth about it. Her dominance does not imply a disturbance of communication, or a final break. The interruption and aggression present in the exchange lead, not to a dead-end, but to a deepening examination of the features of the exchange.

The aim of the interruption is not, in my view, fundamental denial, nor a design finally to dumbfound the protagonist. Rather, the fundamental intention is to provoke the protagonist. And that is what happens. The protagonist throws the conception of conversation, as a factor, into the game. His reaction is a process of change, forced on him by the child's dominance. He has to do something – define the situation he has got into. The awakening of the protagonist's reflective thinking reveals the dynamic side of the conversation. The conversation's power structure is not static, or determined in advance, for the speakers are all the time negotiating their relationship to each other. The birth of contact between the protagonist and the 'beautiful child' is shown in the child's response where she defines herself with the greatest multifacedness:

> I'm having a row with myself
> and full of opposites; I converse about everything,
> I'm a girl and a boy, one and two
> and are you night or day? (T, 30)

The child is beginning to communicate with the protagonist, and a shared language is beginning to arise. The child receives the concept offered by the protagonist (conversation) and adopts it, making it part of her own vocabulary. The conversation makes an addition to the child's existing language. The child's earlier self-assessment – 'I'm two children and I lead myself by the hand' (T, 29) – grows richer through the concept of the conversation. At the same time, in the child's language the conversation acquires meanings the protagonist has not put into it. The child pictures herself as a sovereign conversationalist and announces that she converses 'about everything' (T, 30). The child also says she is 'having a row with herself' and is 'full of opposites' (T, 30). The child's role as a conversationalist unites her feminine and masculine sides. The role consists of a kind of divided being who fashions for herself her own opposite.[6]

Basically the conversation seems to signify self-disputation: a collision of statement and counter-statement, in which the speaker is both one person and another. As the dialogue between the protagonist and the child has demonstrated, the one having a row with herself ('the beautiful child') is not, in spite of that, self-sufficient and closed in on herself. She is thoroughly active in holding on to her part as an interlocutor in the dialectical mechanism, and in adopting from it the language she needs for self-definition.

So far, at the beginning of the conversation, the child has been in complete control; but when the middle is reached, the cards are dealt anew. This change is brought about by the common language that has been generated between the parties. Having adopted the concept of conversation provided by the protagonist, the child turns, for the first time, with a reciprocal gesture to the protagonist. This move has immediate consequences. The protagonist takes over the power position from the child and defines himself:

> I'm a poor robber, a productive consumer
> > seeking honest work,
> I want to go back where I was born,
> > either/or or and/or
> the outside walls can have vertical boards or
> > horizontal or/or not... (T, 30)

In his self-definition the protagonist arrives at a multifacedness comparable to the child's. The protagonist also learns the distinctive feature of the child's use of language: how to involve himself linguistically through opposites. In spite of the complicating divisions referred to, he sees his own dividedness as no split. What he says about the structure's boarding is connected to his architecting of the poetic language. At the same time, the child's language becomes a target for sarcasm. The protagonist's use of 'either/or or and/or' (T, 30) takes up the divisions used in the child's language ('are you night or day') (T, 30) and takes them forward to newer and more complex structures.

In addition to these characterisations, the protagonist depicts himself as a robber: someone at once producing and consuming, and 'seeking honest work'. (T, 30) This remark is a sarcastic observation about the protagonist's adopted role as a writer: writing would not seem to be a 'respectable' role or source of income. With other names – 'poor robber' and 'productive consumer' (T, 30) – the protagonist shows he interprets the recent turn in the conversation less favourably. By learning the child's language, the protagonist 'consumes' the child's linguistic resources and 'produces', by exploiting them, his own self-definition based on opposites.

In spite of the negative side in this language-learning, the conversation has been, as a whole, constructive. Above all, the conversation's most important aim has been achieved: the protagonist has learned his interlocutor's way of linguistically analysing one's own self through opposites. Having solved his problem concerning self-definition, he can now concentrate on his other important task: the construction of the *Winter Palace*, his palace of poetry. The 'Fifth Poem' is, as regards the plot of the poetic series, situated at the most important turning point; for the effect of the feminine begins to grow along with the creation of the poem. A feminine effect is going on in the 'Sixth Poem', and its most decisive impact is in the 'Seventh Poem'.

Before proceeding further, I want to focus briefly on how the feminine and the creation of the poem are coupled together. The presence of the feminine is an absolute necessity for the construction of the poem: the creation of the poem, in the last analysis, rests on images alluding to the feminine. It is therefore of decisive importance that the poem and the woman should suit each other. In adopting a writer's role, the protagonist labours simultaneously with two tasks: the construction of his poem, and the shaping of a woman-character to suit his purpose. In other words, feminine material is to be used in the manufacture of a structure reflecting the creator's intentions. The work unlooses the tensions between the sexes; and it unlooses the contest between the creative, manipulative writer and his feminine raw material.

Nikolai Gogol's imaginary married life

Clarification of the tension between the sexes in *Winter Palace* is shown by the play *The Puppets*,[7] which is close in time to the poem. As regards *Winter Palace*, the most interesting point is the play's meta-theatrical theme, and the associated power-struggle of the sexes. Haavikko's play emphasises a male writer's desire to evolve a creation that corresponds to his own ideal of a woman. This semantic stratum in the work I term the theme of 'the home-made woman'.[8] Behind the theme is the story of Pygmalion in Ovid's *Metamorphoses* (Book X, 243–97). A sculptor carves a marble statue representing a woman, and he falls in love with it. The Pygmalion story was later reworked into several different versions. A common denominator in many is the notion that the artist, as the creator of his ideal, or as the fashioner of a woman, organises raw material into the creation he desires. Haavikko's play, however, does not depict a statue coming to life; instead, the idea of a man creating his woman, or wife, is specifically pointed up.

The Puppets is a fictitious relation of the Russian writer Nikolai Gogol's life. The persona of Gogol captivated Haavikko when he read Vladimir Nabokov's hilarious biography. Gogol's tragicomic life-story has many points of comparison with Gogol's own stories. His *Dead Souls* in particular, and its characters, offer fruitful material for Haavikko's play, with its black humour and grotesque details.[9]

To clarify the background significance of *The Puppets* for *Winter Palace*, I shall briefly examine the play's plot and the significance of its events. The title *The Puppets* is metaphorical, as it refers to characters in a play supposedly written by Gogol and given their words, gestures and life by the author. Gender is the factor that brings into view the differences in the writer's relationship to his creations. The writer himself becomes aware of the existence of these differences. The play's male characters are allowed to act out their own story independently and need not utter the dialogue written for them. On one occasion, the writer makes the mistake of ordering his chief character, Tšitšikov, to obey him – and thus loses a pillar of the plot when the character gets into a fury and exits from the play.

The writer's most personal and obsessive relationship is with his puppet- or doll-wife, whose existence he continually needs to shape. The doll is a composite of two roles. One of them is a woman who appears at the beginning of the play and disappears in the middle phase, coming back into the action at the end. After her departure it becomes evident that the writer has replaced his wife with a doll called Caracas, whom he calls his wife. The doll-wife is not a character in the sense of being an independent personage with a will of her own. Instead, she is freely shapeable. She is a creation the man puffs air into – literally: Caracas is an inflatable rubber doll. The writer plays with his doll, continually altering her outside appearance. He dresses and undresses her, blows her up fully and deflates her, fits her out with new clothing, changes the colour of her hair, and, turn and turn about, insults and fondles her.[10]

The play centres on depicting the writer's attempts at reshaping her, and the rebounds that come from the doll-woman's gradually increasing resistance. The decisive reversal occurs when the doll starts to become independent. The writer notices that this mirror-image of his own will has an independent side, which he now cannot reach. Independence is a trait the writer calls the doll's 'character'. As her character grows the doll begins to acquire the outlines of an independent subject. Growth in independence also has its price, as it means the end of the doll. The writer destroys her by first throwing her out into the frost to freeze to death. After this the doll is tipped onto the rubbish heap.

The play ends with the return of the writer's wife to replace the doll. Caracas's clothes are already being adapted for the wife. Evidently it will not be long before Caracas's fate is in store for her. At the dénouement, the writer announces to his wife, who is on her way home, a line that focuses the play's ruling thought: 'it's no use asking you, since you're my voice, the mirror facing me...' (M/N, 271). A mirror is a very apt image for the woman-character's role, which is to be dependent and reflecting her creator's intentions.

The story of this play prepares the ground for the questions I shall consider in my next section. How does the relation between the artist and his feminine material take shape in *Winter Palace*? Is anything possible between an author and his material other than one person's power of command?

The Women's Act

The relative roles of the sexes are tested in *Winter Palace* within a framework of drama, literally on the stage of the poem. This stage is set up in the 'Sixth Poem', where the protagonist generates a group of feminine characters for an audience. The protagonist's use of 'you' (singular 'thou') is addressed to the audience. The audience's identity is open to interpretation, as the audience remains inarticulate and does not reply to the questions put by the protagonist. In my view, the poem makes it possible to suppose that, apart from the protagonist, there are no other persons present. Quite likely, the protagonist is creating the act for himself. In line with this, the speech situation may be interpreted as a dialogue in which the protagonist addresses himself as 'you'. The protagonist creates the characters, advances the performance and aspires to keep the strings of the performance in his own hands. He repeatedly emphasises that the woman-characters are his creation and that he is bringing them into the poem. The characters are subject to the protagonist's authority and are thus puppet-like objects he can control. The situation puts the characters in a subordinate position – or does it?

For an answer one must study the sort of characters the protagonist is presenting. The poem starts with an interesting character: the first of the cavalcade of women represents an ideal of feminine beauty linked to the Helen of antiquity. The protagonist introduces her by comparing himself to a river that flows into the sea. The action makes, as it were, more dark flow into the darkness:

> And everything's ordinary here, except
>   the thousand ships and the topless towers,
> I like a river to the sea
>   bring total darkness to the night,
>
> a woman whose dress is blooming with flowers
>   unfading,
>   the scent gone
> she'd burst out laughing like a bad dream
>   And smile with her teeth,
>
> no, I'll pass this one by.   (T, 35–36)

The protagonist brings an element of impenetrability and strangeness into the night and the poem. Implicitly he 'flows' it in. This is in two senses: the flow brings the darkness into view, to be observed; and the flow allows connections with Heraclitus's famous fragment, 'One cannot step into the same river twice.' (YS, 23) Heraclitus gives the expression 'the same river' two different meanings. The river is and is not the same, depending on the point of view. It is at once the channel and the channel's changing current. The river comparison introduces the notion that everything is in flux. Nothing stays still: it is always changing into something else.[11] This principle of flux and change is realised in the poem's feminine character. The character is a twofold manifestation. First she shows her charming and ideal side. But when the character surprisingly changes her being, the whole earlier illusion is exploded. The details of this change further develop the notion of flux, and so I shall give them closer consideration in the following.

Primary attention is focused on the idealisation and mythologisation of the woman character. The flower-motif on her dress has bloomed with unfading blossoms. The poem begins by conjuring up eternity and beauty for the reader. The protagonist emphasises the exaltation of the woman into the band of the immortals by alluding to Helen of Troy. The protagonist's words – 'And everything's ordinary here, except / the thousand ships and the topless towers' (T, 35) – adapt Faustus's outcry on seeing Helen in Christopher Marlowe's *Dr Faustus*: 'Was this the face that launched a thousand ships / And burned the topless towers of Ilium?'[12] Helen's beauty had fateful consequences: the voyage against Troy was set in motion through her abduction. The long siege of Troy finally brought victory to the besiegers and the torching of the whole city.

The act's electrifying atmosphere comes from the protagonist's insertion of a fateful and destructive woman character. He retains, however, the ability to handle the force he has summoned up: to tame it and keep it safely at a distance. But something unexpected and remarkable ensues. In the midst of it all, the woman character changes her being. In astonishment, the protagonist tries to describe the nature of the change:

'the scent gone / she'd burst out laughing like a bad dream.' (T, 35). He has himself brought ('like a river', T, 35) the character into view, but the choice of a flowing river to represent the flux of everything has surprising consequences. What looked at first like unfadingness betrays the observer by turning into a nightmare. Also, the woman's dress is a bluff: 'the scent's gone' (T, 35) from the flowers; deathlessness and eternity are impossibilities. In place of the exploded illusion there is a demonic manifestation: it looks as if she will 'smile with her teeth' (T, 35). The protagonist, however, hastily wrenches himself free from the enchantment of the woman who will smile with her teeth: 'no', he bursts out, 'I'll pass this one by' (T, 36). The dangerous situation is quickly by-passed.

Along with Helen, other woman characters appear in the poem. These are visualised doing different things, and in different positions – undressing, for example, or getting out of the bath and drying hair. The characters suggest a group of live paintings, or tableaux, introduced into the poem by the protagonist. The way they are presented is associated with a long tradition of pictorial representation in painting. The background they are placed against suggests an intimate private environment: a bedroom or bathroom.

The protagonist uses a mirror image to introduce one of the women: 'a woman would like to be as blind as a mirror / and undress alone.' (T, 36) The comparison of a woman to a mirror recalls the mirror metaphor in *The Puppets*. In the play, the mirror was used as a trope for the doll's subjection to the author. The woman was the writer's voice: the mirror facing him. In *Winter Palace*, however, the mirror does not represent voice or speech, but reflectivity. The mirror-woman is created as a reflection of the protagonist's purposes and will. What are the traits in the mirror-woman's delineation that are intended to charm the observer? The protagonist's lines imply that eroticism presumably charms the audience. The woman 'undresses alone' (T, 36) but is in actual fact brought before the poem's audience.

Nevertheless, mirroring and blindness have their reverse side, freed from passive reflectivity: the mirror of desires and hopes may be thought of as a prism, which splits the reifying look into alternative modes of observation. The prism-image enables one to construe the characteristics of the passive object in a different way: they modulate into their opposite and thus query the petrifaction of a woman into a thing. The woman, who takes no look around herself, does not want to establish eye-contact with the audience, and she does not want to participate in the role-playing created by the visible world. Her own will rejects passivity and promotes the observed person's equality in the eyes of the observer. This role-change can be expressed in concepts derived from *The Puppets*: the observed object has her own 'character' and 'independence'. She is able to turn down in advance her agreed role as a charming object. Putting an active mirror before an audience denies the observer an easy road to the pleasure of looking. The mirror reflects back the observation directed at it – showing the observer to himself. Thus, at least for a moment, the mirror reverses the power relations. It forces the observer into self-reflection.

Interesting differences in the ways of depicting the woman-characters are observable in the poem. The protagonist does not describe and present all his visual objects as reified, turned into things. In certain situations no hierarchical stance develops between the describer and the described. The changes of stance towards the observed are illustrated in the following extract, where the protagonist renounces his way of putting his characters on show:

> What about this one? An upturned tortoise will always try
> to turn on its belly
> but this doesn't,
> wouldn't she like to be as beautiful as a rose
> closed up at night?   (T, 36–37)

The woman is first presented reifyingly: shown to the audience, by the protagonist, as an upturned tortoise: 'What about this one? An upturned tortoise will always try / to turn on its belly / but this doesn't.' (T, 36) The indicator of a change in the method of description is the change in the mode of reference: she is first referred to with the pronoun 'this'; at the end of the extract the protagonist nevertheless starts to replace 'this' with 'she': the observed is presented as a person rather than an object, in the third person. The protagonist propounds his question to the audience, suggesting that the observed woman could choose her role for herself. Along with this, he approaches his object of description with oblique negotiation: 'wouldn't she like to be as beautiful as a rose...' (T, 37)

The poem's final woman character differs from the others in not containing conflicting tensions that lead in other directions. The woman is revealed as personable and worthy of close observation:

> And the woman rose from the bath and bows
> under her hair's weight,
> she's drying her hair
> and a pretty dimple rose on her shoulder and disappeared:
> her limbs smiled. (T, 37)

Play of feature and loquacity are usually linked to the human face. The poem nevertheless reveals that her expressiveness is not simply limited to one part of the body: it is created throughout the whole being. The portrayer succeeds in catching a flickering moment, as the dimple appears and disappears on her shoulder. In that captured moment, 'her limbs smiled' invitingly, as if unaware.

The last example helps to reveal the different ways of imaging in the 'Sixth Poem'. The image of the woman who dries her hair does not offer her to anyone. As an object she preserves her integrity and is respected on her own terms. She is not forced into a pose. The earlier instrumentality does not operate here. Observation itself is the heart of this image, and the joy it brings.

The theatrical act set up by the protagonist has clearly shown how the variation in his stance has changed the situation, making it sometimes observational, sometimes objectifying. Seeing the poem as one where the protagonist is setting up a theatrical scene for himself gives the whole poem a profound basic irony. Addressing the audience, the protagonist is all the time addressing himself and making himself two different people. His questions and commentary circle round a desire for women and a liking for them. In addition, he props up his position by emphasising the doll-likeness of his objects.

Considering the poem from a meta-lyrical point of view, it is evident that the poem, in concentrating on performance and putting on show, is an experiment in drama. The protagonist is outlining a form where the depiction of women anticipates the scenes of a play. Partly, however, the dramatisation into scenes conflicts with itself. The necessity of pleasing is a particular target of the protagonist's self-irony. It is clear that the woman-images do not fulfil their task. The women do not charm the audience, because, to begin with, they dig their heels in, or because (which is more evident) the desire to please parodies itself. In vain the protagonist makes calculated efforts to charm his audience. The audience's presumed opinions become obvious from the protagonist's reactions. Again and again, his words reveal that the attempts to charm are not succeeding. He confirms this directly: 'Two women I've engraved on the night / but you're not charmed.' (T, 36)

Inversely, the lack of success hints at the sort of woman-characters the protagonist is really seeking. Although a dramatic poem requires a suitable woman-character, she cannot be a puppet created to charm. The protagonist drives this idea onto the rocks. The final outcome of the protagonist's experiments leads us to infer that his attempt at one-sided domination will not, where the creation of a poem is concerned, be fruitful. The woman has to be allowed to keep her integrity. This point also provides a good way forward.

The feminine s a model for the male writer

In the 'Sixth Poem' the protagonist was experimenting with various modes of feminine presentation. Since he had to depend on feminine images for the creation of his poem, these could not be mere clothes-changing puppets: they had to be characters strong enough to support a poetic universe. In this section I shall further clarify the kinds of images the protagonist depends on. In *Winter Palace* two feminine principles appear, carrying mythic authority: in the 'Fourth Poem' there is an imaginary 'region that's not a place', to be identified with the womb; and in the 'Seventh Poem' there is a world-supporting caryatid. Each feminine principle, in its own way, enables the creation of the male poetic architecture: the womb forms a prototype for the poem to imitate; and the trope of a dancing caryatid creates a model for the poem's dramatic structure.

I shall first examine the 'Fourth Poem', where the feminine is not personified but is manifested as a space. The poem's plot advances as follows: a uterine space is preceded by being called 'an exalted being' and 'a rose'; and the poem itself is anticipating later feminine characters such as the 'beautiful child' in the 'Fifth Poem' and the 'dancing caryatid' in the 'Seventh Poem'. The image of 'the region that's not a place' is a mythical and utopian attempt to go back in time, to determine the protagonist's birth. Travelling back towards his own origin also supports the protagonist's meta-lyrical aims: the writer, constructing the poem and creating something new from line to line, goes backwards while he does so. He is seeking his own birth, and the source of the birth of poetry. The protagonist aspires to reconstruct his return with the help of fantasy. In imagining and describing 'the region', the protagonist sets himself on a stage, which is also set before the reader's eyes:

This dense forest, rare trees that are scared
                                     and in this wood
the voice is wet with sweat,

this is a region where the trees burgeon and in here
    a blind tree forgets its visibility,
it's hollow, this place, and all else too, the forest
    burgeoned flowers, embarrassing me,

and should I compare myself to the unborn
    it went so badly with,
the one the flesh swallowed, pliant and soft
    and wholly female.

I didn't know what it was like to be,

I wanted to be quiet,
I wanted to eat the words and change
by compulsion as I did when I was born.... (T, 24)

The flowers burgeon, the abundance of natural elements and the hollow space enclose the protagonist in a bodily space that creates a uterine environment around him. The natural objects landscape a womb; the burgeoning flowers and the trees are important because their organic growth demonstrates fruitfulness. This feminine space also contains the protagonist's mental reality within it. The description of this 'region' employs humanising concepts – thinking, forgetting, and feelings. The simultaneous density and sparsity possibly concretise changes in mental tensions.

The feeling of discomfort transmitted by the landscape gives way before long to more pleasant feelings. At the end of the description the tension and the burgeoning of the flowers cause a burst of embarrassed delight. The protagonist asks himself whether he should compare himself 'to the unborn' (T, 24). When, through the role of the unborn, he reveals his desire, his words show he is feeling a transparency characteristic of the imagination: 'I didn't know what it was like to be, / I wanted to be quiet. ... eat the words and change / by compulsion as I did when I was born' (T, 24). He puts his changeableness in a wide scale: the change from the state of non-being to that of being. Birth, according to him, is one such compelled change. Eating words and falling silent signify, inversely to birth, a 'compelled change' back into a place preceding existence.

The concept of a landscape's anthropomorphic femininity appears in the birth-myths of many cultures. Ancient philosophy also provides a version. In Plato's *Timaeus* a feminine origin is in many ways paralleled with *chóra* (space). Timaeus refers to *chóra* in terms indicating femininity: as a suckler and children's nurse. He also describes *chóra*'s indefiniteness, its unconfinableness to a certain place. The source of existence cannot be situated in a certain place because it is everywhere. Timaeus also states that *chóra* 'offers a location for everything that is born' (52b).

The notion of *chóra* creates a background for the *Winter Palace* protagonist's aspiration to imagine a mythical origin, one which would be indestructible and limitlessly fruitful. According to the *Timaeus*, *chóra* gives birth to the original forms of all beings. Just for this reason *chóra* is an important model for the protagonist's meta-lyrical intent. How does the meta-lyrical intent show itself concretely in the poem? In describing the 'region' – 'it's hollow, this place, and all else too' (T, 24) – the protagonist links it to the description of St Petersburg's Winter Palace in the 'First Poem':

> The old wing (1754–1762) is the Winter Palace
> and all else too, the roof, the floor and
>   the walls are full of exalted beings: Venus, Jupiter
> and women of full-bodied vintage. (T, 10)

In the description of St Petersburg's Winter Palace there is a significant phrase: '... all else too...' (T, 10) Repeated in the 'Fourth Poem', the same expression creates a juncture at which the poem's mythical, philosophical and meta-lyrical patterns converge. When the protagonist has journeyed back to his origins he encounters, in a blossoming and opening space, the prototype for meta-lyrical structures: a hollow interior where the gods, the myths and femininity are present in full manifestation. The hollow womb of 'the region' is a bodily and mythical prototype containing the germ of the structure for a work of verbal art.

The womb is the model also for the house erected by the writing male. The protagonist's place for writing is situated at a sort of self-created place of origin at the centre of the world: 'This is how far I've got: / the house is in the centre, as far as the table, as far as the paper...' (T, 25) A house as the centre of everything is an archetypal image. In many cultures the symbolism of a house is linked to a cosmic conception. In myths and religions a house is a trope for the universe, believed to be situated at the centre of the world (Chevalier-Gheerbrandt 1982, 603).

In the 'Fourth Poem' the writing-protagonist is evidently revealing his aspiration to imitate such a conception. The mythical and philosophical significances linked to the house throw light on how the protagonist is seeking, as if from a higher quarter, the fundamental principles of writing poetry. He seeks help by calling on, for imitation, powers traditionally thought to have preserved a spark of the original creative energy. In the mythical world-order the erection of an abode (or house) is an imitation of a superhuman work of creation (Eliade 1957, 34). The protagonist as it were sees before him a hollow, feminine, concave space that brings all things to birth. – And this he aspires to imitate.

The writing-process is placed within co-ordinates of time as well as space, both times of day and seasons. The protagonist imagines it as follows: '… and this is a poem I'm writing autumn, at night, alone…' (T, 25) The autumn theme contains thoughts of running out of things to say: it is an autumn of writing and of the mind.

Autumn in *Winter Palace* forms the opposite of spring. Spring is the season of burgeoning green, and birth. These features are particularly evident in the 'First Poem', whose world is as far removed as possible from the conclusion's autumnal atmosphere. An early section makes a particularly good point of comparison: it is filled with greenness, bursting out everywhere. The coming of spring happens at a breathless pace: the chief effect is of a peremptory birth, hurry:

> And it was spring again. Long weeks the woman breathes
> into it and it wails:
>   I'm born, I'm a girl
> and I'll go out alone and play in front of the house. (T, 8.)

Fertile spring is doubtless very far from the autumnal mood the protagonist writes in. But it is precisely the difference that draws him. The spring's vital abundance is an object for imitation: a model for artistic creation, and the erection of a house. The house is also a significant distinguishing factor for the sexual roles. Writing, which is a male activity, takes place in the house, inside four walls; but when, in this section, a ßwoman gives birth to a girl, the house is place to emerge from.

Winter Palace's dramatic structure reaches its culmination in the 'Seventh Poem', which takes the form of a play in five acts. The 'Seventh Poem' creates a world that advances from scene to scene to form a whole. In this poem *Winter Palace* modulates from an epic and narrative poem into a dramatic one. Along with the 'region' reminiscent of a womb, the caryatid is the most effective of the meta-lyrical images created by the protagonist:

> … soft is a woman's skin, when out of her eyes look
>   three unborn ones
> and she doesn't have a name for herself; perhaps
>
>   dancing caryatid, a world-upholding pillar
>   that never wearies. (T, 42)

The 'dancing caryatid' is a character the protagonist creates to uphold the work's verbal architecture. The caryatid sheds light on woman's essential task as a pillar supporting the poem's structure. The woman is a world-upholder in two senses. First, she is the principle of giving birth, a being endowed with mythical dimensions, an Ur-mother; next, she is the supporting structure of the world. She upholds the world and prevents it from collapsing. The caryatid's dance indicates that the foundation moves by rule, according to a certain plan or form; also, perhaps, to a certain rhythm. This rhythm, the arrangement of the parts into a whole, organises the poem into dramatic form.

As it moves forward scene by scene, the poem forms a unified organic body, about which one cannot know '... where the shoulder ends and the breast begins...' (T, 43) The scenes interconnect, forming the poem's unifying bonds, like the limbs of a single body. This integrity and harmony of form is undoubtedly what the world-upholding feminine principle contains and the protagonist aims for. The caryatid's idealised character unites both the demand for solid structure and the necessary mobility. The protagonist fuses the ideals of his world-view with the form of a dramatic poem: the Poem is firm but has a springy rhythm. It speaks to the reader through its animated wholeness.

From a dramatic poem to the threshold of drama

The supporting pillar of the 'Seventh Poem', the dancing caryatid, is presented here as, in my view, the most concrete of the woman-characters that guarantee the poem's unity and wholeness. The caryatid was preceded by a group of other unifying feminine characters that helped the protagonist on his journey through *Winter Palace*. These agents, which influence the plot at its turning points, are either powerful and benevolent oracles ('the exalted being' and the 'rose'), or teachers, like the loquacious and tactical 'beautiful child'. In tracing the conversations between the child and the protagonist I pointed out how learning to converse, and considering conversation conceptually, teach the protagonist how to identify himself.

In studying the conceptions of the feminine in *Winter Palace* I have looked at the occurrences that are most important from the point of view of the plot, those that reveal the changes and the progressive development of the relationships between the sexes. Haavikko's play *The Puppets* has supported my thesis. Comparing the images of women in *The Puppets* and *Winter Palace*, I concentrated on the charged content of the intersexual relations. In particular, the male writer's desire to mould a woman to a 'home-made' ideal is depicted, in both works, with unconcealed irony. The male's attempts to get a durable hold on femininity fail. These tensions ease off when the integrity of the feminine is acknowledged. *Winter Palace*'s links to drama are not confined to the thematic similarity of the female characters and the dramatic form of the 'Seventh Poem'. A closer examination of the work soon shows that several of the poems in fact make use of dramatic structures: dialogues between characters occur, and many stages and stage-sets are erected.

The unifying of poetic and dramatic methods also takes on significance when *Winter Palace* is set against Haavikko's early volumes of the

1950s. Initially Haavikko was identified by the reading public as a purely lyrical poet. After his four volumes, *Tiet etäisyyksiin /Road into the Distances* 1951, *Tuulioinä / On Windy Nights*, 1953, *Synnyinmaa / Homeland*, 1955 and *Lehdet lehtiä / Leaves Leaves*, 1958, there was a surprise. The dramatic *Winter Palace*, and the plays that came out at the same time, *Münchhausen* and *Nuket / The Puppets*, defeated expectations. Now, as contemporary readers, we obviously have a perspective on the writer's subsequent development.[13] It is surely no exaggeration to say that *Winter Palace* already demonstrates the way forward: to the important theatrical and radio plays published in the 1960s.[14]

Translated by Herbert Lomas

NOTES

1. To avoid overlapping concepts this study mainly employs the concept 'feminiiniys' (here translated the feminine). It is a unifying concept, covering both generic and feminine connotations.
2. *Winter Palace* is one of the most important works in post-war Finnish poetry. It received international recognition with the 1984 Neustadt Prize. Regardless of receiving appreciation it has carried for several decades the reputation of being a mysterious and impenetrable work. The poem's thematic material, irony, protagonist, polysemousness and consciousness of tradition have received short allusions and observation in general works on Finnish literary history, but there is an absence of analyses of the work as a whole.
3. The stressing of the factors creating unity does not however imply sealing up the text's semantic openings and hiding them from view. The fragmentation, contrast and breaks are building components of the work. My conclusions concerning *Winter Palace's* structure and interpretation are contained in my study: *A Palace of Words. A Definition of the Protagonist in Pauvo Haavikko's Winter Palace and an Outline of the Work's Unity.*
4. From the point of view of the work's plot, the being's rosaceousness points forward to the 'Fourth Poem', where, in 'the region that's not a place', giving birth and rosaceousness are given the characteristics of inspiration and artistic creation.
5. 'Dialogue' refers to the form of interlocution found in the poem. The terms 'conversation' and 'conception of conversation' are employed when I analyse the exchanges using conversational analysis.
6. Both sexes are contained in the child-character. Femininity is however the dominant facet.
7. When *Winter Palace* were published, *The Puppets*, dated in the late 1950s, had its first night at the Finnish National Theatre on 29 February 1958. It received publication in 1960.
8. The term is a borrowing from Haavikko's prose poem *Age of Iron*. In this poem set in the world of the *Kalevala* the smith Ilmari personifies the artist's, the sage's and the craftsman's hubris. Ilmari wants to conquer death itself: from dream and silver he forges a woman for himself to make up for his dead wife. The fundamentals of Ilmari are basically the same as those of Haavikko's character Gogol in *The Puppets*.
9. The male characters in the play share the names of *Dead Souls*. Another text behind Haavikko's is Tommaso Landolf's short story 'Gogol's Wife', which

Haavikko at first mistook for a genuine biography. The story gives Gogol a blown-up doll as a wife. Landolf's text, however, is a fiction in the form of a biography. For more on Haavikko's play and Landolf's story, see Laitinen (1961) and Vartio (1961).

10 The writer's sharply bipolar relationship to his doll is recorded in the name 'Caracas'. Caracas is a slightly altered version of the English word 'carcass', or its alternative 'carcase'. 'Cara' is Italian for 'beloved'. The termination of the word – 'racas' – is pronounced like the Finnish 'rakas', meaning 'darling'.

11 Continual change characterises *Winter Palace*. I initially pointed out the mutability of the feminine characters and the swift changes in the speech situations, contexts and time relations.

12 It was Tuomas Anhava who pointed out (1973, 415) that the lines contain this allusion.

13 His copious production over five decades has taken ever new directions, including not only poetry volumes and plays, but collections of aphorism, prose, studies of historical themes, biographies and pamphlets on contemporary subjects.

14 *Lyhytaikaiset lainat / Short-term Borrowings* (performed as a radio play 16.9.1966), *Pelto / Field* (performed as a radio play 19.6.1967), *Audun ja jääkarhu / Audun and the Polar Bear* (performed as a radio play 18.12.1967), *Ylilääkäri / The Senior Physician* (published 1968), *Agricola ja kettu / Agricola and the Fox* (first performed at the Helsinki City Theatre 21.11.1968), *Kilpikonna / The Tortoise* (performed as a radio play 6.5.1968) and *Brotteruksen perhe / The Brotterus Family* (first performed at the National Theatre of Finland 19.9.1969)

WORKS BY PAAVO HAAVIKKO

Printed

1951 *Tiet Etäisyyksiin / Roads in the Distances.* WSOY, Helsinki.
1953 *Tuuliöinä / On Windy Nights.* Otava, Helsinki.
1954 *Synnyinmaa / Homeland.* Otava, Helsinki.
1958 *Lehdet Lehtiä / Leaves Leaves.* Otava, Helsinki.
1959 *Talvipalatsi. Yhdeksän runoa / Winter Palace, Nine Poems.* Otava, Helsinki.
1960 *Münchhausen, Nuket / The Puppets. Two Plays.* Otava, Helsinki.
1966 *Puut, kaikki heidän vihreytensä / The Trees, All Their Greenness.* Otava, Helsinki.
1967 *Ylilääkäri / The Senior Physician. Two Plays.* Otava, Helsinki.
1968 *Agricola ja kettu / Agricola and the Fox.* Helsinki, published in the previous volume.
1969 *Audun ja jääkarhu / Audun and the Polar Bear.* In *Kahden vuoden äänet / Voices of Two Years. Finnish Radio Plays 1966–1968.* Ed. Jyrki Mäntylä. Otava, Helsinki.
1970 *Kilpikonna / The Tortoise* In *Äänet myöhässä / Voices Late. Finnish Radio Plays 1966–1968.* ed. Jyrki Mäntylä. Otava, Helsinki.
1982 *Rauta-aika / Iron Age.* Otava, Helsinki.

Duplicated

1966 *Lyhytaikaiset lainat / Short-term Loans.* Radio play. Yleisradio.
1967 *Pelto (Freijan pelto) / Freya's Field.* Radio play. Yleisradio.
1968 *Brotteruksen perhe / The Brotterus Family.* A Play in Three Acts. The Society of Finnish Dramatists.

BIBLIOGRAPHY

ANHAVA, TUOMAS 1873 'Haavikko and the Antique'. *Parnasso* 1973/3.
CHEVALIER, JEAN-GHEERBRANDT, ALAIN 1982/1995 *Dictionnaire Des Symbols. Mythes, rêves, coutumes, gestes, formes, figures, couleurs, nombres*. Éditions Robert Laffont S.A. et Éditions Jupiter, Paris.
ELIADE, MIRCEA 1957 *Das Heilige und das Profane. Vom Wesen des Religiosen*. Rowohlt, Hamburg.
HERACLITUS 1971. *Yksi ja sama / One and the Same*, trans. Pentti Saarikoski. Otava, Helsinki.
KAUNONEN, LEENA 2001 *Sanojen palatsi / Palace of Words. The Definition of the Protagonist and the Outlining of the Unity of the Work in Paavo Haavikko's* Winter Palace. Finnish Literature Society (SKS\ Editions 852, Helsinki.
LANDOLFI, TOMMASO 1958 'Gogol's Wife'. *Encounter*. February 1958.
NABOKOV, VLADIMIR 1944. *Nikolai Gogol*. New Directions Books, Norfolk, Conn.
OVIDIUS NASO, PUBLIUS 1986 *Metamorphoses*. Trans. A.D. Melville. OUP, Oxford, New York.
PLATON 1999 'Timaios'. Translated into Finnish by A.M. Anttila. *Teokset V*. 2nd ed. Otava, Helsinki.

Unpublished Sources

LAITINEN, KAI 1961 'Gogolin nukkevaimo / Gogol's Doll Wife'. Unpublished MS. Summer 1961. SKS Literary Archive.
VARTIO, MARJA-LIISA 1961. Letter 196.1961. SKS Literary Archive.

ABBREVIATIONS (Referring to Finnish editions)

MM =   Ovidius Naso, Publius 1986 *Metamorphoses*
M/N =   1960 Haavikko, Paavo *Münchhausen, Nuket*. Kaksi näytelmää
PKV =   Haavikko, Paavo 1966 *Puut, kaikki heidän vihreytensä*
SKS =   Suomalaisen Kirjallisuuden Seura
T =   Haavikko, Paavo 1959 *Talvipalatsi. Yhdeksän runoa*
YS =   Herakleitos 1971 *Yksi ja sama*. Aforismeja

AULI VIIKARI

Poetics of negation

The forest state

The Horseman (1974)[1], a libretto by Paavo Haavikko, tells the story of a peasant rebellion taking place in Novgorod, between Russia and Sweden. The location identifies the region as Savo, in eastern part of Finland. The leader of the rebels presents his political utopia:

> Thus we will capture the king's manor of Liistonsaari
>   And all that we get
> will be divided at once equally.
>   And the taxes will be paid to the forest state
> which is founded between Russia and Sweden.
>   Its territory will move, move.
> When Russia comes, it will move to the Swedish side,
>   When Sweden comes, it will move to Russia.
> The forest state will move like the forest. (TH, 110)

This story belongs to the tradition of 'writing the nation', beginning with the 19th century classics *The Stories of the Field Surgeon* (1853–1867) by Zachris Topelius and *Seven Brothers* (1870), by Aleksis Kivi and continuing in e.g. the postmodern picaresque novel *Kreisland* (1996), by Rosa Liksom. In *The Horseman*, writing the nation extends to actors and events more or less capable of inhabiting the unrecorded Finnish past. The utopia of the horseman does not come true. His strategy comes to nothing: the rebels bearing branches to resemble a moving forest are shot at the gate of the castle.[2] The sheriff has two hundred grotesque rat-chewed candles, which are lit on the ground for the rebels, in a mock funeral rite attended by fifty armed soldiers.

The Horseman opens the stage for a central theme in Haavikko's output since the sixties – an analysis of power and history, often enacted by a cast of 'real' actors in the history of Finland. This theme occurs frequently in the genres of dramatic, narrative, historical and polemical writings.

The plots of power and history make their first full-scale entry in the 'Finnish Suite' in *Leaves Leaves*[3], 1958, confronting Czar Alexander I, his Grand Duchy and his Finnish subjects. 'Sveaborg', the last poem in the cycle, pleads for freedom of thought as an inalienable human right: "the hen and the sheep agree, / we disagree, so be it, a unanimous nation is out of its wits, / it goes where the horses, hens and sheep are taken" – apparently to the slaughterhouse of history.[4] The poem ends with a statement which may be interpreted as a programme for both politics and poetics: "let the mind (– –) be all clarity and a sheltered unconquerable fortress which surrenders."[5]

For Haavikko, the project of writing the nation has during the last decades moved from historical themes to more recent matters. In 1977, Haavikko published a book called *The Nation's Line. Comments on the Unknown History of an Unknown People 1904–1975.*[6] The manuscript was commissioned by TV channel 2, to celebrate, in the form of a TV series, the 60 years of Finland's independence. The story begins with a short history of settlement and the conflict between two spheres of interest, Novgorod and Sweden – two churches and two future states.

The Nation's Line is, as it were, a more detailed factual version of 'the forest state' in *The Horseman* – with a crucial difference: the story has a happy end. According to Haavikko, the rise of industry, and the national awakening during the age of autonomy as a Grand Duchy of the Russian empire, fostered the art of negotiation and the belief in written documents and treaties in politics. In this reading of Finnish history, Finnish political thought and the current Finnish policy of neutrality both have their origins in the 19th century.

The genre of biography is also used by Haavikko in his project of writing the nation. The voluminous biography of president Urho Kekkonen (*This Stern Century of Mine. The Life and Work of a Statesman 1918 – 1981*, 2000[7]) is his most interesting work in this genre. The role of the writer and the hybridity of the genre itself are announced on the cover. Instead of the usual name of the author, this is a book 'Written down and edited by Paavo Haavikko'. The biography is written in the first person, with quotations from articles, columns and letters written by Kekkonen. The would-be distance between the scribe-editor Haavikko and Haavikko, the Finnish author is emphasised by references to "new literature" (aphorisms by Haavikko) 'cited' by the president; moreover, the president gives his evaluation of the first performance of *The Horseman*: "The music and scenography were good, but the libretto was weak and loosely constructed."[8]

My task of writing a short introduction to Paavo Haavikko's work is doomed to failure by its very volume. Haavikko has published about one hundred books in different genres – lyrical and narrative verse, novels and short stories, aphorisms, biographies and autobiographies, dramatical works for theatre and television, libretti for opera, polemical books, enterprise histories – and the enigmatic radio genre of *Kullervo's Story* – "A Polyphonic Monologue"[9]. Luckily, Haavikko is one of all too few Finnish writers whose works have been translated into foreign languages.

This paper will concentrate on Haavikko's poetry. To begin with, some historical context for discussion is useful.

The opening of the Finnish Mind

The history of the nation retold in *The Nation's Line* concentrates on the political and economic history of Finland. It does not deal with the history of Finnish literature, nor the Finnish language, although these would be the topics usually discussed in an analysis of nation building during the 19th century.

Risto Alapuro, in *State and Revolution in Finland* (1988), while discussing political and cultural modernisation in 19th century Finland, counts Finland among the 'latecoming nations' of Europe – though "a developed region" when compared to Russia[10]. In Finland, the literary establishment itself – secular literature and newspapers, their publishers and the reading public – was a latecoming phenomenon as well. *Seven Brothers* by Aleksis Kivi, the first novel in the Finnish language, was published in 1870 – a fascinating robinsonade of seven brothers to the wilderness and their development into model citizens, thus anticipating the conflicts in the process of modernisation.

A decisive change which took place in Finnish literature in the 1890's was the opening of the Finnish mind to contemporary European culture, as testified by many articles in the present volume. In Finland, cultural and social autonomy preceded national independence fostered by the strengthening measures of Russian regime. During the years of oppression characterised by censorship and measures of Russification, literature, music and the visual arts were important fields of political action, creating new emblems, motifs and characters representing Finland and the Finns. The Paris world exhibition in 1900 showed the artistic independence of the Grand Duchy of Finland, represented by the frescoes of Gallén-Kallela and the music of Sibelius.

As far as poetry is concerned, discussion of the symbolist movement in Finnish periodicals began in 1896. Stéphane Mallarmé's *Crise de vers* (1886) and its call for freedom and individuality of verse language were analysed with insight and enthusiasm in the academic dissertation of Emil Zilliacus as early as 1905. According to Zilliacus (NFPA 283)[11], Mallarmé was the first exemplary representative of "modern symbolism". In her landmark study of French symbolism and Finnish fin de siècle, Annamari Sarajas (EM 102–106)[12] argues, referring to intertextual evidence, that Mallarmé's poetry was known to the major Finnish fin de siècle poets Eino Leino and Otto Manninen.

In the mid 19th century, another opening took place – an opening to the past, to the heritage of oral folk poetry. Its poetics, its metre including alliteration, motifs and generic repertoire gave an imposing lesson in the poetic resources of Finnish language and mythology. In the 1890's, the new generation of poets set out to cultivate new idioms for Finnish verse language. Eino Leino mastered both Kalevala metre and the 'new' folk song earlier neglected – skills which produced both individual innovations and a school for would-be poets. Without this polyglot period, the rapid rise of Finnish poetry from the thicket of translations and adaptations to the Gold Age of the fin de siècle would perhaps not have been possible.

Two poets of the period have since then inspired Finnish poets: Eino Leino and his *Whitsongs* (1903, 1916), their richly orchestrated archetypal images; Otto Manninen and his *Lines* (1905, 1916), exploiting all resources of Finnish in his enigmatic and musical verse. In Manninen's poetry, the obligatory parallelism of traditional Kalevala metre and the sound patterns of alliteration were taught to serve modern verse language and its complexities of meaning.

In Finnish poetry, the meeting of the national and international incentives for 'making it new' recurred once again after the Second World War. In addition to the highly valued 'voice of one's own', in the stock formulation of 1950's, both the fin de siècle and the post-war modernists shared an interest in history and the work of their predecessors. New readings of Finnish classics were on demand – one of the characteristic results were new histories of Finnish literature. The literary life and contacts between Finnish and Finland Swedish writers flourished as well as literary debates. In the 1950's, the literary horizons opened to European and Anglo-American modernisms, likewise to classical Chinese and Japanese literatures.

The young generation of writers and critics has often been characterised as the avantgarde of a new scheme of values – dismissing the collective ideologies of left and right prevalent during the war years and the decades between the two wars. One of its targets was the language using 'hollow abstractions' and contrasts – a "black – white, good – bad, sick – healthy language", in a "divided world", according to Mirkka Rekola, one of the new poets and future classics of the early 1950's.[13] The task of the poet was to use and cultivate an idiom to express individual unadulterated experience, as precisely as possible. Philosophy as a fight against the fascination of the language offered a parallel to the fight of poetry against readymade solutions – the spell of rhyme, rhythm and imagery.

The rise of metalyrical poetry bears witness to a new reflexivity – a new awareness of the relationship between poet, reader and poem. Paavo Haavikko, in one of the metalyrical poems In *Land of Birth* (1955), lets the speaker of the poem describe the Emperor to make the reader see the Emperor – only to tell the reader, in the very next lines, the rules of the game called poetry:[14]

> Now, as I tell you about the Emperor, you see him, the Emperor, in the midst of everything,
> as I tell you about the Emperor, you see: it is Winter, the Emperor's lonely,
> the Emperor is an image that becomes clear when darkness descends,
> the Emperor is an image,
> darkness is descending,
> the fallen trees on the slopes are like an eagle's nest, the dense dryness of branches,

>   the Emperor is alone, and he is clear,
>   he is in his pleasure palace, cold in winter,
>   he is the one you see most clearly in the dark, and thought, bird, horned owl,
>   your blindfolded thought still sees, even in the dark
>   the Emperor,
>
>   (– –)

As a warning against the spell of poetry, the poem begins with a long slightly ironic line, mocking the reader. The first line proves to be a false start – it must be repeated. But in the very next lines, the speaker starts to set his snares – visual details, repetitions of phrase, word, sound, and details. The enchantment is at the same time lost and found by the reader – "the Empire is born and falls in the blink of an eye".

The double perspective is a pattern shared by innovations both in the prose and poetry of the 1950's.[15] Having lost faith in one world and one language, the individual and concrete experience of reality provided the starting point for narrating many kinds of stories. Stories myopically writing down perceptions and fragments, stories embedded in stories or inspired by surrealist heritage. Or they might tell ordinary tales in rural settings, but with a difference: avoiding the abstract and conceptual and sticking to the sensual and physical in a degree approaching the metaphysical.[16]

Concentrating on the art and craft of literature, young writers turned away from yesterday's values. The new found right to individual language was first established in poetry, which became a topic of debate. The young generation was accused of escapism and 'l'art pour l'art' attitudes. The skepticism of Haavikko and the outspoken criticism against this attitude, exemplified in the 'Short Cry' by Eila Kivikkaho, went unnoticed:[17]

>   Do you spend nothing but beauty?
>   Do you dig your home in a treasure
>   like rust
>   and eat it through?

Enter: The Poet

In spite of the many young poets entering the scene in the late 1940's and the lively debate about modernism, the first poems published by Paavo Haavikko took the Finnish reading public by surprise. *Roads into the Distances* (1951) was obviously a modernist book of poetry, but did not resemble any earlier modernist poems, neither in translation nor originally written in Finnish. "Haavikko's debut has sprung from the head of its creator like Pallas Athene from the head of Zeus", said Tuomas Anhava, the mentor of the younger generation, a critic and poet himself.

This image is apt, but literary works are not such autochtonous creatures. The newcomer seemed well-versed in history, especially that of classical antiquity. A distinct early old age, a draft of cool and gusty wind seemed to hover around the well wrought-structures (CFP 116)[18]:

> Every house has many builders and is never finished
> and history and mythical aeons are told over again.
> Contradictory corridors lead to a glimpse of error
> and a memory of the only time-immemorial –
> which the rooms will mutter through to the end.
>
> One day flowers will be grown on the abandoned steps.
> A huge water main will burst and the gates will rust too,
>   and a silver pool will spread.
> Someone will marvel at the idiosyncrasy of the machinery
>   and hunt around for tools,
> laugh at a timetable and spend an epoch of a morning.

Some vague allusions to T. S. Eliot were pointed out by critics – a collection of Eliot's poems, including *Four Quartets* and *The Waste Land* among others, had been published in Finnish 1949[19]. Herbert Lomas[20] (CFP 31) though mentioning some similarities in the poetic devices used by T. S. Eliot and Haavikko makes an acute remark on their supposed 'influence': "He [Haavikko] does not write like Eliot, however, and never did. What he must have found was not so much a model as a licence to commit his own thinking and feeling to paper in their spontaneous order, not to fear obscurity, to be paradoxical, to enlist the creativity of the reader."

As far as Finnish poetry is concerned, the 1940's provided Haavikko with fertile formative years. The shortage of everything did not include books. New Finnish literature, new literary magazines and translations were published, including modern classics such as *The Portrait of the Artist as a Young Man* by Joyce (1916/1946), *La Nausée* (1938/1947) by Sartre, *Der Prozess* (1925/1946) by Kafka. The boom in the book market made publishers scrutinise their backlists as well. As a result, collected poems of practically all Finnish classic writers were published. Aspiring young poets, Haavikko included, had easy access to their heritage, challenging them to separate the wheat from the chaff.

In an interview by Hannes Sihvo[21], Haavikko mentions an interesting fact: the excitement caused by the Finnish translation of *The Iliad*, by Otto Manninen (1919). When later[22] asked why the translation made such an impact, Haavikko emphasised the effect of the mutilation of Finnish syntax – a result of Manninen's adherence to the rules of hexameter. Studying *The Iliad* at an early age perhaps made him aware of the possibilities of syntactic foregrounding.

In their search for the literary background of the new generation, neither critics nor researchers have paid much attention to sources beyond Anglo-Saxon modernism. First hand information given by Tuomas Anhava on the new era of Finnish poetry as early as 1960[23] was neglected. According to Anhava, the decisive change occurred with the discovery of the 'autonomous image', based on the surrealist technique of free association – "The most important new method is the use on free association with its roots in surrealism; this well-known process which produces and combines ideas in a chain has turned out to be an exceptionally rich source of material."[24] Jean-Luc Moreau, in his homage to Haavikko celebrating the 1984 Neustadt laureate, also places his poetry in the tradition of surrealism – especially their quality of sketches, of being "drawn blindfolded"[25]. The effect of this hallucinatory touch in his landscapes and images gains more strength by being immediately followed by everyday comments – implying a change of the speaker's position from that of the surrealist seer to that of the exasperated everyman.

In an unpublished paper given in the late 1950's[26], Tuomas Anhava spells out the difference between the Anglo-Saxon heritage of T. S. Eliot and Ezra Pound, the followers of Mallarmé – and The Third Modernism beginning with Rimbaud, continuing in surrealist poetry and flourishing in the 1950's in the poems of Allen Ginsberg and Erik Lindegren. In Finnish poetry, according to Anhava, Haavikko was the clearest example of this surrealist heritage (T 413).The crucial step was to abandon the idea of metaphor and comparison as instances of transferred meaning, and instead to use images based on sense perception. Anhava singles out a further aspect in new poetry: conceptual and narrative statements were used as "comparable to and in the same way as images." (T 416)

Looking back at his lyrical production, Haavikko singles out the years spent in learning the craft. According to his short and severe survey included in a recent selection of his poems,[27] the period of apprenticeship did last from 1951 to 1966, "working hard to build a poem out of autonomous and meaningful images and sentences, based on my own experience", and make the poems "absolutely clear and easy to understand" – "as if immediately received by the senses". (GG 97) In fact, the very goal of "autonomous" images probably made his poems difficult for their first audience, accustomed as it was to abstractions and meanings spelled out – an altogether different poetic language.

An important change took place in *Land of Birth*, 1955. It is "above all, a book of poetry in spoken language", addressing the reader (GG 97). It consists in cycles of thematically connected lyrical poems, a form cultivated by Haavikko already in his earliest work[28]. The name of the book may have struck its first readers as an omen: the land nothing short of a new continent: The Land of Birth of Poetry. The melodious, capricious long lines did not resemble anything written in Finnish. 'Land of Birth', 'Bird Mountain', 'Fruits', 'Coronation Mass' – the very titles connote fertility, ambiance, feast, high poetry.

The next book mentioned by Haavikko in his short presentation is *Winter Palace* (1959) – "a metaphysical book, speaking by negations" (GG 97).[29] Actually, 'speaking by negations'is characteristic of the spoken quality of *Land of Birth* (1955) and *Leaves Leaves* (1958) as well. In *Land of Birth,* especially the metapoetical poems seem to favour sequences where assertions are presented and then annihilated. (Cf. SP 23, 'Now, as I tell you about the Emperor') On the other hand, the essence of poetry as speech and the conscious effort to make poetry "sound like speech" are emphasised by Haavikko, e.g. in an interview in *Books from Finland,* 1977[30]:

> In my own poetry I have always tried to conform to the rhetoric of speech. I've always been quite clear in my mind about this, ever since I was quite young, I try to shape it into speech; I try it out, and listen, until it really sounds like speech, like someone talking. If you put a poem down on paper and look at it, the whole thing so easily becomes theoretical and you start thinking in terms of metres and feet and so on, things which in real speech don't operate in that mechanical way – it's more a matter of the rhythm of the whole sentence governing the way a thing gets said..Yes, certainly, my own poetry definitely follows the rules of speech; but this doesn't apply to all poetry, by any means.

The spoken quality is easily noticed in Haavikko's use of idiomatic expressions and jargon (of business or politics) but is not reduced to vocabulary. The effect of language as spoken seems to depend on the structure of the verse itself, the long lines built of small segments, mini-sentences, images, ejaculations, linked by contrast as well as equivalence. This "rhetoric of speech" seems to be the common ground for both meaning and the 'music' of his poetry. While sharpening its nuances, Haavikko excels in making use of the minimal features of spoken language. These may resist translation, but the dialogue of segments as well as the sense and the ambivalence of pauses are audible in the following poem. Paradoxically, the profuse use of verbal repetition makes the ambivalence of intonation and meaning more, not less prominent (S CFP 117)[31]:

Odysseus:

    Odysseus: I myself am ten suitors
in my own house, ten years have passed and the sea's black,
I 'm ten suitors and I've lost the sea, it's another man's sea,
the sky's in my eyes always, the sky's jealous, like us,
the sky-walking reapers are jealous, not only of this land, but
    of the sky that's empty; the sky of our thoughts.

    Sea: the seafarer's close to the wrecking stars,
his brow bears copper, silver and hallmarked gold,
his voyage is cursed, never to arrive, his ship's the last,
we were jealous of his wanderings all the ten years
    the land waited for his bones to rest.

    there's sea, he has the sea, the sky
and Penelope, all this weighs less in the scale than his grief,
we were jealous most of his grief, the grief off his brow:
guests invited, all welcome, my house is loud with song:
    I'm Odysseus.

The structure of the long line resembles that of the dialogue in Haavikko's early plays – especially in the first sketch for *Baron Münchhausen* published in the literary journal *Parnasso* (1956, 1). According to Haavikko, the early versions of this play are in some respects thematic corollaries of *Winter Palace* – "the omnipresent Fear" as the common background.[32]

"This is Scene Four, and I'm contriving a poem – / from what? from emptiness?"

In Finnish literature, *Winter Palace* (1959) is one of the very few works belonging to world literature – the only work of poetry to join the company of *Kalevala* and Mika Waltari's *Sinuhe the Egyptian*. With three translations in English, two in French and German, it is one of the very few Finnish works of poetry available to a large international audience. In *World Literature Today* (1984), Kai Laitinen characterised it as "a narrative poem about poetry and as such a rarity, one of the few succesful metapoetical works in postwar Finnish poetry [...] what is most startling, however, is the fact that he seems, clearly and ruthlessly, to see through the confusing plurality of things."[33] The reader is among the things ruthlessly confronted, caught by the fury and ambiance of the text.

Being a metapoetical poem, many problems while reading *Winter Palace* are prophesied by the text itself. What about the genre of the text – "this poem is to be sung standing / or read alone"? (WP 124) Isn't it a bit too much to ask the *reader* "what is the theme of this poem, and is this a poem?" (WP 128) – after bashing the reader and crying for money: "Tourist! Perhaps you don't realise I hardly / recover my expenses on these poems." (WP 123)

In fact, the reader has not been cheated. The poem makes difficult reading from beginning to end, agonizing and rewarding at the same time. This is how it begins (WP 120)[34]:

Silver that I chase images into juxtaposed to make them speak.

The multi-gabled roof is clawed by the winds and the birds,
they're going north – the snow, the birds and the grass;
industry minimal;
     an aerial, an airy flourish or
an ear turned to the wind;
     greetings and a goodbye,
tree tree tree after tree;
this is the song:
(– –)

In 1959, a reader of poetry well-versed in the debates on modernist poetry would have probably nodded approvingly at the "images" chased into silver, the landscape with visible details, and the nice pun of "ear turned to the wind". What followed was quite funny, this greeting, tree and song business – perhaps some kind of Surrealism?[35] But there was an uneasy feeling of being made fun of. The shift of register seemed too crude, too childish. Moreover, in Finnish language 'tree' is 'puu', and repeated four times 'puu' resembled, if anything, any old owl wooing. Neither the ordinary reader nor the conservative critic were too enthusiastic.

After having read the 'Second Poem', the reader who noticed the allusion to Achilles' shield chased with scenes and images of an ordered universe, pays attention to the irony of the allusion. The world of *Winter Palace* obviously was, as they say, 'out of joint': a world inhabited by allegorical figures called Exalted Being, Flying Fox, Rose, Mighty Satan and Fear – "his manners foreign office, his memory absolute zero". The hero's journey from line to line is a quest for "a place which is not" which ends "at the bottom of the heaven" – on earth.

As an object of critical readings and research, *Winter Palace* has not been a very enticing task. In the 1980's, it was analysed in two pioneering studies of Finnish poetry – by Maria-Liisa Kunnas (1981) and Hannu Launonen (1984)[36]. The first full-length study of *Winter Palace*, by Leena Kaunonen, was published as late as 2001. The lag in scholarly reception is understandable. *Winter Palace*, in its disarming honesty, blending together eroticism, history and metaphysics, interspersed with fits of fury against the cliches of the imaginary reader's reactions is a provocation against all stock responses to reality and literature.

Leena Kaunonen, in her study *Palace of Words*[37] presents a solution to the crucial problem during the five decades since the publication of the work: the fragmentary nature of the work. Narrative and scenic elements had been pointed out, as well as the abundance of 'imagery' and metapoetical comment. The genre still remained problematic – was it a collection of poems or a narrative poem?

Kaunonen solves the problem of genre by unravelling the structure of the poem as a travelogue in nine 'poems'. In a painstaking step by step reading, the descriptive passages are analysed as elements of frames of reference – building structural coherence instead of destroying it. The metapoetical comments, on the other hand, serve the quest of the hero of the story, his search for identity. (Cf. Leena Kaunonen's article 'The feminine in Paavo Haavikko's *Winter Palace*' in this volume.) After the important study of Leena Kaunonen, one may hope for renewed interest in Haavikko studies. As for *Winter Palace* itself, the discovery and reconstruction of its early manuscript version illuminates new aspects of the poem – and also some 'possible futures' for Finnish modernism in 1959.[38]

Though placed by Haavikko in the 'first', lyrical phase, *Winter Palace* signals a shift toward a more narrative mode (GG 97). In the second phase, it is the dominant mode. According to Haavikko, narrative poetry is formally the most difficult genre of verse: "It presupposes, that there exists something concretely there to be narrated and that it is narrated in detail, without letting the text submit itself to the lyrical, to nothing."(Ibid 98)[39] In fact, the modal reigns overlap: there are cycles of narrative poems in the last collection of the lyrical phase *The Trees, All Their Greenness*, 1966[40] and aphorisms, characteristic of the third phase in the mainly narrative *Poems from a Journey Across the Straits*,1973.[41]

The first full-length epic poem *Fourteen Rulers*, 1970,[42] begins with a metapoetical speech act: bidding farewell to the muse of poetry. To settle the case for good, the speaker gives his opinion on the impossible task of lyrical poetry: "to combine and collect such difficult things, / as robbing and getting rich, as withering, as flourishing, / being eternal order, unbridled forest, great bitch, / summer grass, barn, barn, apple, pear and brown horse". In *Fourteen Rulers,* the lyrical is tantamount to nothing, a doom repeated in the epilogue for the recent German edition quoted earlier.

The last phase, beginning with *The Darkness* (1984)[43], marks, however, a partial return to the lyrical reign, with aphoristic texs predominating. In *The Poems of Prospero* (2001)[44], lyrical texts no longer strive to obey the impossible commands of the muse. The poems are short, more concentrated, subdued in tone – different from those dominated by the effort to combine incompatibles, characteristic of the first lyrical phase. According to the writer, "their author is extinguished, he is etched by the image, only the poem remains". (GG 98)[45]

Between the camps: the narrative poems

To survive in a bipolar world, one must have a thorough knowledge of the adversary camps, their policies and ways of speech – diplomatic rather than soldierly skills. The basic elements of this scheme of values are presented in the narrative poem *Fourteen Rulers* (1970) by its speaker. His model is Psellus, writer of *Chronography*[46], chronicle of the domestic policies and upheavals under the rule of five 11th century rulers of Byzantium.

Tuomas Anhava, in 'Haavikko and Antiquity'[47], 1973, analyses at length the character of Psellus, as Haavikko's alter ego. According to Anhava, the chronicle and comments of Psellus serve as the most detailed exposition of the survivalist doctrine in Haavikko's writings. The central theme is the analysis and opposition of fascism. In the retrospective analysis of his career as a poet, Haavikko (GG 98) states that *Fourteen Rulers* (1972) and *Poems from the Journey Across the Straits* (1973) are "in their Byzanthine thematics a protest against the political orthodoxy of their time" – against the leftist pro-Soviet movements of the Finnish 1970's. The poem makes a reference to the Year of the Rat in Chinese astrology; as a way of political thinking and strategy – 'the new fascism'. "It was easy to see that the Rat means / direct action, short circuit reasoning, effectivity, / belief in the existence of circumstances and their solution by sleight of hand"[48]. This analysis has perhaps not lost its significance – striking as it does a common chord with the public and private 'anything goes'tendencies of recent times.

For the generation of modernists, the survivalist strategy of Psellus might have served as a model. "His cherished region is the no man's land, deadeningly dangerous yet a soil of possibilities to survive and keep one's ability to act, as far as the narrow site may offer." (Anhava 1973/2002, 452) In addition to individual strategies of survival, the trope of 'no man's land' may refer to the international context of Finnish postwar politics of neutrality.

In his study of Haavikko's plays (*Deep Laughter*, 1977[49]), Aarne Kinnunen points out the decisive role of determinism, cyclicity, and belief in fate in the early plays of Haavikko. These patterns of thought also fashion the plot in the narrative poem *Twenty and One* (1974). It is a chronicle recounting the unholy crusade of 21 Finnish peasants rowing to Byzantium to rob its money-making machine. For Haavikko, *Twenty and One* is the first of his works to recycle the rich material of the national epic *Kalevala* – and perhaps the most adventurous of its kind.

The machine is easily recognised as the Sampo of *Kalevala* – the enigmatic mill forged, stolen and lost in battle between the opposing camps of the epic, led by the mistress of Northland and the heroes of Kaleva.[50] The iconoclast poet turns the world upside down – Northland, 'The North', of *Kalevala* is Byzantium in the south; the robbing crusade lasts three hundred years. Its cast consists of both historical persons (e.g. the two Byzantium empresses Zoe and Teodora, and the Czar Peter) and the twenty-one unknown heroes with archaic names – e.g. Crow's Son, Crooked, Dead Man's Son, Mast, Watercape, Black Cock.

Membership of the crew diminishes throughout the journey, one by one. In contrast to *Kalevala*, where the story ends when the Sampo is lost in a battle at sea, the new heroes continue their quest for easy riches. They set out on a journey to find the source of the Nile, to win the reward promised by Byzanthine emperors. The return home through three centuries of Russian history is an excentric chronicle crowded with personified powers – Tver, Novgorod, Moscow – and actors, tales, details and so on.

The diminished number of the crusaders has been augmented by wives. The four men returning bear the names of their ancestors – Man's Forest, Big Toe, and the Son of the Grandson of Crow's Son. The leitmotif, the moral of the story, is repeated by the chronicler: "Do not hope! / Hope is the most cruel, the most treacherous, the most unyielding among the monsters, / fear the most useful, / hubris destroys everything, / do not hope!" (KY 42)[51]

Some aspects of the moral are developed further in *Poems from a Journey Across the Straits* (1973), the third book of poems with Byzanthine themes and settings. In the cycle of aphorisms called 'In Praise of the Tyrant', the moral is taught in the form of epigrams – here some examples translated by Anselm Hollo (SP 1991, 125–127)[52]:

1.
Twice, three times
    may Fate strike. Thereafter
it's the numb beating the numb.

7.
Plant trees. Exactly against this tree
    may Fascism decisively strike its head.

10.
It has been proposed that the stars should be removed from sight.
    No one has been against that. The proposal has already been accepted.

12.
How decisively
    one's brief moments of clear insight
are ameliorated
    by a good, plausible ideology.

Twenty and One ends quoting the traditional last lines of the Sampo-cycle in its different variants – "That's why this world is poor, the sea rich, because the Sampo fell into the sea."[53] *Twenty and One* makes use of a version of the poem performed in Ingrian dialect – to convey the archaic flavour of the original, some elements of *Beowulf* English might be helpful. The closure mirrors different aspects of the poem, the mixture of languages reminds the reader of the mixture of stories and cultures in the poem. The last lines also present a summary of the plot and moral of the story – history as a story of mankind's futile search for riches and luck existing in the imagination only.

Comparing these two narrative poems, one might ask whether this genre with Homeric and Finnish epic poetry as role models in itself invites a certain world view – perhaps the slightly tautological trinity of determinism, cyclicity and belief in fate analysed by Aarne Kinnunen. Within the genre of narrative poems, *Fourteen Rulers* and *Twenty and One* certainly exemplify different types or variants – the former using the elements of didactic poetry, the latter mixing elements of chronicle, fantasy novel and travelogue – perhaps with a finishing touch of melodrama.

While admitting the factual, Psellus, however, is an exponent of an ideology opposing that of the hope-ridden crusaders of *Twenty and One*. Psellus is by character and profession working within the field of the possible. According to Tuomas Anhava, Psellus is "a personification of Haavikko's ideology of negotiation"(T 452). Which mean that his 'ethos of will', his proairesis, must be realistic, realisable, possible – by more or less impossible means (NH 17): "One has to analyse the situation, set the goals, notice the variables. / And perhaps, if I really think about it, perhaps with acute arguments / it might be possible to twist the wind slightly. / Or at least turn the sails."[54] The counsellor trying to twist the wind with arguments is certainly a pathetic figure. But he is ready to turn the sails, in contrast to the twenty and one crusaders.

The "realm of the possible"– to use an expression coined by the Finland-Swedish author Gunnar Björling – does not sound a glorious enterprise. In *Fourteen Rulers*, Psellus the speaker calculates that his strategy might allow for adaptations on the scale of "perhaps two percent". In the wanderings of the Ugrian proto-Finns – in contrast to the learned counsellor from the centre of Byzantium – destruction, total failure is the fate of impossible yearnings.

In addition to the two epic poems *Fourteen Rulers* (1970) and *Twenty and One* (1974), and the 'metapoetical travelogue' *Winter Palace* (1959), narrative structures appear in cycles of poems –actors, events, the narrator. 'June', a cycle of ten poems in *The Trees, All Their Greenness* (1966) narrates a mental process: becoming aware of the finality of death. The reader participates in the process, unaware of the final absence of the addressee.

The first poem of the cycle sounds like an extract from a casual phone conversation with somebody casually absent: "Do you know, summer's so late / that many trees are still in full bloom."[55] There are frequent references to time in the short poems beginning the cycle – "still", "already", "since then", "now", "Call. Write some time." The places and objects mentioned are also situated in time, in terms of future plans: "I was going to have one drink a night / sitting at that marbletop table, / you were going to keep your things / in the cabinet painted to look like rosewood." (J 102) The cherished details and unrealized plans prepare the reader to the final nevermore. In the fifth poem of the cycle, the outcome is settled by a cliché widely used: "We were always in such a hurry."(J 105)

The next poem places the cycle in a new generic context – the lament songs of Finnish folklore. Laments sung by women while preparing the dead to be buried had two functions: to assist the dead in crossing the final border and accepting its finality, and to provide the community with ways of overcoming the loss and grief. The traditional content of laments, expressions of grief, is here transformed into an inventory of personal memories connected with material objects (J 106)[56]:

> You have that graphite-grey suit, jacket and skirt,
>   the jacket a little pleated, spherical mother-of-pearl buttons
>   on the cuffs,
> the same shoes, stockings, garter belt
>   with embroidered flowers,
>   dark blue bra.
> Not very logical.
>   I also put in the leather-covered powder compact, a stick of black
>   for the eye-brows.
> Even though that always was like blackening the night.
>   But no lipstick, nor any money,
> no comb.
>   Now those appear, and clothes appear,
>   not so many but as if
> many women had suddenly left this place.

The fact of personal and shared memories is expressed with the fewest possible means – one deictic pronoun ("that graphite-grey suit") and some definite articles. This poem is to remind the absent addressee of those memories, not to tell them to those present.

The speakers and narrators of the poetry and fiction written by Haavikko usually assume a male point of view. In 'June', the very details of clothes to be worn when buried indicate a woman's gaze – an intimacy rarely shared by the opposite sex. The same gift of intimacy is characteristic of the novel *Another Heaven and Earth* (Toinen taivas ja maa, 1961). Performing the traditional role of lament singing women, while retaining the male perspective, 'June' reminds the reader of the role-models implied by the lament genre of the cycle. Becoming a shaman, lament singer or writer is not tied to gender: the shaman, the lament singer and the writer share the task of negotiation between the visible and the unvisible world.

The grain of voice

Uniting the genres of Haavikko's poetry, there is a basic unity of voice. It does not mean stylistic unity of texture; rather, it has to do with rhetorics based on temperament and perhaps as well on 'ethos of will' characteristic of Haavikko[57]. To get a new grasp of this aspect, a short discussion of the texture may be useful.

In Haavikko's poetry, the analytic insight of the peculiarities and seeming irrationalities of spoken language is striking. To get a grasp of it, I begin with an example in which the results of his analysis are enacted in an encounter between the leading personae of *Winter Palace*: She and I, the speaker of the poem. I apologise for inserting numbers in order to clarify the following discussion (for the unmutilated text, read WP/SFP 130)[58]:

(– –)
1) I:

2) This is Scene Four, 3) and I'm contriving a poem –
                                      4) from what? 5) from emptiness?
6) A short poem to recite standing up 7) or lying down and alone,
8) and aren't you your house?

9) She:

10) How unsheltered I am, 11) as a world: 12) build the house at once!
(– –)

The exchange is a part of a longer conversation in the 'Seventh Poem', beginning where the narrative mode of presentation of speech gives way to the dramatic mode of oratio recta. Within the exchange between man and woman, other exchanges occur.

The I, as a personal pronoun, identifies the speaker (1), addressing the audience as the party knowing what's going on (2) and announcing his intention of writing a poem. (3). His presentation is cut short by a doubt concerning its topic (4), resulting in self-irony (5). After the 'asides' (4–5), the genre of poem in progress is clarified (6) with alternatives running counter the earlier description (7). In the next move, the male speaker finds a way to answer the earlier request of the woman ("Make this poem into an inexpensive winter home for me"), having postponed the answer while bolstering his position in a simultaneous exchange with his imagined audience [59] (2,3,6,7). Answering a request with a question "aren't you your house?"(8) might be an effort at e.g. moving the discussion from the concrete to the existential level, an effort at taming the shrew ("*aren't* you") or getting rid of the whole issue.

In the first section, there is an unruly shift from one addressee to another – addressing the imagined audience, himself, and the woman. The same restlessness seems to structure the woman's speech. The woman, however, is identified by the other, not by herself (9). Her answer makes clear that she has accepted the first, existential option. The anxious exclamation (10) is followed by a self-description (11) which comes as an after-thought, addressing both the other and oneself – "How unsheltered I am, *as a world*". The equation of the unsheltered subject and the unsheltered world is unexpected and powerful – referring perhaps to human kind in general, not to the power struggle between the sexes.

The next move, the command to "build the house at once" (12) restores the original roles – with a difference. According to Leena Kaunonen in her analysis of 'Seventh Poem', "The feminine power endows the speaker with the the creative power he needs"[60] – after the dialogue discussed above, the speaker makes a promises to build the house and surround it with the sun and the moon and the points of the compass. Moreover, the problems of the work in progress (3–7) seem to be solved (WP 131)[61]:

(– –)
I'm walking through a poetry as open, closed as the decades;

and this was Scene Five; the Seventh Poem.
   The play is over.

The dialogue in seven lines between two participants gives room for voices which imply changes of role, strategy, or world of discourse. The dialogue, however, seems to have one element in common: the assertion is followed by its negation, particularly in the sequence of addressing the other followed by addressing oneself. In the quoted dialogue, the change of addressee is implied by a change of footing from the 'concrete' situation to the metaphysical or existential ("I'm contriving a poem, / – from what? from emptiness?", 3–5, "How unsheltered I am, as a world", 10–11).[62] Turning inward, a shadow of irony, despair, or doubt seems to fall between the assertion and its voicing, making the line bifurcated, double-voiced.

In fact, the role of inner speech and its function as self-criticism seems to be a structure based on Haavikko's idea, or philosophy, of communication. In an interview[63], Haavikko discussed the dialogue in his dramatical texts:

> I realised that a line in drama cannot be as it always was told to be, short, short lines, because no contrast or structure is born that way. My idea is that no tension in dramatic texts is born from talk between people, it is born from everybody's own speech. Disagreeing is fake dramatics, but it's no fake dramatics if I disagree with myself. If I say 'yes, of course', and you say 'no', that's just nothing. I just happened to notice that the tension must be structured in my own speech.

The idea of tension structured in the speaker's own speech is relevant beyond dramatic texts. The monologic sections of *Winter Palace* are nearest at hand. 'Fourth Poem' is the most 'monologic' of the eight long poems – no adressees nor antagonists are mentioned. No 'She', no 'you', 'Flying Fox', 'Mighty Satan' nor 'Beautiful child' around. This is how the poem ends (WP 125)[64]:

(– –)
1 what I want to say is:
2 a small house, narrow, high, and the room I'm writing this in –
3 exaggeration!
4   but I imagine it all happening,
5 and who's not alone and who is not a world?

6 I want to be silent about everything language is about.

7 I want to go back where I belong.

The passage begins energetically (1), in contrast to the apparently futile introspection of the preceding lines – "my ungovernable greed looks sad suddenly, it poured rain / and what is poetry?" Time for something real, e.g. a piece of description! (2) But the effort is offhand dismissed as exaggerated (3). Next, the speaker reminds the reader of something shared by humanity in general "– who's not alone and who is not a world?" – which does not frequently take place in Haavikko's work. The two concluding lines present markedly individual decisions. In the quoted sequence, the contrast of the beginning ('I want to say') and end ('I want to be silent') follows the pattern of affirmation -negation which gains additional emphasis by being part of the closure of 'Fourth Poem'.

Reading *Winter Palace* seems to be a work in progress which might make some progress when studied on interdisciplinary basis. 'Poetics of negation' might also serve as a hypothesis for comparative studies in stylistics and literary history. A recent thesis by Sari Salin[65] on irony and doubling in Jorma Korpela's novels written in the 'no man's land' after the Second World War, pays attention to "the peculiar ironic style, in which the narrator (or character) first affirms and then negates (or vice versa) the one and the same thing" – an interesting parallel to the 'poetics of negation'

The epigram is the traditional stage for 'disagreeing with oneself', a genre favoured by Haavikko since the 1970's. The first epigram in the cycle 'In Praise of the Tyrant' (cf. 1, p.16) begins with a remark on the habits of bad Fate; the 'negation', the characteristic point of the epigram mocks the "numb" Fate: no use beating a victim already numb. The genre gives room for spoken language intimacy as well (RMSY 47)[66]:

> Good night.
>   Yes. Plenty of darkness.

Here, the few words leave the voicing of the words and the pauses completely up to the reader. The effort at filling the gaps with more words would be beside the point. Everyday language, its cliches, meanings, with their from tender to morbid options, are written down in the polyphony of the texture. As usual, the polyphonic text is open to a variety of individual performances. Due to the minimalist text, the point of the epigram 'lasts' longer. [67] In contrast to some poets of his generation, the Japanese haiku or tanka have not inspired Haavikko as generic models.

Markku Envall, in his study of Finnish aphorism, the prose parallel of epigram[68], pays attention to structures resembling the 'poetics of negation' in *Winter Palace*. Haavikko's irony, e.g. is "illustrated in the way he disappoints the reader's expectations by turning the titles of his books upside down in the text"[69]. *Speak, Answer, Teach,* 1972, exploits the venerable didactic tradition of the genre by a title 'promising' to speak, answer, and teach, in order to reveal its 'true' nature.

Dionysos Orpheus Psychopompos

In *Fourteen Rulers* (NH 5), the speaker dismissed the muse of lyrical poetry, and its task to combine incompatible things – "as robbing and getting rich, as withering, as flourishing, / being eternal order, un

bridled forest, great bitch, summer grass" and so on. Some of the combinations are antithetical in the same manner as 'wanting to say' and 'wanting to be silent', or 'poetry open, closed'(WP 130). They are oppositions anticipating each other as withering and flourishing do.

In spite of the delight of the epigram writer at nasty antitheses, the muse of Haavikko's poetry seems to want something else as well. What about the tensions within the speaker's own speech, this "saying against oneself" – wouldn't they foster the same kind of fake dramatics the writer now condemns? In that case, the decision "to be silent about everything language is about" (mentioned in 'Fourth Poem') would be the solution. The problem with fake dramatics and 'poetics of negation' is apparently the same as with their philosophical counterpart, contradiction. Both tautology and contradiction fill "the whole logical space and leave[s] no point to reality."[70]

Instead of reality, world is a recurring concept in Haavikko's poems. One of them, included in many editions of a secondary school coursebook of Finnish and Finnish literature, may be the best known and most analysed poem by Haavikko – "as a world comparable to other worlds / I am shipwrecked against other worlds" (*Roads to Distances,* 1951)[71]. In the following poem, reality is palpably present in the encounter of the speaker with a non-allegorical creature[72] (PKHV/TATG 138):

> You can be certain that it itself,
>   not another,
> no one else,
>   has been introduced to you:
>
> the world itself:
>   it's not some allegorical creature
>   celebrating ancient rites,
> and that's why you couldn't quite catch its name,
>   sfor it talks confusingly fast
> and about everything at once.

But didn't we quite recently meet something similar, some*one* of the same kind? It was in fact the dismissed muse of lyrical poetry, that fluent all-embracing babbler. The difficulty of jotting down this world broadcast was bravely faced by Haavikko in the interview quoted earlier (p. 206): "OK, I thought, people, events, things always interrupt each other, but a long line is the only possibility to tell something about the world, those people and the tensions between them."[73]

How to solve the problem of writing the world language, how to equal its confusing fastness and incompatible couplings? One solution is presented in the very beginning of 'First Poem' – the well-wrought 'chased images' followed by nonsense strings of language – "tree tree tree and tree" and so on. (WP 120) Later on, e.g. in 'Eighth Poem', this dimension is fostered by surrealist chains of images – "I'm here already, / a walking plant, a cock's stride and a soul, with no children." (WP 132) In the same poem, nonsense jingles with a foregrounded sound pattern serve the same function.[74] They perform one aspect of world language: discontinuity, the abortive interruptions. On the level of poetics, these language strings are autonomous segments, 'speech acts'of verbal play comparable to autonomous images.

For vernacular readers of Haavikko, the sound patterns in his poetry open access to the simultaneity of world language. However, the examples above show that sound patterns may also function as an independent level of poetic structure in Haavikko's poetry. They represent the Orphic and Dionysic dimension of his verse, in service of the capricious muse of lyrical poetry herself – in service of the poetic function, to put it more crudely. This gift as well as the power of images has inspired the poem 'Dionysos Orfeus Psykhopompos' dedicated to Haavikko by Eeva-Liisa Manner[75] – a visionary and innovator of Finnish poetry herself.

Due to the volume and scope of his work, the Finnish readers probably have quite different versions of the author called Paavo Haavikko – varying from the modern classic to the writer of polemical columns. In this special case, the experts are not different from the the Finnish reading public. *World Literature Today, Homage to Paavo Haavikko, Our 1984 Neustadt Prize Winner* (Autumn 1984) is not an exception.[76]

Kirsti Simonsuuri, in 'The Lyrical Space of Haavikko's Poetry', presents an interesting argument. Following distinctions presented by Jean Paulhan, she compares Paavo Haavikko, Pentti Saarikoski and Eeva-Liisa Manner on the basis of their use of language. The "terrorists" exemplify "pure and original inspiration at the expense of language", exemplified by surrealists and symbolists. The "rhetoricians"emphasize mutual understanding, taste and decorum. According to Simonsuuri, Haavikko, "in contrast with most modernists in Finland such as Saarikoski and Eeva-Liisa Manner, would be in the category of the 'rhetoricians'" (WLT 525).

Is Haavikko "Finland's classical poet par excellence"? In fact Haavikko, on condition of forgetting the latinate superlative, exemplifies some classical virtues – above all, the clarity of expression. The "world itself" may speak confusingly fast, but all things considered, Haavikko's effort to master world language aims at clarity. On the other hand, his generic repertoire includes the classical genres 'par excellence' – the didactic epigram and satire. His gift as a writer might be his readiness to use the means of verbal 'terrorism' in the service of classical virtues.

NOTES

1 Paavo Haavikko, *Ratsumies / The Horseman* (Lahti, 1974). Translated by Philip Binham.
2 The 'moving forest', an allusion to the 'moving' Lusignan forest in *Macbeth*, acts as a prophesy of the Horseman's fall, and perhaps as well to the 'driftwood theory', used to characterise Finnish foreign policy in 1941.
3 Paavo Haavikko, 'Suomalainen sarja', *Lehdet lehtiä* (Helsinki, 1958) = LL
4 The original Finnish quote: "kana ja lammas yhtä mieltä, / olemme erimieliset, hyvä niin, yksimielinen kansa on mieletön, / se menee kunne hevoset, kanat ja lammas viedään". (LL 30)
5 The original Finnish quote: "olkoon (– –) mieli täynnä kirkkautta ja varustettu valloittamaton / linnoitus joka antautuu." (LL 30)
6 Paavo Haavikko, *Kansakunnan linja. Kommentteja erään tuntemattoman kansan tuntemattomaan historiaan 1904–1975* [The Nation's Line. Comments on the Unknown History of an Unknown People] (Helsinki, 1977) = KL
7 Paavo Haavikko, *Tämä minun ankara vuosisatani. Valtiomiehen elämä ja toiminta 1918–1981*. Kirjannut ja toimittanut Paavo Haavikko [This Stern Century of Mine. The Life and Work of a Statesman] (Helsinki, 2000) = TMAV
8 The original Finnish quote: "Musiikki ja lavastus olivat hyviä, mutta teksti eli libretto oli heikko ja hatara." TMAV 250.
9 Paavo Haavikko: *Kullervon tarina Kullervo's Story*. Moniääninen monologi. A polyphonic monologue. Translated from the Finnish by Anselm Hollo (Helsinki, 1989).
10 Cf. Risto Alapuro, *State and Revolution in Finland* (Berkeley and Los Angeles,1988), 19–39.
11 Emil Zilliacus: *Den nyare franska poesin och antiken* [New French Poetry and Antiquity] (Helsingfors, 1905).
12 Annamari Sarajas: *Elämän meri. Tutkielmia uusromantiikan kirjallisista aatteista.* [The Ocean of Life. Studies in the Literary Ideas of Neo-romanticism] (Porvoo, 1961).

13 Mirkka Rekola, 'Kehä joka murtuu'. *Muistinavaruus. Kirjoituksia, puheenvuoroja 1959–1999.* ['The Breaking Circle'. In: The Space of Remembrance.] (Juva: 1999), 97–98.
14 Paavo Haavikko, *Synnyinmaa.* Runoja. (S.a./S.l.), 21. [Land of Birth. Poems.] The original Finnish quote: "Kun nyt kerron keisarista näet hänet, keisarin, kesken kaiken, / kun nyt kerron keisarista, näet: talvi on, keisari yksinäinen, / keisari on kuva joka käy selväksi hämärässä, / keisari on kuva, / hämärä on tulemassa, / on ryteikkö rinteillä kuin kotkanpesä, oksien tiuha kuivuus, / ja keisari on yksin ja hän on kirkas, / hän on huvilinnassa joka on kylmä talvella, / hän on se jonka näet pimeässä selvimmin, ja ajatus, / lintu, huuhkain, sokko ajatuksesi sentään näkee myös pimeässä / keisarin.(– –). Translated from the Finnish by Anselm Hollo, in *Selected Poems* (Manchester, 1991), 23.
15 Auli Viikari, 'Ei kenenkään maa'. *Avoin ja suljettu. Kirjoituksia 1950-luvusta suomalaisessa kulttuurissa.* Toim. Anna Makkonen.(Helsinki, 1992) ['No Man's Land'. Open and Closed. Essays on the 1950's in Finnish Culture] Ed. Anna Makkonen.
16 Cf. Tuula Hökkä, 'Modernismi: uusi alku – vanhan valtaus'. In: *Suomen kirjallisuushistoria 3 Rintamakirjeistä tietoverkkoihin.* Toim. Pertti Lassila (Vammala, 1999) ['Modernism; a New Beginning – Occupying the Old'. In: Finland's History of Literature 3. From Letters from the Front to the Web.] Ed. Pertti Lassila (Vammala,1999), 68–89.
17 Eila Kivikkaho, 'Välihuuto'. *Niityltä pois* ['Short Cry'. Out of the Meadow] (Porvoo, 1951). The original Finnish quote: "Pelkkää kauneuttako kulutat? / Aarteeseenko kaivat asuntosi / kuin ruoste / ja syöt sen rikki?" Translated by Herbert Lomas in CFP, 63.
18 Paavo Haavikko,'Jokainen talo on monien rakentama' *Tiet etäisyyksiin* [Roads into the Distances] (Porvoo,1951), 19. The original Finnish quote: "Jokainen talo on monien rakentama eikä koskaan valmis / ja historia ja myyttiset vaiheet kerrotaan uudelleen. / Ristiriitaiset käytävät johtavat tajuamaan erehdystä / ja muistamaan ainoata muinaisuutta, / jota huoneet kaikuvat lävitse loppuun saakka. // Kerran kasvatetaan hylätyillä portailla kukkia. / Suuri vesijohto halkeaa ja portit ruostuvat kiinni / ja hopeainen lammikko laajenee. / Joku ihmettelee koneistojen yksilöllisyyttä / ja etsii työkaluja, / nauraa aikatauluja ja viettää aamupäivän aikakautta." – Translated from the Finnish by Herbert Lomas.
19 T. S. Eliot, *Autio maa.* Neljä kvartettia ja muita runoja.[The Waste Land. Four Quartets and other Poems] (Helsinki, 1949).
20 Herbert Lomas, Introduction. In: *Contemporary Finnish Poetry.* Edited and translated by Herbert Lomas (Glasgow,1991) 31.
21 Interview of Paavo Haavikko by Hannes Sihvo, 25.2.1978.
22 Interview of Paavo Haavikko on the rhythmical structures in his early poetry, April 1984, recorded by the writer.
23 Tuomas Anhava, 'Den finska diktens förnyelse' [The renewal of Finnish Poetry] *Horisont* 1960, 2. The original Swedish quote: "Den mest betydande nya metoden är bruket av fri association, vilket ursprungligen utgått från surrealismen; den för alla välbekanta process, i vilken föreställningar föds och förenas i en kedja, har visat sig vara en oerhört givande källa till stoff."
24 Cf. Auli Viikari,'Ei kenenkään maa'. *Avoin ja suljettu. Kirjoituksia 1950-luvusta suomalaisessa kulttuurissa,* toim. Anna Makkonen (Helsinki, 1992) [No man's land'. In: The Open and the Closed, Essays on the 1950's in Finnish Culture, edited by Anna Makkonen].
25 Cf. Jean Luc Moreau, 'Premier pas vers les lointains' *World Literature Today,* Autumn 1984, 533.
26 The paper is published posthumously in Tuomas Anhava, *Todenkaltaisuudesta. Kirjoituksia vuosilta 1948–1979.* Toim.Helena ja Martti Anhava (Keuruu, 2002) [On Verisimilitude. Writings from the Years1948–1979] Edited by Helena and Martti Anhava. The original Finnish title of the paper 'Selittämättä selvää' resists translation; some approximations: 'To put it straight', 'Just plain facts'.

27 Paavo Haavikko, 'Nachwort 14.3.1996'. *Gedichte! Gedichte.* Aus dem Finnischen von Gisbert Jänicke. (Salzburg und Wien, 1997), 97–98.
28 'Earliest work' refers to two cycles included in the edition *Runot 1949–1974* [Poems 1949–1974] (Keuruu, 1974): 'Sillat' [The Bridges] (1949–1950), 'Maanosa'[The Continent] (1951–1952) and 'Juhlat' [Feasts], published earlier in *Runot 1951–1961* [Poems 1951–1961] (Helsinki, 1963).
29 *Leaves Leaves* (1958) is not mentioned in this presentation. Its ironic comments e.g, on the writer's craft, erotics, historical and global themes and personages mark the way to *Winter Palace* (1959) and the later books of aphorisms.
30 Aarne Kinnunen, 'The writer and his work. An interview with Paavo Haavikko' *Books from Finland* XI:3, 1977.
31 Paavo Haavikko, 'Odysseus'. In: *Synnyinmaa* [Homeland] (Keuruu, 1955), 7. Translated by Herbert Lomas CFP 117. The original Finnish quote: "Odysseus: minä itse olen myös kymmenen kosijaa / omassa talossani, kymmenen vuotta on kulunut ja meri on musta, / minä olen kymmenen kosijaa ja meren olen menettänyt, se on toisen miehen meri, / taivas on silmissä aina, taivas on kade, meidän kaltaisemme, / taivaalla kulkevat elonleikkaajat kadehtivat, paitsi nyt tätä maata, myös / taivasta joka on tyhjä: ajatuksemme taivaalla. // On meri, merenkulkija on lähellä turmion tähtiä, / hänen otsallaan on kuparia, hopeaa ja leimattua kultaa, hänen retkensä on kirottu, hän ei tule koskaan, hänen laivansa on viimeinen pursi, / me kadehdimme harharetkiä kaikki kymmenen vuotta, / jotka maa odotti hänen luittensa lepoa, // on meri, hänellä on meri, taivas / ja Penelope, kaikki tämä ei paina vaakakupissa enempää kuin hänen murheensa, / enin kadehdimme hänen murhettaan, murhetta hänen otsaltaan: / vieraat kutsutut, kaikki tervetulleet, taloni on laulukas: olen Odysseus."
32 Haavikko in an interview on 21.3.2003. When asked to specify "the fear", Haavikko reminded me of the fairly recent presence of the Soviet military authorities in Helsinki and the fear of communist take over.
33 Kai Laitinen, 'Introduction to Paavo Haavikko's Poetry', *World Literature Today* 58:4, 521 –524.
34 Paavo Haavikko, *Talvipalatsi. Yhdeksän runoa* (Helsinki, 1959)=T [Winter Palace. Nine Poems] Translated by Herbert Lomas, in *Contemporary Finnish Poetry* (Glasgow, 1991) 120–133. =WP – The original Finnish quote: "Hopeaa johon pakotan kuvia vierekkäin / niin että ne puhuvat; // monitaitteinen katto raatelee tuulet ja linnut, / pohjoiseen menee lumi, linnut ja ruoho, / teollisuus vähäistä, // antenni, ilmava koukero tai / tuuleen viritetty korva, / terveisiä ja hyvästi, / puu puu puu ja puu, / tämä on laulu:" (T 1959, 7).
35 In Finland, surrealism in poetry had been discussed by Aaro Hellaakoski in his article 'Vapaasta ja sidotusta'. *Kuuntelua. Esseitä teoksista ja tekijöistä* (Porvoo, 1950) ['On Free and Bound'. Listening. Essays on Works and Authors.]; the term had been used as a positive characterisation by literary critics in the leftist periodical *40-luku* [The 40's] 1945–1947.
36 Maria-Liisa Kunnas, *Muodon vallankumous. Modernismin tulo suomenkieliseen lyriikkaan 1945 – 1959* [The Revolution of Form. The Arrival of Modernism in Finnish Poetry 1945 – 1959] Suomalaisen Kirjallisuuden Seuran Toimituksia 372 (Helsinki, 1981). – Hannu Launonen, *Suomalaisen runon struktuurianalyysia. Tutkimus Jaakko Juteinin, Aleksis Kiven, Otto Mannisen, Eino Leinon, V.A.Koskenniemen, Uuno Kailaan, Kaarlo Sarkian, Tuomas Anhavan, Paavo Haavikon ja Pentti Saarikosken lyriikasta.* [An Analysis of Some Structural Features in Finnish Poetry. A Study in the Poetry of Jaakko Juteini, Aleksis Kivi, Otto Manninen, Eino Leino, V.A.Koskenniemi, Uuno Kailas, Kaarlo Sarkia, Tuomas Anhava, Paavo Haavikko and Pentti Saarikoski.] Suomalaisen Kirjallisuuden Seuran Toimituksia 396 (Helsinki, 1984).
37 Leena Kaunonen, *Sanojen palatsi. Puhujan määrittely ja teoskokonaisuuden hahmotus Paavo Haavikon 'Talvipalatsissa.* [Palace of Words. Problematics of

the Speaker and Textual Coherence in *Winter Palace* by Paavo Haavikko] (Helsinki, 2001).

38 Due to Haavikko's almost illegible handwriting, the published reconstruction by the author *Talvipalatsi. Varhaisversion rekonstruktio vuodelta 1959.* [Winter Palace. Reconstruction of the Early Version from 1959] (Jyväskylä, 2001) is incomplete. Moreover, an earlier manuscript of the work, 634 pages, also written in 1959, has been delivered to the archives of The Finnish Literature Society. – For comments on the manuscripts, cf. Auli Viikari, *Jälkisanat* [Afterword].

39 For a comprehensive analysis of the sources used by Haavikko while working on *Fourteen Rulers* and *Twenty and One,* see Hannes Sihvo, *Soutu Bysanttiin. Paavo Haavikon metodin ja maailmankuvan tarkastelua.* [Rowing to Byzantium.A Critical Study of Paavo Haavikko's Method and World-View] Suomalaisen Kirjallisuuden Seuran toimituksia 356 (Joensuu, 1980).

40 Paavo Haavikko, *Puut, kaikki heidän vihreytensä.* [The Trees, All Their Greenness] (Helsinki, 1966) =PKHV.

41 Paavo Haavikko, *Runoja matkalta salmen yli.* [Poems from a Journey Across the Straits] (Helsinki, 1973).=RMSY.

42 Paavo Haavikko, *Neljätoista hallitsijaa.* [Fourteen Rulers] (Keuruu, 1970).=NH. – The original Finnish quote: "yhdistellä ja koota niin hankalia asioita, / kuin rosvota ja rikastua, kuin kuihtua, kuin kukoistaa, / olla ikuinen järjestys, hillitön metsä, suuri narttu, / kesäinen heinä, lato, lato, omena, päärynä ja ruskea hevonen". Translated by the writer.

43 Paavo Haavikko, *Pimeys* [The Darkness] (Porvoo, 1984).

44 Paavo Haavikko, *Prosperon runot* [The Poems of Prospero] (Pieksämäki, 2001).

45 The original German quote: "Ihr Autor ist ausgelöscht, aus dem Bilde geätzt, nur das Gedicht ist übrig." Aus dem Finnischen von Gisbert Jänicke. – This essay concentrates on the poetry of the first and second phase, available in English. *The Poems of Prospero* are available in German, translated by Gisbert Jänicke in *Gedichte! Gedichte* (Salzburg, 1997).

46 Mikael Psellus, *Fourteen Byzantine Rulers. The Chronographia of Michael Psellus.* Translated, with an introduction by E,R,A. Sewter (Bungway, 1966).

47 Tuomas Anhava: 'Haavikko ja antiikki' (1973/2001) *Todenkaltaisuudesta. Kirjoituksia vuosilta 1948 – 1979.* Toim. Helena ja Martti Anhava, s. 435–454. ['Haavikko and Antiquity'. On Verisimilitude. Writings from the years 1948–1979. Ed. Helena and Martti Anhava] (Keuruu, 2002).

48 The original Finnish quote: "Oli selvästi nähtävissä että Rotta tarkoittaa / suoraa toimintaa, lyhyitä johtopäätöksiä, tehokkuutta, / uskoa että on asioita ja että ne ovat nopealla liikkeellä ratkaistavissa", NH 16.

49 Aarne Kinnunen: *Syvä nauru. Tutkimus Paavo Haavikon dramatiikasta.* Suomalaisen Kirjallisuuden Seuran toimituksia 331 (Forssa, 1977). [Deep Laughter, On the Dramatic Works of Paavo Haavikko].

50 For a short introduction, see *Finnish Folk Poetry Epic*, Commentary. The Sampo. (Helsinki,1977), 525–529.

51 The original Finnish quote: "Älä toivo! / Kaikista hirviöistä toivo kaikkein julmin, katalin, / sitkein, / pelko hyödyllisin, hybris kaiken tuhoava, / älä toivo!" *Kaksikymmentä ja yksi* [Twenty and One] (Keuruu, 1974), 42. Translated by the writer.

52 'Tyrannin ylistys', in: *Runoja matkalta salmen ylitse.* ['In Praise of the Tyrant', in: Poems from a Journey Across the Straits] (Helsinki, 1973), 29–36. The original Finnish quotes: "1. / Kahdesti, kolmesti voi kohtalo lyödä. / Sen jälkeen lyö tunnoton tunnotonta." // "7. / Istuta puita. Juuri tähän puuhun / voi fasismi ratkaisevasti lyödä päänsä." / "10. On ehdotettu että tähdet olisi poistettava näkyvistä. / Sitä ei ole vastustettu. Se on jo hyväksytty."/ "12. Miten ratkaisevasti lyhyitä selvänäköisyyden hetkiä / lieventää hyvä, uskottava ideologia." Translated by Anselm Hollo (SP 125–127).

53 The quote in original Finnish: "sendäh on tämä maailma köyhä, meri pohatta, / kun samppu mereh kaatui." The quote apparently is a hybrid construction of dialect and Finnish. The closing formula – as well as the plot – differs from those of the versions quoted in FFPE 110–134. The outcome in the KY version echoes the earliest forms of the poem which "appear to refer to the fertility of the sea (– –) and the implication that the sea is more fertile than the land" (FFPE 526). – According to Johanna Pentikäinen, in *Myth and Mythic in Paavo Haavikko's 'Kaksikymmentä ja yksi', 'Rauta-aika' and 'Kullervon tarina'* (Ph.D.Diss, University of Helsinki 2002), "the use of archaism (*sendäh on tämä maailma köyhä...*) connoting poverty makes the mythical darkness of Pohjola cover the known reality in its entirety" (MMPH 119).
54 The quote in original Finnish: "On tavoiteltava mahdollista. Käytettävä mahdottomia keinoja. / On katsottava tilanne, asetettava päämäärä, todettava muuttujat. / Ja ehkä, jos mietin tarkoin, on selvin argumentein / mahdollista hiukan kääntää tuulta edullisemmaksi. / Tai ainakin purjetta." *Neljätoista hallitsijaa.* [Fourteen Rulers] (Keuruu, 1970) 17. The quote translated by the writer.
55 Paavo Haavikko, 'June'. *Selected Poems* (Manchester, 1991), 101–110. Translated from the Finnish by Anselm Hollo. Carcanet 1991, 101.
56 The quote in original Finnish: "Sinulla on se grafiitinharmaa puku, jakku ja hame, / pieni rypytys jakussa, pallomaiset helmiäisnapit hihansuissa, / ne samat kengät, sukat, sukkanauhaliivit / joihin oli kudottu kukkia, / tummansiniset rintaliivit. / Ei kovin paljon johdonmukaisuutta. / Panin mukaan nahkapäällysteisen puuterirasian, puikon mustaa / kulmakarvoja varten. / Vaikka ne olivat aina kuin olisi mustannut yötä. / Mutta ei huulipunaa, eikä nyt rahaa, / ei kampaa. / Niitä löytyy nyt, ja tulee esille vaatteita, / ei niin paljon mutta niin / kuin monta naista olisi äkkiä lähtenyt täältä." *Puut, kaikki heidän vihreytensä* (Helsinki, 1966) 124.
57 'Ethos of will' is a concept coined by Tuomas Anhava (T 443/2002), in his article 'Haavikko and Antiquity', to characterise the dimensions of motion and space in early Haavikko.
58 The quote in original Finnish: "Minä: // Tämä on neljäs kohtaus ja minä rakennan runoa, / mistä? tyhjästäkö? / lyhyttä runoa puhuttavaksi seisaalta / tai makuulta ja yksin, / ja etkö sinä ole talosi? // Se: // Miten turvaton olen, maailma, / rakenna äkkiä talo." *Talvipalatsi* [Winter Palace] (Helsinki, 1959) 43–44. Translated by Herbert Lomas WP/CFP 130.
59 In original Finnish, the 'I' is "building", not "contriving" a poem, which makes (3) sound more of an answer to the woman's request.
60 Leena Kaunonen: *Sanojen palatsi. Puhujan määrittely ja teoskokonaisuuden hahmotus Paavo Haavikon 'Talvipalatsissa'.* [Palace of Words. Problematics of the speaker and textual coherence in *Winter Palace* by Paavo Haavikko.] Suomalaisen Kirjallisuuden Seuran Toimituksia 852 (Helsinki, 235).
61 The original Finnish quote: "runoutta minä kuljen lävitse, avointa, suljettua / kuin vuosikymmenet, // ja tämä oli viides kohtaus; seitsemäs runo, / näytelmä on lopussa." (TP 45)
62 My discussion of the conversational encounters in Haavikko's *Winter Palace* is inspired by Erving Goffman's approach and analysis in *Forms of Talk* (Oxford, 1981).
63 An interview with Haavikko on the rhythmical structures in his early poetry, April 1984, recorded by the writer.
64 The original Finnish quote: "minä tahdon kertoa: / pieni talo, kapea, korkea ja huone jossa / minä kirjoitan tätä, / liioittelua! / mutta kuvittelen että kaikki tapahtuu / ja kuka ei ole yksin ja kuka ei ole maailma? // Minä tahdon vaieta kaikesta mistä kieli on. // Minä tahdon takaisin sinne mistä olen kotoisin." (TP 25–26) – In the late 1950's, with recent articles on Wittgenstein's *Tractatus* and *Philosophical Investigations* by Jaakko Hintikka, *Winter Palace* (e.g. "I want to be silent about everything language is about.") also aroused interest due to its 'philosophy of language'.
65 Sari Salin, *Hullua hurskaampi. Ironinen kahdentuminen Jorma Korpelan romaaneissa.* [Holier than Madman. Irony and Doubling in Jorma Korpela's nov-els] (Vantaa, 2002).

66 The examples mentioned have been published in Paavo Haavikko, *Runoja matkalta salmen ylitse* (Keuruu, 1973). For quotes (1,7) in original Finnish see p. Translated by Anselm Hollo in SP 125, 126. For 'Good night', the quote in original Finnish: "Hyvää yötä. / Niin. Paljon pimeyttä." RMSY 47, translated by the writer.
67 Cf. Barbara Herrnstein Smith, *Poetic Closure. A Study of How Poems End* (Chicago, 1968), 196–218.
68 Markku Envall: *Suomalainen aforismi. Keinoja / Rakenteita / Lajeja / Ongelmia* [Finnish Aphorism. Means / Structures / Problems] Suomalaisen Kirjallisuuden Seuran Toimituksia 450 (Helsinki, 1987).
69 Markku Envall: 'Haavikko the Aphorist: Philosopher, Ironist and Oracle'. In: *World Literature Today*, 58:4 (Norman, Oklahoma, 1984), 556–557.
70 Ludwig Wittgenstein: *Tractatus Logico-Philosophicus*. 4.463, third chapter: "Tautology leaves to reality the whole infinite logical space; contradiction fills the whole logical space and leaves no point to reality. Neither of them, therefore, can in any way determine reality."(London, 1958) 99.
71 Paavo Haavikko, *Tiet etäisyyksiin. Runoja* [Roads into the Distances] (Porvoo, 1951), 41. The original Finnish quote: "maailmana maailmojen veroisena / haaksirikkoudun muita maailmoja vastaan."
72 Paavo Haavikko, *Puut, kaikki heidän vihreytensä* [The Trees, All Their Greenness] (Helsinki, 1966), 112. The original Finnish quote: "Voit olla varma että se itse, / ei joku toinen, / on esitelty sinulle, / maailma itse, / se ei ole joku allegorinen olento / joka suorittaa vanhoja menoja, / ja siksi sinä tuskin olet saanut selvää kun se on sanonut nimensä, / sillä se puhuu, epäselvästi ja nopeasti ja / kaikista asioista yhtä aikaa."
73 Interview on the rhythmical structures in Haavikko's early poetry, April 1984. Recorded by the writer.
74 E.g. "On KURKi aRKa KyLmÄLLe ja hUUteLI tÄnne pUIta." (TP 51) In English: A crane is shy of cold and was calling the trees to come. (CFP 132) – In Finnish, the jingle quality of the language string is produced by its mainly iambic metre, deviating from the free verse context.
75 Cf. Herbert Lomas, 'Introduction' CFP 19–23.
76 Further reading with interesting writers and topics (e.g.Tuomas Anhava on Haavikko's prose, Hannes Sihvo on Haavikko as a renewer of the Kalevala myth) in *World Literature Today*, 58:4.

PRIMARY SOURCES

Works by Paavo Haavikko

Tiet etäisyyksiin [Roads into the Distances] (WSOY: Helsinki, 1951).
Synnyinmaa [Land of Birth] (Otava: Helsinki, 1955).
Lehdet lehtiä [Leaves Leaves] (Otava: Helsinki, 1958).
Talvipalatsi [Winter Palace] (Otava: Helsinki, 1959).
Puut, kaikki heidän vihreytensä [The Trees, All Their Greenness] (Otava: Helsinki, 1966).
Neljätoista hallitsijaa [Fourteen Rulers] (Otava: Helsinki, 1970).
Runoja matkalta salmen yli [Poems from a Journey Across the Straits] (Otava: Helsinki, 1973).
Kaksikymmentä ja yksi [Twenty and One] (Otava: Helsinki, 1974).
Ratsumies / The Horseman (Esan kirjapaino: Lahti, 1974). Translated by Philip Binham.
Kansakunnan linja. Kommentteja erään tuntemattoman kansan tuntemattomaan historiaan 1904–1975. [The Nation's Line. Comments on the Unknown History of an Unknown People] (Otava: Helsinki, 1977).

Tämä minun ankara vuosisatani. The Life and Work of a Statesman 1918–1981. Kirjannut ja toimittanut Paavo Haavikko. [This Stern Century of Mine] (Art House: Helsinki, 2000).
Talvipalatsi. Varhaisversion rekonstruktio vuodelta 1959. [Winter Palace. Reconstruction of the Early Version from 1959] (Art House; Helsinki, 2001).
Prosperon runot. [The Poems of Prospero] (Art House: Helsinki, 2001).

Translations of works by Paavo Haavikko

Anselm Hollo, *Paavo Haavikko. Selected Poems.* Translated from the Finnish by Anselm Hollo.(Carcanet: Manchester, 1991).
Herbert Lomas, *Contemporary Finnish Poetry.* Edited and translated by Herbert Lomas. (Bloodaxe Books: Newcastle upon Tyne, 1991), 114–150.
Gisbert Jänicke: *Gedichte! Gedichte,* Aus dem Finnischen von Gisbert Jänicke. (Residenz Verlag:Salzburg und Wien, 1997).

BIBLIOGRAPHY

ALAPURO, RISTO 1988: *State and Revolution in Finland.* University of California Press: Berkeley – Los Angeles – London.
ANHAVA, TUOMAS 1960: 'Den finska diktens förnyelse' [The Renewal of Finnish Poetry] *Horisont* 2/1960.
ANHAVA, TUOMAS 2002: *Todenkaltaisuudesta. Kirjoituksia vuosilta 1948–1979.* [On Verisimilitude. Writings from the Years 1948–1979.] Edited by Helena and Martti Anhava. Helsinki: Otava.
ENVALL. MARKKU 1984: 'Haavikko the Aphorist: Philosopher, Ironist and Oracle.' In: *World Literature Today,* 58:4. Norman, Oklahoma: University of Oklahoma.
ENVALL, MARKKU 1987: *Suomalainen aforismi. Keinoja / Rakenteita / Lajeja / Ongelmia.* [Finnish Aphorism. /Means / Structures/ Genres/ Problems] Suomalaisen Kirjallisuuden Seuran Toimituksia 450. Helsinki: SKS.
GOFFMAN, ERVING 1981: *Forms of Talk.* Oxford: Basil Blackwell.
HELLAAKOSKI, AARO 1950: 'Vapaasta ja sidotusta.' *Kuuntelua. Esseitä teoksista ja tekijöistä.* ['Free and Bound'. In: Listening. Essays on Works and Authors.] Helsinki: WSOY.
HÖKKÄ, TUULA 1999: 'Modernismi: uusi alku – vanhan valtaus.' *Rintamakirjeistä tietoverkkoihin. Suomen kirjallisuushistoria 3.* Toim. Pertti Lassila. 'Modernism: a New Beginning – Occupying the Old.' In: Finland's History of Literature 3. From Letters from the Front to the Web] Ed. Pertti Lassila. Helsinki: SKS.
KAUNONEN, LEENA 2001: *Sanojen palatsi. Puhujan määrittely ja teoskokonaisuuden hahmotus Paavo Haavikon 'Talvipalatsissa'.* [Palace of Words. Problematics of the speaker and textual coherence in 'Winter Palace' by Paavo Haavikko] Suomalaisen Kirjallisuuden Seuran Toimituksia 852. Helsinki: SKS.
KUNNAS, MARIA-LIISA 1981: *Muodon vallankumous. Modernismin tulo suomenkieliseen lyriikkaan 1945–1959* [The Arrival of Modernism in Finnish Poetry 1945–1959] Suomalaisen Kirjallisuuden Seuran Toimituksia 372. Helsinki: SKS.
KINNUNEN, AARNE 1977: 'The Writer and his Work.' An interview with Paavo Haavikko. *Books from Finland,* XI:3. Helsinki: SKS.
KINNUNEN, AARNE 1977: *Syvä nauru. Tutkimus Paavo Haavikon dramatiikasta.* Suomalaisen Kirjallisuuden Seuran Toimituksia 331. Helsinki: SKS.
KUUSI, MATTI et.al. 1977: *Finnish Folk Poetry Epic. An Anthology in Finnish and English.* Edited and translated by Matti Kuusi, Keith Bosley and Michael Branch. Publications of the Finnish Literature Society 329. Helsinki: SKS.
LAITINEN, KAI 1984: 'Introduction to Paavo Haavikko's Poetry.' *World Literature Today,* 58:4. Norman, Oklahoma: University of Oklahoma Press.

LAUNONEN, HANNU 1984: Suomalaisen runon struktuurianalyysia. Tutkimus Jaakko Juteinin, Aleksis Kiven, Otto Mannisen, Eino Leinon, V. A. Koskenniemen, Uuno Kailaan, Kaarlo Sarkian, Tuomas Anhavan, Paavo Haavikon ja Pentti Saarikosken lyriikasta. (An Analysis of Some Structural Features in Finnish Poetry. A Study in the Poetry of Jaakko Juteini, Aleksis Kivi, Otto Manninen, Eino Leino, V. A. Koskenniemi, Uuno Kailas, Kaarlo Sarkia, Tuomas Anhava, Paavo Haavikko and Pentti Saarikoski.] Suomalaisen Kirjallisuuden Seuran Toimituksia 396. Helsinki:SKS.

LOMAS, HERBERT 1991: 'Introduction.' *Contemporary Finnish Poetry,* 10–48. Edited and translated by Herbert Lomas. Newcastle upon Tyne: Bloodaxe Books Ltd.

MOREAU, JEAN-LUC 1984: 'Premier pas vers les lointains.' *World Literature Today.* 58:4. University of Oklahoma Press: Norman, Oklahoma.

REKOLA, MIRKKA 1999: 'Kehä joka murtuu.' *Muistinavaruus. Kirjoituksia, puheenvuoroja 1959–1999.* ['The Breaking Circle.' In: The Space of Remembrance] WSOY: Helsinki.

SALIN, SARI 2002: *Hullua hurskaampi. Ironinen kahdentuminen Jorma Korpelan romaaneissa.* [Holier than Madman. Irony and Doubling in Jorma Korpela's Novels] WSOY: Helsinki.

SARAJAS, ANNAMARI 1961: *Elämän meri. Tutkielmia uusromantiikan kirjallisista aatteista.* [The Ocean of Life. Studies in the Literary Ideas of Neo-Romanticism.] Helsinki: WSOY.

SIHVO, HANNES 1980: *Soutu Bysanttiin. Paavo Haavikon metodin ja maailmankuvan tarkastelua.*[Rowing to Byxantium. A Critical Study of Paavo Haavikko's Method and WorldView] Suomalaisen Kirjallisuuden Seuran toimituksia 356. Helsinki: SKS.

SIMONSUURI, KIRSTI 1984: 'The Lyrical Space of Haavikko's Poetry.' *World Literature Today.* 58:4. University of Oklahoma Press: Norman, Oklahoma.

VIIKARI. AULI 1987: *Ääneen kirjoitettu. Vapautuvien mittojen varhaisvaiheet suomenkielisessä lyriikassa.* Suomalaisen Kirjallisuuden Seuran Toimituksia 488. Helsinki: 1987.

VIIKARI, AULI 1992: 'Ei kenenkään maa.' *Avoin ja suljettu. Kirjoituksia 1950-luvusta suomalaisessa kulttuurissa.* Toim. Anna Makkonen. ['No Man's Land' In: Open and Closed, Essays on the 1950's in Finnish Culture] Ed. Anna Makkonen. Helsinki: SKS.

WITTGENSTEIN, LUDWIG 1958(1922): *Tractatus Logico-Philosophicus.* International Library of Psychology Philosophy and Scientific Method. London: Routledge and Kegan Paul Ltd.

ZILLIACUS, EMIL 1905: *Den nyare franska poesin och antiken.* [New French Poetry and Antiquity] Helsingfors: Aktiebolaget Handelstryckeriet.

CONTRIBUTORS

Haapala, Vesa
Research fellow, Department of Finnish Literature.
University of Helsinki.

Kaunonen, Leena
Research fellow, Department of Finnish Literature.
University of Helsinki.

Lyytikäinen, Pirjo
Professor of Finnish Literature.
University of Helsinki.

Molarius, Päivi
Lecturer. Department of Finnish Literature.
University of Helsinki.

Nummi, Jyrki
Professor of Finnish Literature.
University of Helsinki.

Parente-Čapková, Viola
Assistant, Department of Finnish Literature.
University of Turku.

Rossi, Riikka
Research fellow, Department of Finnish Literature.
University of Helsinki.

Viikari, Auli
Professor emerita of Finnish Literature.
University of Helsinki.

www.ingramcontent.com/pod-product-compliance
Lightning Source LLC
Chambersburg PA
CBHW080805300426
44114CB00020B/2832